Alien Woman

The Making of Lt. Ellen Ripley

Ximena Gallardo C. and C. Jason Smith

continuum
NEW YORK • LONDON

2004

The Continuum International Publishing Group Inc
15 E 26 Street, New York, NY 10010

The Continuum International Publishing Group Ltd
The Tower Building, 11 York Road, London SE1 7NX

www.continuumbooks.com

Printed in the United States of America

Library of Congress Cataloging-in-Publication Data

Gallardo C., Ximena.
  Alien woman : The making of Lt. Ellen Ripley / Ximena Gallardo C. and C. Jason Smith.
    p.   cm.
  Includes bibliographical references and index.
  ISBN 0-8264-1569-5 (alk. paper)—ISBN 0-8264-1570-9 (pbk. : alk. paper)
  1. Ripley (Fictitious character)   2. Alien films—History and criticism.
3. Sex role in motion pictures.   I. Smith, C. Jason.   II. Title.
PN1995.9.A475G35   2004
791.43'651—dc22
                                                          2004001216

Contents

This book is for the women in our family, especially our mothers, Ximena and Janet, who always believed anything was possible.

Acknowledgments

We would like to acknowledge the institutions whose financial support helped offset our research: the West Virginia Humanities Council for their generous fellowship and Glenville State College for the Presidential Faculty Scholar Award, which assisted with the later stages of our writing.

Our research was made possible by the assistance of many dedicated individuals in libraries, museums, and specialty video stores across the country. We are particularly in debt to the staff of the R. F. Kidd Library at Glenville State College, the West Virginia State University Library, the Louisiana State University Library, the Queens Library at Astoria, the New York Public Library, the Museum of Sex, Towne Bookstore, and Kim's Video.

We have been fortunate to enjoy the support and assistance of colleagues, friends, and family, and we would like to express our gratitude to all of them. First and foremost, we are deeply indebted to the readers who patiently waded through rough drafts and gave us many helpful remarks: the inimitable Geoff Klock, author of *How to Read Superhero Comics and Why*; our editor, David Barker, and the crew at Continuum; and George S. "Pop" Smith, Likourgous "Luke" Vassiliou, Tom Trice, Richard Tuerk, David Mazel, and Robin Reid.

For their encouragement, arguments, rants, and sudden insights, usually late at night on Fridays, we would like to thank Nancy Zane for front-porch beach parties, Ralph Bauer and Grace Crussiah for a long weekend at Chincoteague, Wayne deRosset for punny, oh so punny stories, and Sara Reiss for being her beautiful and feisty self.

ACKNOWLEDGMENTS

A very special thanks to the mentors who made us think and care—Anna Nardo of Louisiana State University; John Locke (in memoriam), Kay Pritchett, and Luis Fernando Restrepo of the University of Arkansas; and Bo Grimshaw and Gerald Duchovnay of Texas A&M University-Commerce.

Last, but not least, a heartfelt thanks to all the presenters and audience members in the Science Fiction and Fantasy Area at the Southwest and Texas Popular Culture Association/American Culture Association over the last five years who sat through papers on *Alien* again and again, particularly to Susan J. Wolfe and David J. Carlson for always being interested.

Foreword

I met Ripley during a visit to my grandfather's house in Temuco, the main city in what used to be the land of the Mapuche Indians in the south of Chile. *El Chanfle*, starring the Mexican slapstick comedian Chespirito (the little Shakespeare), whom I worshiped, was playing at the local *rotativo*. *Alien: El Octavo Pasajero* was "the other" feature. My older cousin got us tickets (I was thirteen at the time) and promised we would leave immediately if I became too scared. I cannot for the life of me remember whether *Alien* scared me or not, because all my memories of the movie had to do with its ending—you know, the one where the captain comes from nowhere at the last minute and saves the girl. I remember insisting to my cousin that the captain was not really dead, that he would come and rescue Ripley. But—oh, wonder!—he never did, and I walked toward the theater exit in a daze.

The next *Alien* movie that affected me deeply was *Alien³*. I had just moved into a new city in a strange country, and now my only hero was gone. I walked back to my student apartment on the "bad side" of Baton Rouge, Louisiana, in pure desolation. I compensated by watching every single Sigourney Weaver film that came out and was rewarded with *Death and the Maiden*. I felt that I had been touched personally by this actress who not only had portrayed the only female hero I had ever cared for but also had given voice to all the women, all the people, who had suffered so much under the dictatorship of Augusto Pinochet. Certainly, *Death and the Maiden* does not mention the country where Paulina Escobar lives, but I already knew the play the film was based on, written by the Chilean Ariel Dorfman.

So when Ripley was reborn in *Alien Resurrection*, I decided to write this book. It has taken several years and the optimism and patience of my cowriter to bring you *Alien Woman*, for cowriting is very much like watching an *Alien* sequel: you love parts of it, you hate others, and, sucker that you are, you would do it all over again.

—*Ximena Gallardo C.*

I was eleven years, eight months, and some odd days and hours old when *Alien* hit the theaters. I was almost twelve and felt I deserved the rite of passage of a horror film. Good or bad, it didn't matter. What mattered was that I could say I had been there, seen it, and survived. My father and I were science-fiction buffs, so I immediately saw an opening. *Alien* was horror and science fiction, so I figured I could slide one by and be the first kid under sixteen to see the film and enter the preteen hall of fame.

"Can we go *together* to see the new science fiction film?"

"Which one?"

"You know, the *Alien* one."

"No."

My father never said just "no." He was always interested in *why* I wanted to do something.

So, I asked Mom to ask Pop for me and listened from down the hall.

"The kid can't see it until he's thirty. And for that matter, neither can you."

Now firmly in my thirties, I find myself completing a book on not one *Alien* film but four.

I do not distinctly remember the first time I actually saw the film, nor the second or third. Each viewing blends into a continual stream of horror. It scares me every single time. What I do remember distinctly is meeting a young woman from Chile who had just completed her Ph.D. in English and had a thing for both *Star Trek: The Next Generation* and the *Alien* film series. She will tell you (anyone, actually) that the film didn't scare her. Now that I know her better, I believe it, but I don't see how it is possible. That essential difference between my experience and hers became the point of origin for this book.

Finally, I would like to say that cowriting is never easy and inevitably takes longer than a solo project, where the author has to contend with only one set of "voices," not two. Left to our own devices, I think we each would have written quite different books, but those books would never have been written. Nor is this book a hodgepodge of those unwritten books. What has emerged from our collaboration is something different all together. I dislike authors who compare writing a book to giving birth, but at least now I understand them.

—*C. Jason Smith*

INTRODUCTION

Can't Live with Them, Can't Kill Them

Sexploration

> One is not born, but rather becomes a woman.
>
> —Simone de Beauvoir, *The Second Sex*

Since *Le voyage dans la lune* (*A Trip to the Moon*, 1902), the science-fiction film has depicted the human male as the hero of its narratives. Whether a heroic astronaut or a cool scientist (and sometimes both), it is Man who embodies the superior rational-humanistic qualities of the species as he boldly travels the deep, dark, limitless depths of space. Human females in these narratives mostly complement the males in distinctively secondary roles as love interests, nurses, counselors, and low-ranking officers. Even the few extraordinary women who manage to rise above the glass ceiling are inevitably undermined by various devices in plot, characterization, and cinematography during the course of a standard science-fiction film. In *Them!* (1954), for example, the audience's first view of the smart and gutsy Dr. Patricia "Pat" Medford (Joan Wheldon) comes in the form of her well-turned legs sexily descending from an airplane; in *It! The Terror from Beyond Space* (1958), the scientist Dr. Mary Royce (Ann Doran) cheerily cleans up the dinner table and serves

1

coffee to the male astronauts. This trend, unfortunately, continues into our more "enlightened" times. The formidable Dr. Beverly Crusher (Gates McFadden) of the *Star Trek: The Next Generation* television series, who in the show has whole episodes devoted to her and who regularly uses her authority as a medical doctor to order even the captain about, has been almost completely written out of the *Next Generation* films.[1] The beefed up Sara Connor (Linda Hamilton) of *Terminator 2: Judgment Day* (1991), though more prepared to fight the machines from the future than in the first film, has become a whacked-out bad mother who pales in comparison to Arnold Schwarzenegger's android in both killing and parenting skills. Even in *Contact* (1997), the motivation of the protagonist, Dr. Eleanor Ann "Ellie" Arroway (Jodie Foster), centers on a father fixation. When Dr. Arroway finally does get to go into the alien machine after her male boss is killed (it seems Tom Skerritt is always in the way of some woman) and travels the cosmos at faster than the speed of light to meet the aliens, the alien she encounters takes the guise of her father, and, of course, no one believes her story. Such is the usual lot of women in the science-fiction film.

Science fiction also offers a variety of nonhuman females. Exotic and seductive, the weird and wonderful fem-alien comes in a variety of sizes, shapes, and colors. Sexy and dangerous, she is Phena from constellation Hydra (*Star Pilot*, 1965), Ursa from Krypton (*Superman*, 1978), V'ger as Lieutenant Ilia (*Star Trek: The Motion Picture*, 1979), the treacherous and scantily clad Aura (*Flash Gordon*, 1980), the xenomorph Sil (*Species*, 1992), and the Borg Queen (*Star Trek: First Contact*, 1996). Sometimes good, more often evil, the female alien always heralds danger. Her exotic Otherness—whether it be her gigantic size, green skin, violet eyes, or three breasts—marks her as the true test of the male astronaut and, ultimately, humanity. If he can survive *her* (after a romantic interlude perhaps), he can survive *anything*.

And then there is Ripley. Born of the long and uncomfortable association between science fiction and horror, Ripley combines the survivor of slasher with the heroic astronaut of science fiction. Her confrontation with the monstrous creature includes the requisite running and sweating, but she substitutes the shrieking of her predecessors for some understandable swearing, and, in the end, she vanquishes her foe on her own.

Though Ripley was, as many critics have pointed out, a product of masculine discourse, in the sense that the role was originally written by males for a male actor and *Alien* (1979) was directed and produced by males, the character Ripley as she appeared on the screen is, nonetheless, the product of 1960s and '70s Second Wave feminism. Ripley may not be "feminist" per se: she does not, for example, actively fight for women's equality, and none of her arguments with the men draw attention to their misogyny, even though she is clearly the object of gender bias. However, one cannot easily dismiss the fact that her presence on the ship and the rank she holds (and eventually wields) is surely "forward looking" for the time and genre. Neither Ripley nor *Alien*'s other female crew member, Lambert, are secretaries in space: they do not serve coffee, they do not receive special treatment or deference as "girls," and they do not pander to the egos of the men; and, as we shall see, if Lambert betrays a tendency toward hysteria, so does her macho captain, Dallas. In essence, feminism created the context in which a female could be considered not only for the post of commanding officer (a concept that Gene Rodenberry had tried to sell a decade earlier in the pilot episode of *Star Trek* [1965], only to be told nobody would believe a woman could command a starship), but also as the lead in a science-fiction film. Without feminism, there would be no Ripley.

The Ripley of *Alien*, though not necessarily a feminist icon, filled a need among women for a strong female protagonist, and her debut made an understandable impression on many female viewers. Winona Ryder, Sigourney Weaver's costar in *Alien Resurrection*, recalls how exciting it was to see Ripley triumph over the Alien in 1979:

I was about eight. But I remember the impact it had on me. I had never seen a female character like that. It was the first female action hero that I had and that any of us had. It was a huge impact. . . . I mean, she was the survivor. . . . I can't think of a movie before where it was a woman. . . . That whole last sequence where she is trying to blow up the ship and make it to the other ship, she goes back for the cat, she's running with the cat, and then she thinks she's safe and then she realizes the alien's on board . . . If you talk to anybody of my generation, they can recount that scene frame by frame, because it's such a classic scene. And of course we've seen guys do that a lot. Guys surviving, being the hero. Girls really just being mostly the victim. And this time it was great to see a woman really, you know, kick ass for the first time.[2]

Alien was not the last time Ripley dominated the screen. Left to grapple with a strong female protagonist, subsequent writers and directors in the 1980s and 1990s reenvisioned Lieutenant Ripley to fit differing social, political, and cultural imperatives for women, but they never diminished her heroic role. Again and again, Ripley proved to be smarter, stronger, more courageous, and humane than the Colonial Marines in *Aliens*, the double-Y chromosome convicts of *Alien³*, and the scientists, army men, and pirates of *Alien Resurrection*. As such, she continues to speak to female viewers of science fiction, whose only other options still range between identifying with Claire Danes as the love interest Kate Brewster or Kristanna Loken as the vain femme fatale Terminatrix (*Terminator 3: Rise of the Machines* [2003]).

Ripley was, and continues to be, something new. A bastard child of science fiction and horror, she is also the proto-slayer: long before Buffy, there was Ripley. But she is much more: a woman who thwarts the destructive patriarchal desire, faces her shadow self again and again, embraces it, and ultimately incorporates the monstrous feminine into her very being. A creation of men, Ripley nonetheless rattles her chains loudly, filling the void of silence imposed on women by male narratives. She may not get entirely free, but she is seen, she is heard, and she is remembered.

4

A New Breed

> I expect Woman will be the last thing
> civilized by Man.
>
> —George Meredith

Because the exploration of space is pitted as a sexual enterprise (Man defining himself against the mysterious Feminine), it is not unusual for science-fiction films to depict close encounters of any kind in sexual terms. The canonical *2001: A Space Odyssey* (1968), for example, uses blatant reproductive metaphors to illustrate the evolution of humanity (represented by male scientists and astronauts) as it goes into the womb of space. Early on in *2001*, the viewer witnesses an extended docking sequence between a tiny phallic space shuttle and a gigantic, wheel-shaped space station: the entire sequence is staged as a cosmic dance to the tune of a waltz. This scene prefigures *2001*'s climax, in which the pod that contains astronaut David Bowman (Keir Dullea) flies into a psychedelic, vaginal space vortex that transports him to a stark white chamber, where he dies and is reborn as a new organism, the Star Child.

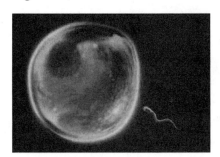 

Death ovum meets space sperm: the sexploration of space.

Lest we think Stanley Kubrick's film an isolated case, a decade later the space opera *Star Wars* (1977) staged the Rebel attack on the Empire's Death Star as so many sperm assaulting an egg. In this case, the feminine form is depicted as lethal, for the Death Star, a spherical, dark gray battle station the size of a small moon, is capable of destroying entire planets with one fatal blow of its main laser. Flying a sleek

5

X-wing starfighter, the Rebel hero Luke Skywalker (Mark Hamill) must hit a small port on the Death Star's surface with his proton torpedoes to begin a chain reaction in the station's central reactor—a fatal implantation that does not fertilize, but rather destroys the monstrous space egg.

Little wonder, then, that the image of the egg represents the extra-terrestrial menace in *Alien*'s poster and trailers. Such a common image would seem silly if not for the fear of monstrous birth it evokes: the shell of the egg is cracked in a grotesque parody of the vaginal cleft or a cruel acidic grin. The Alien egg advertises, first and foremost, the evil ur-womb: it gives birth, and men die.

The creature that will spring from this egg is a nightmare vision of sex and death. It subdues and opens the male body to make it pregnant, then explodes it in birth. In its adult form, the Alien strikes its victims with a rigid, phallic tongue that breaks through skin and bone. More than a phallus, however, its retractable tongue has its own set of snapping, metallic teeth that connects it to the castrating vagina dentata. The vagina dentata, a symbolic expression of the male fear that a woman's genitals may eat or castrate her partner during intercourse, is tied to the image of the phallic woman (i.e., a woman with a knife) and the monstrous generative mother, whose vagina threatens to devour and reincorporate her offspring.

Unlike most nightmarish creatures, then, the Alien is not only a killing machine but also a relentless reproductive machine, seeking hosts to bring forth more of its species. It is the Alien reproductive drive and its consequences that both the characters in the series and the audience fear most—the impending moment when the dark creature will emerge from within. Inevitably, then, an *Alien* narrative engages a wide range of female body narratives such as rape, pregnancy, birth, and mothering, bringing the Otherness of the otherwise repressed and denied female body to the fore. That in the *Alien* series many of these traditionally female narratives can be acted out on the male body broadens the discursive space to address issues of sex, gender, and the body. As males are penetrated, impregnated, and give birth, the distinction between the male body and the female body, upon which our entire culture is based, begins to blur. This is the site of the *Alien* horror: faced with the Alien, we are all feminized.

Alien Woman explores how the conflict between the female protagonist and the monstrous feminine set up in the first film operates throughout the *Alien* series. With a female protagonist in the role of the traditional male lead, we are able to see more clearly how the same gender codes operate differently for the protagonist and the antagonist. Although the series explores the similarities between Alien and Woman starting with *Alien*, director James Cameron made the parallelism literal by creating a female Alien as the embodiment and originator of the entire species. Ripley's mirroring of her dark Other becomes more complex in *Alien³* because she is herself first identified as the monstrous feminine by the men of the narrative even before she learns she has been infected with an Alien Queen. By *Alien Resurrection*, however, the female protagonist has integrated the monstrous feminine into her very DNA, emphasizing the interchangeability of Alien and Woman.

Thus, the title of this introduction, "Can't Live with Them, Can't Kill Them" (taken from a misogynistic joke about women), not only refers to the relationship Man has to Woman and Human has to Alien, but also signals Ripley's conundrum, for the monstrous feminine has given her new life, and so destroying the Alien completely would be destroying herself.

Acts of Theory

This book is not an application of theory. Beyond our admitted interest in the formation of sex and gender, we do not bring any particular theorist or set of theories to bear on these films as an exemplum of a predetermined thesis. Rather, *Alien Woman* is an act of theory where we, the authors, actively engage in a dialogue with the texts of the films, the historical contexts of their making, and one another. Readers who would like to learn more about the theoretical background that informs this text will find ample material in the notes and bibliography.

A Note on VHS, DVD, and Cinematic Releases

As we discuss the films as not only a text but a historical process, we occasionally make forays into materials not included in the films as originally shown, such as outtakes and scripts, but we take great pains to make it clear that these materials are not part of the text of the film per se.

In the case of *Aliens*, however, several scenes excised from the original theatrical release to shorten the run time were later included in *Aliens: Special Edition* at director James Cameron's request. This widely available version of *Aliens* (also marketed as the *Director's Cut* [1991]) is the only one included in the box set *The Alien Legacy: 20th Anniversary Edition* (1999); both versions are featured in the 9-disc *Alien Quadrilogy* (2003).[3] The difference between these two versions of *Aliens* is important: in *Aliens: Special Edition*, Ripley *had* a daughter, Amy, while in the cinematic release, no mention is made of a daughter. To help the reader understand the difference between both versions, we have included a comparative plot summary of the films in chapter 2.

Aliens is thus unique to the series in that the reintegrated scenes present a more firmly grounded vision of the motherhood/maternity theme that drives the film. As a biological mother herself who lost a daughter, for example, alternate explanations arise for Ripley's quick attachment to the girl-child Newt. She acts maternally because she is suffering the loss of her own daughter and not simply because she is a woman. Our reading of *Aliens* thus engages in a bit of double vision: we read the film as originally released with the added scenes as overlay. It is our contention that although Cameron did cut the scenes, the maternal theme remained in the text of the film, as evidenced by the numerous reviews and articles written after the cinematic release of *Aliens* that focus on Ripley and the Alien Queen as mothers.

Chapter Outline

Chapter 1, "Men, Women, and an *Alien* Baby," examines the resolute yet feminine protagonist of *Alien* and the cultural context of her creation. Originally written for an all-male cast, the script for *Alien* (1979; Dir. Ridley Scott) changed dramatically when the then president of 20th Century Fox, Alan Ladd Jr., asked if the protagonist, Ripley, could be played by a woman. By conflating the typical male hero of science fiction with the female survivor of slasher films, *Alien* became the first science-fiction film in which a female (rather than a male) represented humanity, effectively destabilizing gender difference. Ripley is third officer of the spaceship *Nostromo*, whose crew is awakened from its cryo-sleep to answer a distress call from an unexplored planet. After discovering a derelict spaceship, a crew member is attacked by an alien life form, whose parasitic progeny later bursts through his chest. With this scene, *Alien* effectively erased the basic sexual distinction between men and women, and invoked cultural anxieties about the subversion of male power by visually representing the male body as a site of rape and birth.

Freed from the human body, the Alien escapes, and, one by one, kills the crew. Ripley discovers that the very company that hired them has determined to bring back the Alien for its "weapons division." She, then, must fight the Alien *and* a calculating patriarchal system (represented by the Company's robot, Ash, who tries to dispose of Ripley in a telling mock-rape scene). Ripley's confrontation with, and final destruction of, the Alien becomes the major theme of the film (and the series), and thereby gives voice to the contemporary feminist goal of saving humanity from the destructive impulses of patriarchy.

Chapter 2, "Ripley Gets Her Gun: *Aliens* and the Reagan Era Hero," traces the revision of "Ripley" into "Ellen Ripley." For this second installment, writer/director James Cameron rewrites Ripley as an action hero, as *Aliens* (1986) is a military expedition/combat film. At the same time, the political climate of the Reagan era informed the film's conservative revision of Ripley into a socially authorized female role: the "mother" Ellen Ripley. Her nightmares of the Alien bursting through her chest not only allude to fears of giving birth to a monstrosity (and of dying in the process) but also serve as counterpoint to the loss of Ripley's own natural daughter (a theme made clear in the director's cut version of the film). Although Ripley returns to the alien planet (now named LV-426) to confront her fears, once there her strength and motivation come from her maternal instincts toward the orphaned child and surrogate daughter, Newt. The maternal theme is mirrored in grotesque form by the introduction of the Alien Queen as a monstrous mother who dominates the Alien drones and, by extension, the macho Marines who fight them. The theme of monstrous birth set up in the first film is reified in the second, and birth and rebirth become the central recurring themes of the series with the conflict between mothers at the core.

Like the hero of many '80s action films who fights, at least in part, to get his wife, lover, or family back (i.e. *Die Hard, Lethal Weapon*), Ripley fights to recover her lost daughter, and, importantly, binds a male to her quest, creating an impromptu family. We get the sense that Ripley is, in Reagan era terms, "fulfilling her inner destiny" as the mother who destroys the Alien threat to her family. Furthermore,

Ellen Ripley stands for the redeemed American who has returned to the hard-body politics of right and wrong, good and evil, us and them. She is in her place, a woman fighting women's battles, not the patriarchy of the Company, as she did in *Alien*. She has a new daughter, a mate, and is heading home to good old Earth.

Chapter 3, "'The Bitch Is Back': The Iconoclastic Body in *Alien³*," posits *Alien³* (1992; dir. David Fincher) as a self-conscious response to the politics of *Aliens*. Where *Aliens* is exhilarating, *Alien³* is introspective; whereas the former emphasizes individual action, the latter emphasizes collaboration and suffering; *Aliens*' heroic Marines and womanly "mother" Ripley aided by a battery of high-tech weaponry are counteracted by *Alien³*'s hysterical inmates and the androgynous "bitch" Ripley bereft of any weapons whatsoever. Ripley's surrogate motherhood is replaced by a forced, biologically determined motherhood. Significantly, Ripley's apotheosis in *Alien³* erases the happy ending of *Aliens*, leaving us with the image of a radically different type of hero: the mother-protector is replaced with the mother-destroyer.

Using Christian iconography, *Alien³* rewrites Ripley as the abject, a liminal woman who will ultimately reject the patriarchal imperatives she defends in *Aliens*. Ripley's violent landing on the hellish prison-planet Fury 161 casts her out from the utopian promise of *Aliens* into a feminist hell, where she is surrounded by fundamentalist Christian misogynist hypermale convicts. There, Ripley is reconstructed as a paradox: she is the virgin/whore, "the intolerable"/object of desire, the savior/destroyer, the hyperfemale/macho bitch, and the self-destructive/reproductive body. Most importantly, within her lurks an embryonic Alien Queen who could destroy humanity once and for all. In the end, she chooses to leap into the burning leadworks, taking her Alien "baby" with her. Her transformation from perennial victim of the Company and the Alien to eternal foe makes Ripley's death a victory, and propels her figure into legend.

Chapter 4, "'Who Are You?': *Alien Resurrection* and the Posthuman Subject," examines Ripley as the dark or monstrous posthuman superwoman. As we have seen, Ripley moves from an arguably genderless role (at least in its conception), through motherhood, to that of a defiant bitch. When she is brought back to life as a clone in *Alien: Resurrection* (1997; dir. Jean-Pierre Jeunet), however, Ripley's gender and sexuality explode to encompass the entire film. Neither horror nor action, this psychological thriller has gender as its focus and parody as its method. From her literal emergence out of the hole left by the demise of Captain Elgin, the conventional hero, to her destruction by fire of her other, cloned, "selves," this Ripley represents a clear threat to patriarchal order. As always, the military-industrial complex prizes the Alien species over humanity, only this time Ripley is also alien: a human/Alien hybrid, a freak treated variously as a pet, a curiosity, or a threat. Gender is most highly interrogated by the birth of a new type of Alien, born not through a host, but from the cloned Alien Queen, which develops a humanlike womb. This new Alien, a product of mixed female (Alien Queen and Ripley) DNA, represents the greatest fear of the patriarchal power structure: a race produced solely of Woman. Although Ripley chooses to "abort" her Alien offspring, she still carries the potential it represented within her. She is no longer human, but she is still female: a complex posthuman female of choice and action. Moreover, she is a superhero in the grand tradition of mutation, and in the film's open ending, she is about to finally come home.

CHAPTER 1

Men, Women, and an *Alien* Baby

Beware the Jabberwock, my son!
The jaws that bite, the claws that catch!
—from "Jabberwocky" by Lewis Carrol

Breaking the Gender Barrier

Like other science-fiction films of the 1960s and '70s, *Alien* (1979) is preoccupied with the future of a humanity faced with the perceived perils of continued exploration and transformation. While some films optimistically explored human transformation as progress in an essentially benevolent universe, others expressed its negative aspect, notably devolution, technophobia, invasion, and infiltration in a brute fang-and-tentacle Nature. Stanley Kubric's *2001: A Space Odyssey* (1968), which features human evolution as alien-inspired—from ape to human and finally into a new form, the "Star Child"—harmonizes quite nicely with the less urbane *Planet of the Apes* (also 1968), which explores the devolution of the human species and evolution of the apes following a nuclear apocalypse. A decade later, Steven Spielberg's *Close Encounters of the Third Kind* (1977) and the unsurprisingly optimistic *Star Trek: The Motion Picture* (1979) navigated the psychological terrain of invasion and first

13

contact with similar results: Roy Neary, the protagonist of *Close Encounters*, ascends into space aboard an alien spacecraft, and Starfleet Commander Decker joins with a machine of humanity's own making, a *Voyager* space probe, augmented by a vastly superior, robotic, alien intelligence.* In each case, humanity is altered by the contact with the cosmos, although the great majority of humans, at least for the moment, are left unfazed. Thus, it would seem that the primary concern of science-fiction films of the 1960s and '70s is to question the primacy of the rational-humanist subject—what it means to be "human"—in order to reinforce that primacy or horrifically deconstruct it.

Although *Alien* certainly grew out of this tradition, no one was quite ready for its approach to human transformation, and therein lay its terrible beauty. For *Alien* was the first science-fiction film to assault the rational-humanist subject from the basis of biological sex and gender roles: when Kane's chest exploded and that phallic little beastie escaped from the depth of our unconscious and onto the screen, with it went the primacy of the sexed body in science-fiction films.

Alien owes a debt for its uniqueness to the horror genre, particularly to a then nascent subgenre, the slasher. In her groundbreaking critique of the slasher, occult, and rape-revenge film genres entitled *Men, Women, and Chainsaws*, Carol J. Clover unequivocally designates *Alien* "a sci-fi/slasher hybrid," positioning it along the lines of *The Texas Chainsaw Massacre* (1974) and *Halloween* (1978).[1] Indeed, *Alien* does partake of many of the standard elements of slasher as defined by Clover: set in an archetypal Terrible Place, "where no one can hear you scream," its primary characters are an unfathomable Killer and a beautiful Final Girl, as Clover calls her, the one female who has the strength, courage, and wit to survive the killer's on-

---

*A note on usage: We use several different forms of the word *alien* in this text: the lowercase *alien* refers to the dictionary definition, while Alien (capitalized, no italics) indicates the alien species designed by H. R. Giger for the film *Alien* (capitalized, in italics).

14

slaught. Before *Alien*, however, the Final Girl had never defeated the killer alone. Apparently, *Alien*'s grafting of the science-fiction and horror genres yielded an altogether different "voice" from what audiences and critics of either science fiction or horror might have expected.

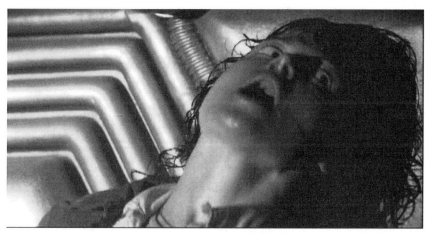

Ripley as the Final Girl:
"In space no one can hear you scream."

As many critics have noted, *Alien* was conceived as a modest "B" movie with a bug-eyed monster theme. Accordingly, Dan O'Bannon and Ronald Shusett's original story, tentatively named *Star Beast*, mostly reprised the rampaging monster from outer space narratives of *The Thing from Another World* (1951) and *It! The Terror from Beyond Space* (1958).[2] But their story had one truly innovative and horrifying scene: the infamous moment when the Alien bursts through the astronaut's chest. Accounts of the filming and screening of this scene are almost legend. Actor Yaphet Kotto, for example, who plays Parker, was nervous for weeks after his close encounter with the Chestburster, while members of the film crew became physically ill after watching different shots of the scene repeatedly.[3] The emotional and physical impact of the scene (particularly in 1979) was undeniable: when *Alien* hit the theaters, adults were daring each other to go to the film and not get sick.

Film critic and author David Thomson recalls audiences' intense gut reaction to the film and attributes it to the frontal assault on the gender barrier:

> What made audiences scream in 1979, what had some people vomiting as they ran away, was the eruption from within. For I think very few people then foresaw that the monster was going to demand birth from Kane's body. We had never seen one body breaking out of another, even if there had been hints of that in *The Exorcist*. We had not really understood the title, *Alien*, until this scene, and the absolute, parasitic subduing of one organism by another. . . . [T]he body seemed more secure then. And the nausea, the gulping and retching, came in the sudden upheaval of understanding, of what had been done down Kane's throat. For the man had been made pregnant.[4]

All this may seem exaggerated to us now, inured as we supposedly are to violence, thanks to special effects developments in television and film; but, even today, viewers watching the film for the first time sometimes cannot get past this moment: no wonder, then, that the Chestburster scene became a synecdoche for the entire film.

After unsuccessfully pitching the original story to 20th Century Fox, O'Bannon turned to Brandywine Productions, headed by Gordon Carroll, Walter Hill, and David Giler. Giler and Hill thought the script had potential, and to convince 20th Century Fox to make the film, they refined the script themselves, most notoriously adding the menace of Ash, the robot. At the request of Alan Ladd Jr., then president of 20th Century Fox, Giler and Hill also made the protagonist a woman. An admirer of Alfred Hitchcock's films, such as *Psycho* (1960) and *The Birds* (1963), Ladd believed that audiences would become more engaged in the story if a woman were in peril. Because O'Bannon and Shusett had stipulated in the script that women could play a couple of the roles "to reach a broader audience," Ripley became a woman.[5] The transformation was, according to producer David Giler, simple: "We really just had the secretary change 'he' to 'she.'"[6]

16

Alien was not the first science-fiction film to feature a serious, strong female protagonist: the studio's decision to cast Sigourney Weaver in the role of Ripley was probably based on the success of female leads such as Katharine Ross in *The Stepford Wives* (1975), Julie Christie in *Demon Seed* (1977), and Genevieve Bujold in *Coma* (1978). In the end, however, every single one of these women either relied on a man or was finally crushed by the evil forces plotting against her. Mainstream Hollywood was ready for a woman hero, particularly if such a choice kept audiences wondering who would survive the onslaught of the creature. What could be more unexpected than making the sole protagonist and survivor a woman? This rationale says much about the times in which *Alien* was being produced: it shows that women as heroic survivors was a concept alien enough to constitute a surprise for the audience while at the same time not so foreign that it would put mainstream audiences off.

In fact, America was already enjoying the New Woman heroes of the television series *Charlie's Angels* (1976–1981), *The Bionic Woman* (1976–1978), and *Wonder Woman* (1976–1979). While men watched these shows to see the "foxy" Farrah Fawcett gallivant around with guns, the athletic Lindsay Wagner running in slow motion, or the gorgeous Linda Carter lasso the bad guys, women watched them for their fantasies of transgression. Writing in 2000, author and social observer Sarah Vowell remembers how shows like *Charlie's Angels* helped to shape her into a feminist: "In 1976, other than my first-grade teacher, every woman of my small-town acquaintance was a housewife or widowed housewife. The Angels not only had jobs, they had jobs within their jobs, often going undercover as hotel maids or race-car drivers or roller-derby players."[7] Vowell's observations accurately record the discrepancy between the public and the private sphere in terms of women's issues. Headlines and news broadcasts reported on important legal decisions and social confrontations furthering women's equality: for example, the Equal Rights Amendment was approved by the Senate and was pending state approval (1972), the U.S. Supreme Court had ruled in *Roe* v. *Wade* (1973) that abortion was legal during the first trimester, and the indomitable Billie Jean

King defeated Bobby Riggs in a "Battle of the Sexes" tennis match (also 1973). Privately, however, the great majority of women in America (which is not to say the world) still led lives centered on their families and homes. Shows like *Charlie's Angels* were the only way girls like Vowell could dream of a future different from what they saw about them.

We should make no mistake, however: *Alien* was never intended to be primarily a feminist movie nor even a movie for women. Rather, as feminist critic Judith Newton explains, "What *Alien* offers on one level, and to a white, middle-class audience, is a utopian fantasy of women's liberation, a fantasy of economic and social equality, friendship, and collectivity between middle-class women and men," where white, middle-class women save humanity "from its worst excesses and specifically from its dehumanization."[8] Woman, allowed freedom from economic constraints, could now "save the day," but the day saved still belonged to the men.

Ridley Scott, who had impressed the executives at 20th Century Fox with his first film, the period piece *The Duellists* (1977), was asked to direct. Excited by the visual possibilities of science-fiction cinema after having watched *Star Wars*, Scott became interested in the project and, following in George Lucas's casting strategy, settled on a then unknown actress, Sigourney Weaver, for the role of Ripley.[9] Scott then filmed several screen tests of Weaver for the studio executives: in one she runs through rather nicely constructed "science-fiction" corridors; in another she asks for sexual "relief" from the captain, removing her top in the process. David Giler recalls that the selection process even included a female audience: "Alan Ladd watched the screen test and had all the secretaries in the building come down and watch it. And then everybody asked—and they got in a big argument—did she look more like Jane Fonda or Faye Dunaway?"[10] The secretaries liked her, so Weaver was in. That Alan Ladd asked the working women in the building what they thought of Weaver indicates his interest in making *Alien* compelling for the female viewer as well as for the male. On the other hand, that the female test audience for science-fiction film's first solo female hero were apparently all secretaries is a very telling sign of the times.

In addition to Weaver, *Alien* was blessed with a cast of veteran actors and a formidable design team. But what truly elevated the movie from the substrata of the "B" science-fiction film was the contracting of Swiss surrealist H. R. Giger as the visual designer of the different forms of the Alien creature and the alien environs. O'Bannon, who had become acquainted with Giger's work during a failed French film production of *Dune*, presented Scott with a copy of the artist's first published book, *H. R. Giger's Necronomicon*. Giger's fusion of the human and the technological, of decay and radiance, of elegance and grotesquerie, and of male and female sexuality in his "biomechanical art" seemed particularly suited for the ferocious Alien of the script. In several interviews over the years, Scott has recalled that the two paintings of biomechanical Giger creatures that really caught his attention were entitled "Necronom IV" and "Necronom V": "I nearly fell off my desk, said 'that's it' and 'why look farther?' I've never been so certain of anything in my life."[11] Originally hired as a concept designer only, Giger ended up working firsthand on the film, designing the alien planet's landscape, the derelict ship, and its occupant—a fossilized creature referred to as the "Space Jockey"—as well as four of the five stages of the Alien life cycle: the Egg, the Facehugger, the adult Alien, and the Cocoon (see the section "H. R. Giger's Biomechanoid Nightmare" below).

Visually based as it was on Giger's nightmare-inspired art, *Alien* predictably attracted the attention of psychoanalytic critics, who regarded it predominantly as a horror movie.[12] Of these, Barbara Creed's feminist reading of *Alien* as "a complex representation of the monstrous-feminine as archaic mother" became a canonical interpretation of the film and an important text in feminist film studies. In her analysis of *Alien*, Creed argues that the figure of the archaic mother—whose central characteristic is her massive generative womb, which gives birth but also consumes—is present throughout the film "in the images of birth, the representations of the primal scene (the taboo fantasy of watching one's parents in the act of procreation), the womb-like imagery, the long winding tunnels leading to inner chambers, the rows of hatching eggs, the body of the mother-ship, the voice of the life-support system, and the birth of the alien." As a negative force, she represents the all-consuming feminine, "the voracious maw, the mysterious black hole that signifies female genitalia which threatens to give birth to equally horrific offspring as well as threatening to incorporate everything in its path." By Creed's reading, the adult Alien's teeth and phallic, toothed tongue could both display and conceal the archaic mother's monstrous vagina dentata (see our discussion in "Can't Live with Them, Can't Kill Them").[13] The horror in *Alien*, then, may be read as the fear of the castrated and castrating feminine Other, whose monstrous reproductive drive threatens to overrun the human, and therefore must be repressed and controlled. Notably, Creed's outstanding analysis of the film prefigures James Cameron's concept and design for the monstrous Alien Queen in *Aliens*.

As for *Alien*'s female protagonist, most reviewers agree that Ripley is tough and that Weaver's performance is compelling. Among the predictable references to Weaver as "sexy" and "pleasant to look at," she is also described as "gutsy," "controlled," "earnest," "intelligent," "impressive," "funny," and "efficient."[14] *Newsweek*'s David Ansen's diminutive labeling of Ripley as a "tough talking astronette" (rather than "tough astronaut"), in particular, reveals a certain fascination with this confident female who is something other than the screaming heroine of the 1950s monster movies that Ansen and others otherwise see as the basis for *Alien*. The consistent praise of Ripley and Weaver indicates an appreciation for the strong woman lead, even if many of the initial film reviewers did not see Ripley as particularly "progressive."

It was not until the late 1980s that critics started to argue for Ripley's importance to science fiction and cinema. Thus, with the benefit of intellectual distance, Rebecca Bell-Metereau cites early reviewers of *Alien* as being unable to see Ripley as a radically new type of female hero because she is, for male audiences at least, "so foreign as to be unrecognizable."[15] Rarely, if ever, had the male audience been asked to identify with the female protagonist.

Bell-Metereau was not alone in this new critical appraisal of Ripley. In *Science Fiction Films of the Seventies,* Craig Anderson remembers Ripley as a "refreshing change from the Princess Leia's and *Close Encounters* wives of previous years,"[16] while *Futurevisions'* authors Douglas Menville and R. Reginald explain the importance of being Ripley:

> One of the most notable features of [*Alien*] is the fact that the "hero" is a woman—a most courageous, bright and entirely logical woman—overturning one of SF pulp fiction's most sacred canons: all heroes are men, sometimes accompanied by clinging cardboard women characters who must be saved or protected. In this case, Ripley saves herself, every bit as effectively as the male heroes of tradition.[17]

As Menville and Reginald note, Ripley was every bit as effective as a male hero, and that fact became the sole criticism aimed at the character. James H. Kavanagh, for example, admits that *Alien* "broadcasts a very sophisticated set of overwhelmingly feminist signals" but only to mask the fact that Ripley still stands for the traditional rational-humanist subject, or, as he puts it, "a tough gal, rather than a tough guy."[18] Judith Newton also reads Ripley as a stand-in for the traditional male hero: "*Alien* . . . is at once wish-fulfilling or utopian and protectively repressive in its thrust. The most obvious utopian element in *Alien* is its casting of a female character in the role of individualist hero, a role conventionally played by, and in this case specifically written for, a male."[19] Kavanagh's and Newton's interpretations of Ripley as a woman in man's clothing coincide with Clover's definition of the Final Girl as a male surrogate, masculinized (as Ripley's name implies) so that the male audience can identify with her. Because Ripley, like any other Final Girl, is meant to stand in for the missing male hero, Clover warns about making her into a prototype for feminism: "To applaud the Final Girl as a feminist development, as some reviews of *Aliens* have done with Ripley, is, in light of her figurative meaning, a particularly grotesque expression of wishful thinking. She is simply an agreed-upon fiction and the male viewer's use of her as a vehicle for his own sadomasochistic fantasies an act of perhaps timeless dishonesty."[20] Ripley's survival, in effect, serves as a justification (and apology, of sorts) for the violence and voyeurism visited upon the crew of the *Nostromo* during the course of the film, since in its final moments the male viewer can relieve his fantasy-induced guilt (of raping and killing) through a false identification with the heroic female.

Ripley the New Woman: Going Full Throttle in 1979.

Even if Ripley were standing in for the heroic male, the fact remains that by the end of Scott's film all the men are dead and a woman is the last one on deck. Prior to *Alien*, a woman might have discovered the beast, run from it, submitted to it, acted as bait, poked it, prodded it, hurt it, even delivered the coup de grâce, but she never, ever did these things alone; some man was always there. The Final Girls of *The Texas Chainsaw Massacre* and *Halloween*, for example, get away just in the nick of time, but in the end both are rescued by men (in *Texas*, by a trucker; in *Halloween*, by the killer's gun-wielding psychiatrist). In her role preceding *Alien*, Veronica Cartwright actually came close as Nancy Bellicec, the sole survivor of an alien takeover in *Invasion of the Body Snatchers* (1978). Nancy, however, survives only to witness the loss of the male protagonist, who in the final moments betrays her presence to the other pod people. In contrast, Ripley saves not only herself, but humanity from the ravages of the beast, blowing up her Company's spaceship and its cargo in the process.

Blame the "empowerment in tiny panties" ending on the contradictory roles women were trying to juggle in the 1970s (and still are today); yet somewhere in the confusion between assertive independent working girl, sex object, and savior of the world, Ripley became something more than a quaint footnote in cinematic history.

H. R. Giger's Biomechanoid Nightmare

> I don't think anybody has come up with a design or an idea as profoundly frightening and dark as Giger's Alien.
>
> —Ivor Powell, *Alien*'s associate producer

The producers of *Alien* might have found H. R. Giger, but Giger had visualized the Alien within us long before. His nightmare visions, collected in *H. R. Giger's Necronomicon*, became, by his own admission, the Bible of the Alien world.[21] During the production of *Alien*, Giger was responsible for the design concepts and much of the construction of the alien planet's landscape, the derelict ship and its pilot, the Space Jockey, and the five phases of the Alien creature: the Egg, the Facehugger, the Chestburster, the adult Alien, and the Cocoon. (An extended, personal account of Giger's work for *Alien* can be found in his book *Giger's Alien*.)

In July 1977, Giger received a letter from Dan O'Bannon commissioning him to create two paintings, of an alien Egg and a Facehugger, to help visualize a yet unsold script he was working on, later to be entitled *Alien*. For the location where the astronauts find the Alien, O'Bannon had settled on a temple created by an "ancient, primitive, and cruel culture."[22] It never made it to the film. Instead, the artist designed and built a skeletal landscape surrounding a gigantic dere-

23

lict spaceship that juts out of the terrain at a bizarre angle, its three entrances clearly reminiscent of giant vaginas. Once inside and past the bony gangway, the astronauts are confronted by a twenty-six-foot-tall fossilized biomechanoid reclining in the middle of the cavernous cockpit. This Space Jockey, as the film crew called it, formed a single unit with its massive seat, as if it had grown out of the chair.

An opening in the cockpit's deck became the way to the Alien egg silo (now looking more like a cargo space) below. Conceived as "Spore Pods" by O'Bannon, the Alien wombs became eggs in Giger's hands: "The story tells of spore-capsules (eggs) inside a pyramid," the artist writes in *Giger's Alien*. "That gives me the idea of using the Swiss egg-box for the basic structure of the pyramid. The eggs themselves, which according to O'Bannon's sketch contain the first nucleus of the *Alien*, the Facehugger, will consequently also be inside the pyramid, in the egg silo." Echoing the entrance to the ship proper, Giger originally endowed the Alien eggs with a "vagina-like opening" complete with "an inner and outer vulva," but the director and producers of *Alien* thought it too obvious, especially for Catholic audiences. Giger, with a masterful stroke of hyperbole, doubled the vaginal opening so that, "seen from above, they would form the cross that people in Catholic countries are so fond of looking at."[23] In some drawings, the phalanges of the Alien Facehugger curl like witch, or vampire, fingers inside the translucent eggs.[24]

For the Facehugger, O'Bannon suggested a "possibly octopoidal" first phase of the Alien to inhabit the pod, which then would leap out and attach itself to the face of the victim. Indeed, Giger's early design of the Facehugger reminds one of a wicked crossbreeding between an octopus and a chicken-turned-slug sticking a penis down a humanoid's throat.[25] A later drawing of the Facehugger (shown below) betrays its transgressive sexuality: this time, Giger imagines the creature shaped like two human hands placed side by side with a vaginal opening between them, from which a phallic appendage emerges—the overall effect is of a fingered testicular sac. When attached to a humanoid head, the Facehugger's dual nature as vaginal and phallic implies both the acts of cunnilingus and fellatio.

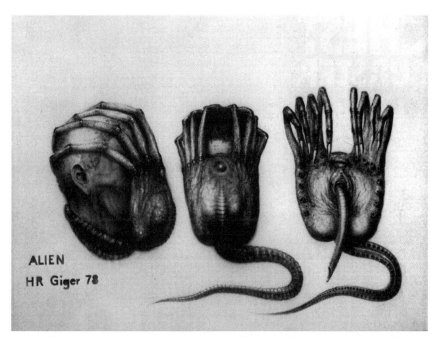

"Alien/Facehugger," 379, 1978, © 2003 HR GIGER, Acrylic, 70 × 100 cm.
Courtesy of www.HRGigerMuseum.com and www.HRGiger.com.

The Chestburster, described in O'Bannon's letter as "a small creature that bites its way out of the victim's body," became the artist's own nightmare. Apparently, Giger was not able to distance himself from the vision of the Chestburster as some form of mutated chicken, and his early drawings seem even to the untrained eye as unfilmable. Giger himself called his model a "degenerate plucked turkey." His frustration was evident: "Even I am not satisfied with my work."[26] His hands full with the design and construction of the alien planet's surface, the derelict spacecraft, the mummified Space Jockey, and every other stage of the Alien's life cycle, Giger gave up the task, and the Chestburster design was given to Roger Dicken, who produced the final Chestburster that explodes from Kane's chest, splattering the crew with blood.

The adult Alien became the production's most trying creation. O'Bannon's letter asked for a man-sized alien that would be "terrifically dangerous," "very mobile, strong, and capable of tearing a man to pieces," that "feeds on human flesh," or, in other words, "a profane abomination." At the producers' suggestion, he added that "something resembling an over-sized, deformed baby might be sufficiently loathsome."[27] Ridley Scott, thankfully, had something other than a gigantic baby in mind: the elegant and fierce form of the artist's bio-mechanoid Necronoms as they appeared in *H. R. Giger's Necronomicon.*

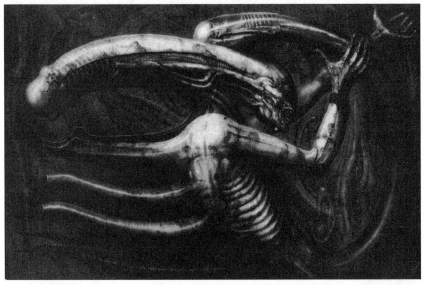

"Necronom IV," 303, 1976, © 2003 HR GIGER, 100 × 150 cm.
Courtesy of www.HRGigerMuseum.com and www.HRGiger.com.

The Alien's head was given "a long tongue, with sharp teeth, which the Alien can flick out like an anteater," while the eyes, "too suggestive of motor-cyclist's goggles," were "replaced by a dark, semi transparent cranium."[28] Special effects wizard Carlo Rambaldi was called in to build the mechanism that animated the head. Appropriately for such an obviously phallic creature, "six stretched and shredded condoms doubled as tendons" to allow the Alien's lips to curl "to reveal vicious teeth fashioned out of polished steel," and its "jaws [were] smeared with KY jelly" before shooting.[29] Its gaunt body was molded after the six-foot, ten-and-one-half-inch-tall actor who would play the Alien, Bolaji Badejo, and given a tail six feet long.[30] Even though it proved impossible to make the Alien transparent, as Ridley Scott had desired, the creature retained its inside-out look with bones and traces of musculature evident on its surface.[31]

As the final phase of the Alien life cycle, the Alien Cocoon is "a stage through which a victim of [the adult Alien] passes before he himself becomes an egg." Giger also developed two kinds of Cocoon: the "fresher," meaning "only partially enveloped," cocoon was built to contain the still recognizable form of actor Tom Skerritt; the "almost completely cocooned" form was made to represent the dreadful mutation of actor Harry Dean Stanton into an Alien egg.[32] These scenes were later edited from the film because, according to Ridley Scott, they slowed down the action.[33]

In 1980, Giger received a much-deserved Academy Award for Best Achievement in Special Effects as part of the *Alien* design team. Since *Alien*, however, Giger's history with the franchise has been a tumultuous one: he was not asked to work in *Aliens*, completed several creature designs for *Alien³* but was not credited properly for them, and was left uncredited in the theatrical release of *Alien Resurrection*.[34]

Giger's influence on Hollywood science fiction and horror did not end with the *Alien* series. In 1986, the artist worked on *Poltergeist II: The Other Side*. In 1995, he designed the beautiful and fierce hybrid female "Sil" for *Species* and *Species II*. His design for the Alien and the spaces it inhabits have become canonical for science fiction-horror, as dozens of copies and even parodies attest. The influence of Giger's vision can easily be located in such diverse films as John Carpenter's *The Thing* (1982), the monolithic Schwarzenegger vehicle *Predator* (1987), and the big bug film *Mimic* (1997), not to mention the many *Alien* rip-offs that immediately followed *Alien*, such as *Galaxina* (1980), *Contamination* (1980), *Galaxy of Terror* (1981), and *Return of the Aliens: The Deadly Spawn* (1983), to name a very few. It is safe to say that, since 1979, every alien must come to terms with Giger's Alien.

Working Girls and Body Snatchers

> Elizabeth: Where are they coming from?
> Nancy: Outer space?
> Jack: They're not coming from outer space.
> Nancy: Why not, Jack?
> Jack: They're not coming from outer space, Nancy.
> Nancy: Why?
> Jack: What are you talking about, a space flower?
> Nancy: Why not a space flower? Why do we always expect metal ships?
> Jack: I've never expected metal ships.
>
> —*Invasion of the Body Snatchers*
> (1978)

Alien opens in the dark, foreboding womb of deep space. The camera pans over the body of an enormous ringed planet as the word A L I E N slowly builds in pieces, like a puzzle or code. Drawing upon *2001: A Space Odyssey*, the eeriness of the setting reminds us that space is an unfathomable place where extraterrestrial life awaits to envelope the human in its terrible embrace. On cue, the image dissolves to reveal the massive spaceship *Nostromo*, a commercial towing vehicle on its way to Earth. The ship's round interiors constitute another feminine structure, a comfortable womb that insulates its human crew from the dangers of outer space. Scott's camera explores the *Nostromo*'s claustrophobic maze-like corridors and spherical rooms as if searching aimlessly for something. Pausing briefly here and there for us to take in the surroundings, it finally stops before an unmanned station on the bridge. A computer screen turns on, and we see some incomprehensible commands flash across a screen and reflect in the faceplate of a lifeless space helmet: the ship, it seems, is running on autopilot without human assistance at all. The camera then moves to another corridor, the tube-shaped lights blink on, and a door lifts to disclose a more spacious circular room, impeccably white, with seven white cryo-tubes arranged in a circle. The cryo-tubes' lids rise in unison, giving the impression of a bird lifting its wings to let its brood out. The soundtrack trills in wonder. Like babies in their cribs, the *Nostromo*'s seven crew members sleep peacefully. The first human to awake—a thin, pallid, white male—is slow to rise, and after gaining his bearings, leaves the others behind to wake on their own.

The image of the individual human slowly moving through the silent ship is, however, quickly replaced by a lively scene where the full crew eats at a table in the ship's mess. In jarring contrast to their peaceful, deathlike repose in the sleeping chamber, the crew members at breakfast are loud, unruly, and very much alive. The viewer, confronted with overlapping and mostly indiscernible dialogue, is left to identify characters by image and body language alone. Two of the crew members are female. One is black. They drink coffee, smoke, shovel food into their mouths as they argue good-naturedly, and laugh. One drinks milk. An orange tabby laps from a bowl next to one of the women. Overall, the scene denotes a carnality that underscores the openness of the body.[35]

In contrast to the disciplined bodies of the astronauts and military men that usually populate science-fiction films, the *Nostromo*'s crew are all dressed differently, and no one style of dress dominates. We get the impression that this is an informal, ragtag bunch with a relaxed attitude toward regulation or hierarchy; as the film progresses, their attitudes and attire will degrade even further. Sure enough, the apparent camaraderie suggested by the joint meal begins to show a sign of wear as the black chief engineer, Parker (Yaphet Kotto), stereotypically the loudest of the bunch, wants to discuss the "bonus situation" with cool Captain Dallas (Tom Skerritt).

Their exchange is interrupted by the dapper science officer, Ash (Ian Holm), who, like a dutiful son, relays to Dallas that "Mother"—the Nostromo's central computer, MU/TH/UR 6000—is calling him. When Dallas—after flipping a requisite number of secret switches—enters the chamber dedicated solely to the computer, he experiences a peaceful envelopment, for Mother's round, creamy room, softly illuminated by hundreds of tiny white lights, emulates a temple of worship.[36] Dallas seats himself in the rotating chair that turns toward one of the several blank computer screens. "What's the story Mother?" he types. Dallas's unusually phrased question (especially to communicate with a computer) carries the weight of unwitting prophecy: she will, in fact, spin him quite a tale.

Tensions rise as the crew members on the bridge learn that they are not in their home system (Sol), and they begin to stake out their emotional territories. The women immediately get catty with each other in a way that suggests that both are efficient and strong-willed but do not think highly of the other's ability to read the future equivalent of a map. Dallas returns from his commune with Mother. The story is, apparently, that Mother has interrupted their journey because "she" has intercepted a systematized transmission that they have to investigate. Dallas's use of the feminine pronoun indicates the level of emotional investment the crew has in the computer. After all, Mother has their lives in her figurative hands every time they enter the cryo-tubes.

Parker wants nothing to do with investigating a signal from an unknown origin. He just wants to "go home and party" or be paid for the extra work. Executive Officer Kane (John Hurt) and Ash begin to explain why they cannot afford to do that, but the chief engineer speaks over them. Raising his voice, Dallas asks him to listen to Ash cite the Company regulation that requires them to investigate or suffer the penalty of not being paid at all. That Captain Dallas defers to the science officer shows that he agrees all Company orders must be followed and establishes the justification for Ash's later influence on his decisions. The quick appeal to money as the main motivator tips off the audience to the dystopic nature of *Alien*'s future and life under the Company: Parker threatens to not work unless he receives more money, and Ash retaliates by threatening him with the loss of money he has already earned. No one bothers to couch the mission in "humanitarian" terms. The effect of this particular scene is to present Parker as a self-serving egotist, even as he points out the inequitable bonus system, which favors the white-collar workers on upper decks of the ship, rather than to show Dallas, Kane, and Ash as being willing to play the heroes simply because they have the luxury (privilege, money, and power) to do so.[37]

When the *Nostromo* lands rather inelegantly on the alien planet, it catches fire and, we learn from Parker over the intercom, suffers some significant damage. They are, at least for the moment, marooned. Parker and Engineering Technician Brett (Harry Dean Stanton), no doubt still incensed by the bonus situation, are passive aggressive, claiming they need more time for the repairs than they really think necessary. Warrant Officer Ripley (Sigourney Weaver)—showing her rank on the ship for the first time—tells them to "get started" and that she will "be right down." Brett and Parker clearly do not want her anywhere near them or their working space. "She'd better stay the fuck out of my way," warns Brett, while Parker derides her ability to fix anything. Ripley, a woman and an officer whose place is "above" on the bridge, is breaking both a class and gender barrier by coming into the masculine space the engineers have created for themselves in the bowels of the ship.

The engineers' anxiety about this transgression of boundaries carries over to the next scene, which opens with a close-up of the worried Navigator Lambert (Veronica Cartwright) silently, slowly smoking a cigarette on the bridge. She is looking out at the howling gale outside, a hostile environment barely contained by the *Nostromo*'s shell. Ash, Kane, and Dallas, on the other hand, are all about risk and exploration. Rather than waiting for the repairs or trying to decipher the beacon's message—or assisting with either, as Ripley does—the men check the planet's climate on the ship's readout and consider the possibility of actually trying to walk to the beacon. Kane, the gung-ho explorer type, volunteers to be on the "first team to go out" (assuming there will be more), and Dallas decides to go as well. They do not even wait for daybreak to get on their way. Dragging the unwilling Lambert along with them seems, in this context, a cruelty: just as they ignore Parker's "equity problem," they discount the woman's poorly veiled fear. Ash, who is monitoring their progress from an observation bay, cutely waves at them with the fingers of both hands as they trudge away through the predawn storm.

Back on the lower decks, a gender battle takes place as Ripley, Parker, and Brett yell at each other through unbridled blowing steam. Parker asks Ripley questions and then pretends not to hear her, so that she finally gets fed up and tells him to "fuck off" and turns to go back to the bridge. As she leaves, Parker chants, "Hey, Ripley, come back here, heyooouu . . ." Once she is gone, Parker turns a valve and the steam dies down. Brett laughs at their clever prank, but Parker seems upset at Ripley's departure. He angrily exclaims, "Son of a bitch," revealing that his macho posturing partly comes from attraction to Ripley, an attraction he can only express through antagonism because, as Judith Newton observes, Parker is "black and working class."[38] Apparently, race and class distinctions are operating in full twentieth-century mode in this future.

The harshness of the alien world assaults the three astronauts as they stumble through howling winds and swirling, frozen precipitation, neither of which can be turned off like the howling steam on the ship. Obviously not thrilled to be part of the scout party, Lambert takes every opportunity to complain, emulating Parker's passive-aggressive attitude, albeit in a feminine way: when told by Kane to "stop griping," for example, she snaps back, "I like griping." Once again, the apparent dichotomy between above and below (white collar/blue collar) is superseded (and obscured) by a "minority" voice that expresses similar distrust of the motives and actions of the white, male professionals. The viewer can tell that Dallas, in particular, often wishes those Other voices would, as he tells Parker, "just shut up and listen to *the man*" (our emphasis). Soon it will be time for Ripley to join the dissenting voices.

When dawn arrives—signaled primarily by a calming of the winds—the landscape is revealed as a forbidding assembly of skeletal rock formations. The stillness is underscored by the discordant, eerie music and the astronauts' amplified heartbeats and heavy breathing. The party spots an uncanny construction: asymmetrical, nonutilitarian, counterintuitive, its enigmatic shape juts out of the landscape in

32

the form of a crescent. Intimidated by its bizarreness, Lambert whines, "Let's get out of here," but Kane opposes her in a strangely adamant voice, "We've come this far. We must go on. We have to go on." Kane's expression of the inexplicable necessity to keep trudging ever onward expresses a pessimistic, anti–*Star Trek* sentiment: an "unboldly going" where no man has gone before.

As the explorers get closer to the peculiar structure, their connection to the safety of the ship becomes even more tenuous: their video and audio feeds begin to break up, and all the audience hears are snippets of conversation and broken images filtered through static. Their minuscule figures are barely distinguishable as they approach three orifices in the center near ground level. A closer shot reveals these to be enormous vaginal openings, making the imagination reel at the structure's colossal size. The explorers climb some rocks and enter through one of the openings.

The astronauts approach the vaginal openings to the alien craft.

The overall impression is that the party has penetrated the body of a gigantic female, whose alienness is represented by its enormous size and the multiplication of sexual organs that write large the absent phallus that marks the Other. The symbolic multiplication of the vaginal orifice also indicates the massiveness of the maternal power contained therein. And just as the multiple hands of the Hindu goddess Kali hold symbols of both her destructive and generative powers, the three orifices of the alien ship represent death and new life.[39] For the mother-destroyer is the image of both life and death, and thereby represents the individual passage into and out of the world. However, from an Occidental, Judeo-Christian perspective based on "God the Father" (who is the originator of all), the dichotomy of a goddess like Kali is usually read simply as a destructive (horrific) figure and thereby loses its positive generative function. What the astronauts enter in *Alien*, then, is the body of what Creed has termed the monstrous-feminine.

We see the difference between the two ships immediately: in contrast to the white interiors of the *Nostromo*, the dark, visceral passage in the alien structure looks primeval. Like a massive grotto, the dark walls seem both constructed and yet strangely organic as shapes reminiscent of bones (and not the panels, wires, and switches of the *Nostromo*) evoke a monstrous rib cage. The grotesque, cavernous, confusing interior of the alien structure connects the monstrous female body with the labyrinth, a simple amplification of the mother-destroyer symbolism, as the labyrinth similarly represents the womb we all navigate on entering this world and the tomb that serves as our entrance into the mysteries of death and the afterlife. As befits its dual function of womb and tomb, the labyrinth is the container of the hidden treasure (the boon) and the guardian monster or demon who remains lost in its convoluted design (as in the legend of the Minotaur). Only the true hero can successfully navigate the labyrinth, destroy (or liberate) the monster, gain his boon, and be reborn.[40]

The ribbed passage leads to a large chamber, where the astronauts find a gigantic, desiccated extraterrestrial, the Space Jockey, whose command chair has become its sepulcher.[41] The chamber in which this colossus lies combines the imagery of the fetus in the womb and of an ancient tomb, imparting a sense of the "curse of the mummy" to the astronauts' incursion. Dallas discovers that the Space Jockey's chest has a rupture—something seemingly pushed its way out of the giant's body—but Kane, who has wandered off, does not see this prefiguration of his own death. Lambert, unnerved at the sight, suggests yet again that they get out of the derelict ship, but now Dallas is distracted by Kane's drive to exploration. The executive officer has discovered a hole about an arm's breadth wide that seems to have been burned in the deck and doggedly thinks it, too, must be investigated.

It is clear by now that the signal intercepted by the Nostromo was not human, but, as in all science fiction-horror crossovers, nothing can stop the inevitable meeting with the monstrous alien. Accordingly, just as Ripley discovers that the unidentified signal *could* be a warning and wonders whether she should go alert the team (Ash rebukes her with an irrational "What's the point?"), Kane descends on a winch into a cavernous space of staggering dimensions. Littering the floor are thousands of large, ovoid shapes. Kane takes a few careful steps over a narrow wall, one tiny man facing thousands of podlike structures (what he calls "eggs or something") in a horrific inversion of human reproduction, where millions of sperm seek out the one ovum. A blue film, giving the impression of a protective layer like a placental wall, covers the eggs near him. Unable to balance himself, Kane falls through the barrier. Again following his impulse to "go on," apparently at whatever cost to himself or others, Kane flashes a light at one of the eggs and detects "organic life" inside it. Like an inquisitive child who has not yet learned the maxim "Look, don't touch," he slowly extends one gloved hand toward the egg, and as his fingers approach the tip, the egg hisses sharply, as if releasing pressure, and opens. Kane leans over and stares in at a fleshy, pink mass inside. In rapid sequence, a long coiled tentacle suddenly springs toward the camera, followed by a crablike creature whose inner member lashes at the viewer. The explorer falls back with the creature attached to his helmet.

Kane has finally found what he was looking for: he has made first contact with an alien life-form, although it did not turn out as he might have hoped. But his exploration has a deeper meaning, for his transgressive actions—investigating the interior of the monstrous female body, looking into the uterus-shaped eggs with a distinctly vaginal opening—point to his encounter with the Alien as an enactment of the primal scene, to which he is a party as well as a witness.[42] Through the first-person camera work, the audience is implicated in

Kane's transgression as well: the viewer partakes of Kane's excited and terrified gaze, only to be punished by becoming the victim of a fleshly flowerlike explosion, reminiscent of the blossoming pods of the 1978 *Invasion of the Body Snatchers*.

The audience does not see how Lambert and Dallas retrieve Kane, nor is it privy to their reaction to his submission by the Alien, but one can imagine Dallas's revulsion and Lambert's high-pitched scream, echoing the finale of *Body Snatchers*. What the viewer does get to see is that after the long walk back with the burden of Kane's body, Dallas and Lambert betray not exhaustion, but thinly veiled hysteria. They demand that Ripley open the hatch, but Ripley will not allow the party back in. The rules, she reminds them, call for twenty-four-hour decontamination (presumably after any encounter with an alien life-form). Quite simply, one does not survive long by breaking the basic rules of survival in space, as Ripley's firm "No" reminds the audience. What happens next is precisely what such rules try to prevent.

After nervously stalking about for a moment, Ash opens the hatch. The audience, like Kane, has been the victim of an assault, and it cannot help but feel for the man, though what horror has been visited upon him is still unclear. Even though the viewer knows that letting the party bring Kane's body onto the ship is unwise (this is, after all, partly a horror movie), it still feels like the right thing to do simply because it seems the most humane action, based, not on quarantine laws, but on solidarity. Compared to Ash, Ripley comes off as callous, as she ignores Lambert's panicked request to open the door, and obdurate, as she does not follow Dallas's direct order to let the party in immediately.

Once Ash removes Kane's helmet in the *Nostromo*'s medlab, we get to see the creature that attacked Kane in detail. Its main body resembles two melded oversized hands with crablike fingers. Sacs hanging from each side of the main body rhythmically inflate and deflate. Covering Kane's face completely, the Facehugger suppresses (or erases) his voice and face and renders him immobile. The overall image is dramatic and repulsive: blanketed in the monstrous flesh, Kane no longer looks human at all.

A scan reveals that the Facehugger has inserted a member down Kane's throat, completing a representation of fellatio, since its "hands" are holding Kane's head to force its appendage deep inside his body. Cowriter Dan O'Bannon, who (years later) termed the image "homosexual oral rape," contends that he created it to "make the men in the audience cross their legs." The action of "crossing one's legs," of course, is a gesture of protecting the penis and testicles that, in turn, points to the Alien assault as castration: Kane is being made "not a man."

The Facehugger's physiology and the effect of its attack also suggest that Kane is under the attack of the monstrous-maternal: a mobile placenta, its underside member acts like an umbilical cord, keeping Kane alive, but in a state of coma. The horror of Kane's situation stems partly from being reduced to a powerless baby: the Facehugger breathes for him, keeps him alive and "asleep," and covers him with its blanket of flesh. Kane has thus regressed to an earlier stage of sexual organization where his body is inseparable from the mother's body: he has been enwombed.[43] This juxtaposition of both masculine and feminine imagery in the body and actions of the Facehugger indicates its transgressive, and thereby horrific, "alien" nature. As a combination of both the masculine and the feminine in one body, the Facehugger is a monstrously embodied sex act: its very existence challenges human notions of biology, sex, and gender.

As always, Parker voices the commonsense question many viewers are asking themselves: Why don't Dallas and Ash freeze Kane? But Captain Dallas ignores the chief engineer and forgoes common sense, for he wants the Facehugger removed from Kane's face right away and readily accepts "full responsibility" for a procedure that could be fatal. Death—for Dallas, at least—is preferable to *this*. Dallas's hysterical response to the Facehugger is understandable, faced as he is with this assault on individuality, the male sex, and ultimately the human species. However, the fact that the cause of his excessive reaction is the emasculation of the male (Kane) links his conduct to the original meaning of the word *hysteria* (literally, "womb-sickness").[44] He is not simply behaving emotionally "like a woman," but his apprehension is caused by a creature that within human experience could best be described as uterine.

The Facehugger has no intention of letting its catch go. When Ash pulls one of the its crablike legs, it reacts by tightening its prehensile tail about Kane's throat. When, at Dallas's prompting, Ash tries to cut a phalange off, the Facehugger spews acid blood that burns through the ship's decks, threatening to breach the hull and kill the entire crew. As Parker astutely observes, the Facehugger has "one hell of a defense mechanism," and so all attempts to remove it from Kane's face stop. At this point, the audience understands that Lambert's fear was right, Ripley's caution was right, and Parker's advice is right— they should freeze Kane for the return trip. Dallas, however, leaves the decision to Ash.

Ripley, on the other hand, is not content to leave Kane in the hands of the science officer, so she goes back to the medlab to get some answers. Her actions once there (asking questions, trying to look at Ash's work and in his microscope) are portrayed as highly transgressive, even though she has every right to inquire why Ash disobeyed her command decision and broke the Science Division's basic quarantine law. Ash becomes agitated, defensive, and inarticulate, babbling excuses like "I forgot." He finally tries a bit of aggression so that Ripley will back off: "You do your job, and let me do mine," he tells her between gritted teeth. Once again, Ripley has seriously unnerved a male crew member by invading his domain and questioning his authority. And although the Facehugger on Kane's face proves that Ripley is right in her caution, compared to Captain Dallas she still seems overzealous. What in a man is appropriate, in a woman is transgressive.

Then, miraculously, the Facehugger is gone. As Dallas, Ripley, and Ash carefully search the medlab for the creature, it falls on Ripley from above, and she yelps in surprise. Suddenly Dallas turns into the gallant protecting the frightened woman, although Ripley has done nothing particularly feminine. He yells at Ash to "cover the goddamned thing," again revealing a hysterical reaction to the Facehugger, which he is masking by "protecting" Ripley. His disgust and horror at the creature's reappearance underscore the nature of its assault: the very sight of its upturned body with the undersides exposed is intolerable. Like the vagina, like the unprepared corpse, the Facehugger is an organ/ism that must be concealed from public view. The Facehugger is thus contextualized as an abject body, an offensive sight in both form and function.

Ash, it seems, takes Dallas's command as something other than a serious order and, rather, pokes its undersides like a boy who has discovered a dead turtle on the road. Its claws close, and Dallas moves forward as Ripley recoils. Ash sighs and, like a beleaguered parent explaining something to little children, tells them that the Facehugger's movement is just a reflex action—it is dead. Ash takes it to his worktable, where we note (with some surprise) that the phallic protuberance it had inserted down Kane's throat seems to have disappeared. On the contrary, the Facehugger's undersides have a fleshy, organic, obviously vaginal appearance, for, as Scott has explained, it was constructed by the film's special effects crew out of shellfish.[45] Ash's poking and prodding into what clearly stands for a vagina, then, mirrors the human intrusion into the derelict ship and Kane's own penetration. The Facehugger's passive state and vaginal look reinforce Ash's hasty declaration of death: the phallic acts, the vaginal (castrated) merely reacts.

Ash's "scientific" conclusion is questioned, however, by Ripley, who understands that the Alien physiology could transgress easy, dichotomous descriptions based on "normal" human anatomy and behavior. Accordingly, when Ash states the necessity to keep the Facehugger, Ripley blurts out, "Are you kidding? This thing bled acid. Who knows what it's gonna do when it's dead." Ash, however, has made an argument Dallas will buy: the Facehugger cannot threaten masculinity anymore, so the captain grudgingly allows Ash to keep it. When the bewildered Ripley tries to make him change his mind, Dallas tells her he cannot meddle with the science officer's decisions (even though he outranks him). Ripley, now truly flabbergasted, asks, "Since when is that standard procedure?" Dallas's answer carries the weight of foreshadowing: standard procedure is whatever the Company tells them to do, which in this case is letting Ash decide the fate of the dead Facehugger. When it comes to Ash, that which claims the right of science, particularly in the name of profit, is the final authority. Ripley, who has all along been following standard procedure, discovers not only that Dallas will make arbitrary decisions based on his personal feelings, but that he will apparently follow any order the Company gives them, even if it threatens their very lives.

For the moment, the narrative seems to support both Ash and Dallas as humane, intelligent authorities. Their actions, no matter how arbitrary and poorly thought out as they were at the time, bear fruit: Kane wakes up and appears none the worse for wear. The assault on the primacy of the masculine body seems concluded, and the corresponding rupture in the male narrative caused by Ripley, Parker, and Lambert is, for the moment, sealed.

Opening the Body

> Giving birth: the height of bloodshed and life, scorching moment of hesitation (between inside and outside, ego and other, life and death), horror and beauty, sexuality and the blunt negation of the sexual.
> —Julia Kristeva, *The Powers of Horror*

> Once the abdomen is ripped open, how can Humpty Dumpty ever be put right again?
> —Harvey Greenberg, "Reimagining the Gargoyle"

Kane wakes up confused and feeling terrible. Dallas cautiously refers to "the planet" to test what Kane remembers about the Alien attack, but Kane does not remember anything about the alien ship or the Facehugger, and the crew does not mention them either. When Ripley asks Kane what he does remember, he tells them he dreamed of "smothering." Playing on the meaning of *other* and *mother*, Kane's definition of his experience confirms the encounter with the Alien as a m/otherly embrace that overwhelms and suffocates the individual, but also leaves room for more radical readings based on the concept of Otherness. The Facehugger's aggressive sexual subjugation and transformation of the male body, for instance, could be interpreted as a type of sexual disciplining, an S&M Othering, that forcibly disciplines the male body into a new type of sexual being.

Kane dispels the uncomfortable mood—no one knows what to say—by brushing away his nightmare and asking where they are. When he learns the crew was planning to go back to hypersleep, he demands to have one last meal—he is starving. Happy to put the incident behind them, they all sit down together to chow down large helpings of what appears to be spaghetti. True to form, the crew members, acting as if nothing of consequence has happened to Kane, chatter around the table as they stuff their laughing faces with food. Parker jokes as usual, this time disgusting Lambert with a barely discernible cunnilingus reference that serves at least two functions in the scene. First, it expresses a defensive reaction formation to Kane's penetration by the Facehugger, as it replicates in word (oral sex) what the Alien apparently did to Kane's body. Kane and Dallas, it seems, are not the only crew members traumatized by the Alien. Second, it exposes the openness of the human body, but deflects that openness onto the female body. At the very moment that Kane's unexpected recovery should restore our faith in the closed body, *Alien* supplies us with a jolly, grotesque scene where the sanctity of bodily boundaries is questioned in both act and word.[46]

As if on cue, Kane starts choking. Parker, thinking his banter has made Kane cough, laughs at him briefly before becoming anxious: the repressed fear of penetration and feminization barely veiled by his joke is about to be made manifest. Kane stands, then falls over the table, convulsing. His crewmates hold him down, Kane's body replacing the meal on the table. Blood suddenly splatters the front of his white T-shirt. Everything pauses. And, in the long silence that follows, horror builds as everyone stares at this unreadable event. What has happened to Kane's body that something could try and push its way out? Kane begins thrashing again, and then the same spot erupts violently, sending a jet of blood onto Lambert's face. The Chestburster—a phallic little beastie with metal teeth—emerges erect from Kane's chest, still covered in blood and other viscous liquids. The table has been remade into an altar of sacrifice, and the male body has given way to the dark child.

Parker is the first to react: he grabs a knife, clearly intending to kill the little abomination, but Ash, fascinated by the Chestburster, stops him. After screeching at the congregation of stunned humans, the creature explosively skitters its way out of the room with its tail madly flailing about, giving the impression of an erection on the loose, the very image of adolescent male nightmare trauma: an erection that is not only painful and evidences a will of its own, but that escapes the body to rampage, rape, and kill.[47] The emasculated corpse is left behind like a husk.

Here is where *Alien* is a radical text, for, as Amy Taubin noticed, the Alien species disregards the sexual difference that is so essential to our definition of what it is to be human.[48] The male body is repositioned to correspond to the female body: the male mouth becomes the vagina, his chest the womb. The dichotomy male/female is broken down, as all humanity is female (a womb) in the face of the Alien.

Horror arises at the sight of the male body ripped open, taken apart, dismantled. To deny the ruptured body, the crew wraps up Kane's corpse like a mummy before ejecting it into space. No one has a word to say: Kane's cadaver as discarded womb is simply too horrific for words. What can one *say* when a feral scream of horror is the only response? Kane's corpse reminds the *Nostromo* crew that exploring space and interacting with the Other is not safe: what happened to him could happen to them, to all of humanity.

Gone but not forgotten, Kane's body symbolically meets the Alien again in Dallas's plan to force the creature into an airlock and then release it out into space. That outer space is both the resting place for the dead and the trash heap for vermin—an all-purpose void—

The "little-dick-with-teeth" is born.

underscores the abject state of Kane's body. The crew desires to expel both the corpse and the Alien from the body of the ship like the human body expels feces.[49] The Alien, however, will turn out to be quite resistant to expulsion.

The crew puts together some basic equipment to help catch the creature. Brett supplies some shock sticks similar to cattle prods and a net to trap it, and Ash supplies a motion detector to find it. They divide into two groups. As Parker, Brett, and Ripley search the dark corridors of the lower decks with flashlights, the motion detector picks up and loses a movement signal. It finally fixes on a locker. The three clump together nervously, get the net ready, and throw open the door . . . only to be scared crazy (along with the audience) by the terrified, hissing Jones, the cat, whose open maw in extreme close-up mirrors the Chestburster's defiant birth screams. Jones escapes, and Brett is sent to find him.

Now firmly in the clutches of a horror movie, the viewer follows Brett as he moves from room to room calling "Here kitty, kitty, kitty." This part of the *Nostromo* resembles the dark, industrial interior of the alien derelict spacecraft, the mood suggesting that the *Nostromo* is infected (rotten on the inside) just like Kane was infected: it has become the dark mother or, alternatively, the archetypal Terrible Place—the woods, the basement, the abandoned warehouse—of the slasher, where the Killer inevitably lurks. Tension builds. The cavernous space fills almost imperceptibly with the sound of a heartbeat. Brett finds the nervous Jones in some type of vehicle. The cat springs. We see something like skin fall, and the cat skitters through two massive doors into the next cargo area. Brett stops for a second to examine the skin on the floor. He seems to understand it indicates the Alien is growing, but nevertheless continues to follow Jones.

Dark, heavy chains sway in the air, their light rattling intermingled with the sound of water falling from above (apparently from condensation). This image, likely picked up from the rattling chains of gothic horror, is later iterated in the horror film, particularly in such body-horror fetish films as those of the *Hellraiser* film series (originating in 1987), where the chains, under the direction of demons, herald not just death but the loss of both body and soul. Brett stands in falling droplets and looks up, allowing the water to drip on his face, and becoming suddenly extremely vulnerable, with his eyes filled with water and his neck exposed. He is the perfect victim. The audience waits for the Alien to strike or for the water to turn into its acid blood, burning Brett's face.

Jones's meow, however, disrupts the scene, and Brett goes to where he is hiding. As he gently entices the cat to come to him, Jones recoils, once again hissing and baring his teeth. Behind Brett a dark hooklike tail that mimics the dangling chains suddenly unfolds, and the Alien descends, spiderlike, from above. Jones growls again, making Brett realize in true horror fashion that something creepy is behind him. He straightens suddenly and, wide-eyed, turns around to witness the dreadful Alien inexplicably grown to gigantic proportions. We get a glimpse of its elongated gray-black aspic head and its vaguely humanoid form. Its mouth opens, revealing two sets of sharp metallic teeth streaming with saliva. Its interlocking jaw (what looks like a toothed, rigid phallic tongue) snaps out and strikes Brett violently in the head, portraying the Alien as animalistic and primitive in its use of the mouth and teeth as primary weapons, and alluding both to the phallus and the vagina dentata simultaneously. The camera films Jones's attentive but unconcerned face in close-up as Brett screams, and the Alien hauls him up and away, making the cat seem maliciously in league with the Alien. And why not? A domesticated predator, the cat makes a logical stand-in for the Alien, operating both as a visual mirror of the creature and as an expression of the Company's desire to "domesticate" the predatorial Alien. The fact that Scott has visually connected Ripley with the cat throughout the film (at the opening breakfast, Ripley pets Jones while she drinks her coffee, and during their forced stay on the planet she falls asleep with the cat on her lap) creates a context for seeing Ripley as a site of fear as well.[50]

Truly scared, Parker reports to the rest of the crew that the Alien is now as big as a man. "Kane's son," murmurs Ash at the news, causing Dallas and Ripley to wince in distaste. Ash's allusion to the biblical Cain plumbs the mythology of the monstrous offspring of men—the "sons of Cain," like *Beowulf*'s man-eating monster Grendel—who were born outside the laws of God the Father and were thereby monstrous in their appetites and appearance. Ash's reference matters, for the crew is not dealing with an infant Alien anymore, but with a full-bodied monstrosity—a hard-core porn version of a vampire whose double jaws drip KY jelly—that has stepped right out of the nightmare of myth onto the deck of the *Nostromo*. Like Dracula, who kills the crew of the schooner *Demeter* one by one as they journey to England, the Alien has become a deadly stowaway.[51] Once unleashed, it lurks in the shadows, unfurling itself to attack those that cross its way. Now, there can be no doubt: the ship is no longer a safe place.

Following Ash's suggestion, Parker arms a couple of flamethrowers in hopes that the creature may fear fire. Dallas, doggedly insisting on his one plan of spacing the Alien, suggests going into the air shafts where it has hidden itself, blocking all exits to trap the Alien into an air lock. Perhaps because he feels responsible for Kane's and Brett's deaths, Dallas decides to go into the shafts himself. The labyrinth will be his test, and he will either triumph and be reborn or die at the hands of the creature.

Crouched down, bent almost double in the oppressive small space, and holding both a flashlight and a fully charged flamethrower, Dallas seems already lost in the darkness of the air shafts. Tension rises as he orders the metallic iris-shaped hatches closed behind him one after another, effectively locking him in with the beast. At each junction shafts extend up and down and in each of the cardinal directions. The inspiration for the layout of these tunnels may be based on one of H. R. Giger's installations entitled "The Passage Temple" and described in *H. R. Giger's Necronomicon*. Essentially a four-sided room with one entrance/exit—the "passage of all becoming, or dissolution"—the Passage Temple simulates the symbolic functions of the labyrinth in that the other three axes of the interior represent birth, death, and the Magician, "the path which must be taken to attain man's most desirable goal and become on a level with God."[52] That Scott would draw upon Giger's own understanding of life as a labyrinth seems even more likely if one considers that the air shaft junctures feature an unusual shape similar to an image that fascinated Giger himself: the rear opening of a German-made trash truck, which resembles nothing so much as a vaginal opening into which the garbage men dump the overflowing cans of trash.[53] This detail, however minor it may seem, reinforces not only the visual influence of Giger's work on the look of the film but also the thematic importance of the evil ur-mother (the filthy, gaping womb that is filled with garbage) to the overall meaning of *Alien*.

Lambert, who has been tracking Dallas's movements on the motion detector, picks up another signal in the junction near him. He surveys the claustrophobic space with the flashlight, scanning first one way and then another, but no Alien. Unnerved, he asks Lambert if he can continue right as she picks up the signal from the Alien again—this time coming toward Dallas. She screams through the radio to him, "Get out of there!" Hurriedly descending one level, Dallas shines his flashlight behind him in time to illuminate the waiting Alien, who unfolds itself from the tunnel, hissing as it flings open its arms for a vampiric embrace.

Dallas fails the test of the labyrinth, just as he failed the test of leadership by allowing Kane to put them all in danger, by bringing in a noxious alien species onboard the *Nostromo* without taking minimum precautions, and by going after the creature himself. His disappearance, like Kane's death, radically alters the traditional male narrative, for now the film is both deprived of the primacy of the white, male body and divested of its cool American hero.

Body Doubles

> One, a robot may not injure a human being, or, through inaction, allow a human being to come to harm. Two, a robot must obey the orders given it by human beings except where such orders would conflict with the First Law. And three, a robot must protect its own existence as long as such protection does not conflict with the First or Second Laws.
>
> —Isaac Asimov, Laws of Robotics from *I, Robot*

With Dallas and Kane gone, Ripley has a rough time convincing the rest of the crew that she is in charge, even though she is now the ranking officer on the *Nostromo*. While the frantic Lambert insists that they take their chances on the *Nostromo*'s shuttle (which, Ripley reminds her, is not designed for four passengers), Parker, angry and scared, keeps interrupting Ripley's arguments for continuing with the captain's plan. Only when Ripley yells at him to shut up does Parker grudgingly accept her authority.

Ash, however, is still a problem, and he is clearly not happy with Ripley's newfound authority. When she asks him what he and Mother have come up with to defeat the Alien, the science officer is reticent, and with his back to her, responds that they are "still collating."

Ripley, now deeply suspicious of Ash, accesses Mother (after a notable failure to get any response from the computer at all) and asks the computer to explain the science officer's inability to help the crew neutralize the Alien. At first, Mother proves unhelpful, and the viewer is reminded that every one of Dallas's queries to the computer before he braved the shafts in search of the Alien was answered with "Does not compute." When questioned further, however, Mother reveals that the Company has given Ash a special order:

Nostromo rerouted to new coordinates. Investigate life form. Gather specimen. Priority one ensure return of organism for analysis. All other considerations secondary. Crew expendable.

Mother's stunning revelation quite abruptly changes the narrative arc of the film from a bug-eyed monster movie to a conspiracy thriller. Ash is a traitor: all along, he has been working against his crewmates. Even worse, the seemingly benevolent Company that ordered Mother to investigate a possible SOS signal, giving the impression that it prioritizes the rescue of lives over its commercial goals, is a ruthless profiteering corporation that does not care about human lives. What is more, Ash is apparently a suicidal minion of the Company, as he too is a member of the *Nostromo*'s "expendable" crew.

Confronted with the fact that Ripley knows his dirty little secret, Ash reacts like a psycho killer. A single drop of ejaculate-like fluid descending from his temple tips the audience that he is undergoing some sinister transformation. He then violently assaults Ripley, ripping a clump of hair from her head. On the floor, Ripley hurriedly moves on all fours, trying to get out of Ash's reach, but he grabs her by the back of her flight suit and, with superhuman strength, throws her against a wall, and after that over a seat. He blinks rapidly and then, as if getting the idea from the hodgepodge of pinup pictures on the wall in front of him, grabs a porn magazine, methodically rolls it up, and shoves it into Ripley's mouth, apparently attempting to suffocate her. His assault mimics the Facehugger's invasive aggression, though this time what is smothering the victim is pornography. Ash's attack is thus coded as a rape, with the added significance of the implied violence against women commonly associated with pornographic material.

Ash goes into a violent paroxysm as he continues to force the magazine down Ripley's throat. Thankfully, Parker and Lambert arrive on the scene. Parker tries to pull Ash's hand back to save Ripley, but Ash easily fends off the larger man with one hand. Parker then grabs a canister and hits the science officer on the neck. Ash goes berserk, thrashing around the room, spewing a whitish liquid, and emitting a high-pitched squealing sound, proclaiming his alienness, as do the extraterrestrials in *Invasion of the Body Snatchers*. Taken aback, Parker hits Ash again, decapitating him. Ash falls and stops moving. His fallen, open body squirting white fluid clearly indicates that he is not human. The audience wonders, could this be another form of the Alien that has replaced the science officer? Parker, blinking hard, solves the mystery by proclaiming, "Ash is a goddamned robot!" He tries to take a closer look at Ash's prostrate body, but it attacks him, its head horribly flapping on its back and white fluid flowing from its neck. Finally, the horrified, weeping Lambert transfixes Ash with one of the shock sticks, putting him out of commission.

Cast violently out of the robotic closet, Ash's behavior is suddenly and irrevocably contextualized in terms of inhuman transgression: as a "goddamned robot," Ash would be capable of anything. This fear of the robot derives from specific cultural concerns about the nature of the subject in a capitalistic, technocratic society. That Ash is also specifically an android intensifies those fears, as the android is not simply a machine, but a machine that passes for the human. As a technology, the android represents the fear that machines in a posthuman world will eventually replace humans. Psychologically, the android represents the possibility that humans (particularly the working class and bourgeoisie) will be (or have already been) turned into machines, that we will be "programmed" to work, make money, shop, make babies, shop, retire on cue, all without complaining. These fears of the robot, of course, are as old as science fiction itself (or much older, if we consider the mythical figure of the Golem), and in science-fiction film they have been superbly articulated by Fritz Lang's *Metropolis* (1927).

As an android, the fact that Ash was constructed and programmed by the Company defines him as a tool of capitalism and suggests the fear that the Company has a similar view of its employees as tools and not persons. The Company does not care about the lives of the crew, it only cares about attaining the creature.

The status of the android as a being created, defined, controlled, and deprived of power (castrated) by the patriarchy marks the android as feminized. In Ash's case, this feminization is represented by his grotesque, exposed, open body—a disgusting mass of white fluid and spaghetti-like entrails festooned with clear grape-sized nodules. Parker's revulsion at Ash's body suggests it not only represents the corruption of the Company, but also Parker's—and therefore the crew's—own potential feminization at the hands of the Company and the Alien. For, as Donna J. Haraway writes in *Simians, Cyborgs, and Women*, "to be feminized means to be made extremely vulnerable; able to be disassembled, reassembled, exploited as a reserve labor force; seen less as workers than as servers."[54]

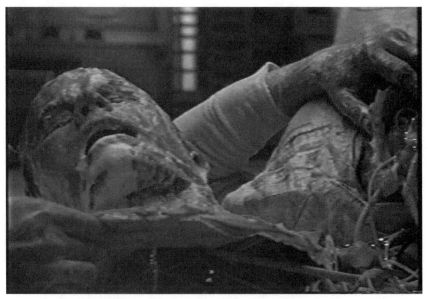

The grotesque simulacrum: Ash's secret self laid bare.

As a feminized male-gendered creation, the android represents a perverse sexuality: a "third sex." Although Ash is gendered male (having the outward appearance and behavior of a human male), he cannot be properly described as having a "sex" at all. Even if he does have a penis and testes, they are not real biological organs and serve no real biological function. His "sex" would serve a performative function only, allowing him to pass as a normal male in tight quarters. (A cut scene had Ripley asking Lambert if she had sex with Ash. Ripley's question implies both her suspicion that Ash is not what he seems and that his secrecy might somehow be related to sex: if Lambert had slept with Ash, she would know more about him in more ways than one.)[55] Ash's attack on Ripley—which Scott called "the closest thing to seeing a robot have sex"[56]—belies his castrated nature, his "lack": like Norman Bates in *Psycho*, Ash must use a substitute phallus to subdue the female. In this context, the fear of the android might be read as a metaphor for homophobia and opens the door for a queer reading of Ash as a villainous homosexual.

As she fiddles with Ash's wiring, Ripley hypothesizes that the Company wants the creature for its "weapons division." An ideal melding of humanoid and machine, the biomechanoid Alien is, as the reanimated Ash describes, a "perfect organism" with no "conscience, remorse, or delusions of morality." The android's avowed admiration of the Alien is based on its opposition to the less perfect human species. The Alien, like the robot, surpasses the human body and also the moral and ethical imperative by which humanity attempts to define itself. The Alien represents not only what Ash would desire to be, but also the ultimate expression of the corporate body of the Company—a well-oiled, amoral machine of flesh with a wonderful defense mechanism to ensure its survival and proliferation.

With a smirk, Ash expresses his deepest sympathies to the three crew members. Fed up with his derision, Ripley responds by deciding to blow up the *Nostromo*. Parker lingers behind a moment, then vents his rage by burning Ash's remains with the flamethrower, in a fitting symbolic gesture to the Company's multilayered betrayal. However, Scott's film never mentions the guilt of the Company again. Instead, it displaces the Company's malevolence on the searing image of the traitorous Ash, the violence of the Alien, and the lethal indifference of Mother, while letting the real villain remain inscrutable and intangibly distant, little more than a word, like God.

Following Lambert's suggestion, the three plan to leave in the shuttle *Narcissus*. Ripley sends Parker and Lambert to gather coolant for the air support system while she preps the shuttle from the bridge. Once there, Ripley hears Jones's cry, finds him, and puts him in his cage. Below, the situation turns grim. As Lambert gathers coolant, she catches sight of the Alien and is horror-struck. Focused entirely on Lambert, the Alien performs an odd, slow-motion dance of death. Parker, unable to use his flamethrower because Lambert is in the line of fire, goes cowboy and charges at it. The Alien dispatches him quickly, as he has done with all the men. In the case of Lambert, it takes its time, moving slowly. Its tail gradually ensnares her leg and moves upward, suggesting penetration. The audience does not get to watch what it actually does to her, but the sounds of Lambert hyperventilating broadcast over the intercom are strongly reminiscent of the grunts and heavy breathing occurring during sex, turning her death into a perverse rape-murder.

Like a true hero, Ripley not only runs toward Parker's and Lambert's screams, she also has the presence of mind to keep to the plan of destroying the *Nostromo* even after seeing the slaughtered bodies of her crewmates. Although it takes precious minutes that she could use to escape in the shuttle, she activates the autodestruct sequence. Mother announces that the ship will explode in ten minutes. Ripley makes for the shuttle, but her way is blocked by the Alien. Terrified, she leaves Jones's carrier on the floor and runs away. The Alien examines Jones with apparent curiosity, yet spares him, strengthening the connection between the Alien and Jones that has led some viewers to believe that the Alien will now somehow be "in the cat."

Clearly not suicidal or foolhardy, Ripley attempts to shut off the autodestruct mechanism to allow herself the time to find another way to circumvent the Alien. Mother, however, has no mercy, and the countdown continues. Ripley vainly tries to reason with the computer, then goes into a rage, screaming, "You bitch!" and slamming her flamethrower against the computer interface. This angry line, which may be amusing in the context of *Alien*, as we know that Mother is not sentient, will be appropriated in all seriousness by *Aliens* director James Cameron to blame another mother for all the death and destruction in his narrative, and, retrospectively, for the death and destruction in *Alien* as well.

Ripley runs back to the *Narcissus*, this time apparently ready to face the Alien, but it is gone. We must wonder: Where is the Alien now? She picks up Jones's cage, gets in the *Narcissus*, and blasts off, in true Hollywood style, with barely enough time to get away. Three enormous explosions mark the end of the *Nostromo*, the destruction of Mother, and, so it seems, the Alien nightmare.

"Kill Me": From the Cutting-Room Floor

We pause here to discuss a scene that did not make the final version of *Alien*, though, ironically, the sequels allude to it more than any other. In this scene, Ripley finds the Alien's nest while running from the Alien during the previously discussed sequences. In the nest, Dallas and Brett are immobilized and in the process of becoming Alien eggs: Brett is almost completely morphed, but Dallas is still half human and alive. He repeatedly begs Ripley to kill him, which she does with her flamethrower. From the scene, then, viewers could extrapolate that the Alien kidnaps its victims and entombs them so that they will become like it (in its egg form). The elimination of the Cocoon scene leaves the fate of Brett and Dallas open, and so it is not strange that some viewers expected Dallas to show up at the very end to save Ripley.

Although the Cocoon scene was not released as part of *Alien*, all three sequels to the film have drawn upon its dramatic impact. *Aliens* borrows the idea of the nest and cocoons, but ascribes them to an Alien Queen. It also draws on it for both Ripley's nightmare sequence, where she begs the nurses to kill her, and a traumatic scene in which a cocooned female colonist infected with a Chestburster likewise asks the rescuing Marines to kill her before she gives birth to it. The suggestion that the Alien incorporates the DNA of its victim-hosts (from the morphing of Dallas's and Brett's bodies)[57] will be taken up in *Alien³*, where an impregnated dog gives birth to a canine Alien. Also in *Alien³*, Ripley begs to be killed to prevent the birth of the Alien Queen inside her. Finally, in *Alien Resurrection*, a grotesque Ripley clone begs her "perfect" counterpart to kill her in order to end her wretched existence as the scientists' forgotten specimen.

The Cocoon scene was reinserted for the theatrical release of *Alien: The Director's Cut* (2003), though its running length was cut almost in half.

Undressed to Kill

> You are my lucky star. . . .
> —Burlesque dancer Dixie Evans doing
> her "Marilyn" routine

Having saved the cat, blown up the ship, and escaped the Alien, Ripley begins to undress slowly in preparation for hypersleep. We are suddenly, and bluntly, reminded of her sex. The sweaty, grimy-fingered, hard-jawed astronaut fighting her way to the shuttle gives way to the supple, creamy female body beneath. The scene is highly voyeuristic, highly sexual, and obviously written for an actress, in contradiction to the assertion by producer David Giler that Ripley's "sex change" had just been a matter of changing *he* to *she* in the script. Twenty-four years later, film critic Pete Croatto would still remember this as "Sigourney Weaver's famous underwear shot, which probably launched millions of now middle-aged men straight into puberty and beyond."[58]

The camera follows Ripley around the interior of the shuttle as she manipulates controls, generously showing parts of her back and legs as well as her erect nipples under her white undershirt. Her white panties seem several sizes too small for her, and, as she leans forward, we can see the upper part of her buttocks. At first, this seems simply what Ros Jennings has called a "token if somewhat blatant" objectification of the female body for the viewing pleasure of the male audience.[59] But as she proceeds with the routine preparations for hypersleep, Ripley is surprised by the sudden drop of a black claw from a niche in the wall where the Alien has stowed itself. The tone of the scene changes: now Ripley is seminaked and being threatened with bodily violation.

Ripley retreats into the archetypal space reserved for the slasher heroine: a closet.[60] Once inside, close-up crotch shots are interposed with the Alien's extending toothed jaw. Scott's camera literally probes toward Ripley's vagina, as if the director were a little boy sneakily lying on the floor looking up a woman's skirts. Harvey R. Greenberg's description of the scene reprises its almost pornographic feel:

Unlike the blinding speed of its earlier assaults, [the Alien] moves slowly, languorously. It stretches its phallic head out, as if preening. Ripley, her horrified gaze fixed hypnotically upon it, retreats stealthily into the equipment locker. It extends a ramrod tongue, tipped with hinged teeth from which drips luminescent slime (KY jelly!), and hisses voluptuously. The very air is charged with the palpable threat of rape—and worse.[61]

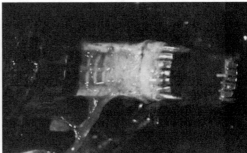

Ripley pants as the Alien's phallic jaw extends.

In fact, the whole sequence illustrates what Andrea Dworkin has called "the male erotic trinity" found in pornography: sex, violence, and death.[62] Several elements specifically reference the "hard-core" film: for example, the threat of violence and rape, and shots filmed with a hand-held camera in extreme close-up focusing on the face, vagina, and phallus, all to which Scott will add a soundtrack featuring panting and climactic screams a bit later.[63] Admittedly, Scott is not making a pornographic film, but a slasher hybrid, and slashers require the combination of eroticism and death. However, Scott's take on the vulnerability of the Final Girl walks the fine line.

Writing in 1998, David Thomson explains that the inherent voyeurism of the scene places the audience in the same position as that of the monstrous Alien:

There were observations in 1979 that the movie's stirring tribute to a woman's courage and effectiveness still reduced the lead actress to the level of a voyeur's delight—and guys do remember this scene. Sigourney Weaver was nothing short of awesome, and her underwear was spotless white, no matter the trying time Ripley had had. Still, her disrobing subtly supports the menace of more to come: she is staked out for us, and for story—and so there grows an inescapable conclusion, that we and the monster are watching her together. Is there glue hanging from our lascivious gaze?[64]

The desire expressed by the camera's gaze is exposed as perverse when the Alien, its voyeuristic evil twin, reveals itself and the camera swoops in for the crotch shots in the closet paired with the extending jaws of the Alien. The male viewers may not be able to identify clearly with the monster, but their dark desires have been identified by it.

Ripley's sex is hidden once again as she puts on an oversized, snow-white spacesuit. Wisely, she arms herself with a miniature harpoon gun (most likely an emergency tether device): the White Knight is ready to take on the Black Beast. She slowly exits the closet and sits down at one of the shuttle's stations, fastens her seat belt, and gets ready to flush out the Alien, all the while repeating feverishly "You are my lucky star . . . lucky, lucky, lucky." The Alien, bothered by her maneuvers, approaches her from one side. As in the case of the Alien's attack on Lambert, the soundtrack (especially taken alone) helps re-create the scene as a sexual encounter: Ripley pants heavily inside her spacesuit, her eyes half closed in what could be interpreted as either terror or ecstasy with very little stretching of the imagination. She turns around to see the Alien's salivating jaws ready for the strike, lets out a piercing scream, and whacks the red button that opens the shuttle hatch.

The great expanse of space is revealed through the open port, and the Alien flies out—only to grab the doorway. Ripley shoots the Alien with the harpoon, casting it across the threshold. She closes the hatch, but the gun slips from her hand and gets trapped, suspending the Alien as if from an umbilical cord (as tethers in space are sometimes called). Ripley quickly ignites the shuttle's thrusters, and the cleansing fire blasts the Alien back into the darkness of outer space.

Safe at last, Ripley dutifully records the last log entry for the *Nostromo* and goes to bed. We get one last glimpse of her lying in the cryo-tube, a peaceful, untouched Sleeping Beauty.

The Outer Limits

> *Star Wars* was the Beatles and we were
> The Rolling Stones.
> —David Giler, Coproducer of *Alien*

As the first film in what would become a high-profile film series, *Alien* set the direction of the *Alien* universe. Subsequent writers and directors attempting to build an *Alien* narrative would have to come to terms with four driving themes of the original film: a dystopic, technocratic future; the attack on the rational humanist subject from both within and without; the use of the word *Alien* to describe a predatory, extraterrestrial species; and a strong female protagonist with little tolerance for the boy's club double-talk.

The Dystopic Future

Alien is like a *Star Trek* episode gone horribly wrong: a less than congenial crew hauls corporate mining facilities around the cosmos for money, gratefully sleeps through most of it, and sees exploration (even when it means possibly rescuing other humans) as a distasteful "duty" at best and at worst a waste of their time and money. The captain is lackadaisical, the engineers are crude and passive aggressive, and the women are obstinate. Their supercomputer does not even talk. Without any real characterization, the entire crew of the ill-fated *Nostromo* seems like so many "ensign-expendables" destined to die before the end of the episode.

In this dystopic, technocratic future—run by at least one megacorporation so omnipresent that its employees only need to call it "the Company"—the corporate machine and its technology have dwarfed humanity, and humans have become passively dependent on both for life and death, never more so than when they lie in their cryo-tubes. The fact that the crew members of the *Nostromo* call their supercomputer "Mother" points to them as the children of technology and also explains the degradation of the relationships on board; after all, they live in a world where the closest nurturer is a virtually silent computer. The fact that one among them is an android that passes for human also points to the blurring boundary between humans and technology.

In a universe where human life is so cheapened, it makes some kind of macabre sense that the employer of the *Nostromo* crew considers their lives worth risking to obtain an extraterrestrial specimen. The dictates of the Company reduce humans to hands for flipping switches, feet to walk the surface of alien planets, and, ultimately, wombs for the Alien species; indeed, for the android Ash, humans are little more than annoying, argumentative beings who must be coddled so he can complete his mission of bringing back an Alien specimen. The fact that Ripley speculates that this specimen could be turned into some kind of weapon (a technology of destruction) underscores the insignificance of the individual human in the *Alien* future. Making war is, after all, the biggest business of them all, and war is never about the rights of the individual subject.

Given the dystopic future of *Alien*, the Alien life-form is, in a sense, assaulting a species that has already been subjugated and feminized by its own social system, and whose technology is rapidly turning it obsolete. The effect of the Alien's attack, then, is to exacerbate (to a grotesque level, no doubt) a condition that already existed. It is the externalized representation of the dehumanizing force of the Company—as a manifestation of its desire, the Alien represents the next evolutionary phase of the human, the perfect combination of man and machine conquering the galaxy without the need of cryo-tubes or remorse.

The Attack on the Rational Humanist Subject

Because the rational-humanist subject is based on the two-sex model, the Alien's attack—specifically coded as a sexual assault—subverts the biological model of humanity and thereby questions what it means to be a man and, by extension, a human being. The Alien's use of the mouth as the port of entry into the human body underscores the unspeakable openness of the body.

That *Alien* features not one meal scene, but two reminds us of the frailty of the corpus, whether it be the family unit or the individual body. Joint meals are bonding rituals between individuals who form a community. After all, one does not eat with an enemy for a reason; to do so would be to admit the similarity of both, the permeability that makes us all essentially the same. Eating is also humanity's daily collective encounter with individual openness, and the only bodily function relatively unrestrained by social performance taboos, particularly when compared to other bodily functions such as defecation, urination, menstruation, and coitus. The communal meals in *Alien* also serve as the occasion for sexual banter. The transgression of the Alien, its radical demonstration of the open body, is sublimated as an act of control: jokes about sex (specifically cunnilingus) both reference and deny the horror of the Facehugger's attack, and preface the appearance of the Chestburster.

The Term Alien and the Species It Defines

Calling the species capable of deconstructing the human simply the Alien was a master stroke. The name implies that the creature is first of all the irreconcilable foe or opposite of humanity: that which cannot be incorporated and therefore must be rejected at all cost.

The name also implies an Otherness that in the context of the film translates as a monstrous-femininity, specifically the mother-destroyer. Much of *Alien* is spent navigating the labyrinthine spaces that represent this monstrous motherhood (outer space, the alien planet, the derelict ship, the *Nostromo*). Ultimately, the passage of the labyrinth is the test of the hero: the beast destroys those who lose their way, but those who solve the intricacies of the maze and defeat the beast are reborn.

As synonymous of what is unknown or unexplored, the term *Alien* also refers to the Jungian Shadow, the darkness that the subject denies in herself. As the shadow of the human, the Alien is cruel, remorseless, and not burdened by guilt. As the shadow of the female protagonist, the Alien represents the monstrous, fetishized feminine. Although the adult Alien is presented as phallic, the creature is not a supermale but that which destroys the very notion of the male. The Alien does not, after all, have a penis and does not procreate in the human way: the primary organ of fascination on the Alien is the fetishized phallic "tongue," which impregnates (in the Facehugger form) and kills (in the adult form). Considered as a unit, the Alien is essentially the monstrous Other that is always feminine by the sheer fact that it is not Man. In the final scenes of *Alien*, then, Ripley meets not just an alien creature, but a dark physical and psychological mirror of herself: like a woman with a flamethrower, the Alien is a phallicized fetish object, a creation of the male psyche, of masculine fear and desire. Thus, the film ultimately pits the female body against her own shadow self.

The Female Protagonist

Although the Alien assaults the sexual difference on which humanity is based, the world of *Alien* is still very much gendered. Consequently, the presence of a female hero is an infiltration or transgression of the status quo that must be either repressed or authorized. The fear of the female hero, of course, is that her presence will bring more like her.

In terms of the horror narrative, Ripley is a castrated being revealed as open and vulnerable in the final scenes, but also capable of castration. Under these terms, she is equated with the monstrous-feminine and pitted against her own monstrous shadow self. The two worst fears of the patriarchy meet: the woman who does not know her place and the all-consuming maw of the creature that represents the womb-tomb. In a universe where men can be subjected to the monstrous-feminine, become pregnant, and give birth to monsters, where women can become the heroes and sole survivors, the male becomes superfluous—a soon to be outmoded form.

Although in the world of *Alien* Ripley is a Company woman, by the end of *Alien* Ripley has purposefully blown up a Company ship to ensure the Alien's demise, and her vehemence in this decision insinuates her intent to pay back the betraying Company as well. In fact, Ripley's confrontation with, and final destruction of, the Alien, the object of desire of the military-industrial complex, becomes the major theme of the film (and the series), and thereby gives voice to the contemporary feminist goal of saving humanity from the destructive impulses of patriarchy.

In the final say, Ripley is not a radical feminist or even a political feminist, she is not a collectivist or a Marxist (she tells Parker to shut up with the rest), she does not burn her bra (though she does not wear one) or speak out about the abuses of the patriarchy. What Ripley does, however, is question laziness, random decisions made from a self-centered autocracy, corporate technocratic capitalism, sexism, subversion, covert operations, and warmongering. She hates nonsense and likes cats. Ripley may not have been a feminist hero, but she was a hero for potential feminists.

CHAPTER 2

Ripley Gets Her Gun:
Aliens and the Reagan Era Hero

I have my veto pen drawn and ready for
any tax increase that Congress might even
think of sending up. And I have only one
thing to say to the tax increasers. Go
ahead—make my day.

> —Ronald Reagan, to the American
> Business Conference, quoting "Dirty
> Harry" Callahan in *Sudden Impact*
> (1983)

Rewriting Ripley:
From Sci-Fi Horror to Action Adventure

By far the most popular film of the Alien franchise, *Aliens*
(1986) continues the transgenre impulse of *Alien* by capital-
izing on the burgeoning action-adventure boom of the
1980s. Blood, gore, and bullets riddled the screen as studios cashed
in on sequels that were often more popular than the originals. "Dirty
Harry" Callahan finds new life in *Sudden Impact* (1983), Rocky
comes out of retirement again to fight the Soviet boxer who killed

62

Apollo Creed in the ring (*Rocky IV*, 1985), and Colonel James Braddock (*Missing in Action*, 1984) and Rambo (*Rambo: First Blood, Part 2*, 1985) go back to Vietnam to rescue MIAs and fight a corrupt system with as many explosions as possible. And what the heck: Ronald Reagan was in the White House. Suddenly everything was a war—the war on drugs, on poverty, on pornography, to name a few—and the war business was good in both Washington, D.C., and Hollywood. Harvey R. Greenberg, writing of *Aliens* in 1988, explained the driving force behind the new national sentiment:

> Jimmy Carter was swept from office; the economy cycled into a semblance of recovery. Ronald Reagan was reelected as oil prices plummeted and stocks soared. The country's renascent patriotism waxed even more fervent. Inevitably, the Vietnam debacle was re-viewed through our reawakened pride and conservatism. Today, it is widely suggested that our forces were vanquished by the fecklessness of liberals at home rather than by the skill or conviction of the Asian enemy. Official rhetoric, as well as much private discourse, now echoes with a high moral tone, with ominous appeals to American manifest destiny, informed by a simplicity verging on the decerebrate. Devil theory is frequently evoked to interpret our adversaries—abetted by a deal of devilish behavior on their part.[1]

Ridley Scott's *Alien*—that dark, sci-fi, alien-among-us, shadow-horror—was to prove the perfect basis for another genre-bending project to explore America's fears during the early Reagan years.

In the previous chapter we discussed how *Alien* uses elements from the slasher, vampire, and monster-from-outer-space films. *Aliens* operates very much in the same vein by grafting action-adventure onto science fiction and horror. The result was a very Reagan era movie, with "our boys" going into the heart of darkness to rescue civilians from the awful Aliens. Needless to say, the mix was highly popular with American audiences.

Director James Cameron was no stranger to the genres he combined in *Aliens*, especially science fiction. His first film was the science-fiction short *Xenogenesis* (1978).[2] He also worked on several science-fiction films, including *Battle Beyond the Stars* (1980; as miniature constructor, miniature designer, and additional photographer), *Escape from New York* (1981; as matte artist, special effects director of photography), the *Alien* rip-off *Galaxy of Terror* (1981; as unit director), and *Android* (1982; as design consultant). Cameron's directorial debut in a major film was with the painfully horrendous "B" movie *Piranha II: The Spawning* (1981), which he described in good humor as "the finest flying piranha film ever made."[3] His real break was as director of the blockbuster *The Terminator* (1984), which he cowrote with Gale Anne Hurd (his then wife and later *Aliens'* producer). *The Terminator*'s themes anticipate those of *Aliens*: the protagonists Sarah Connor, Kyle Reese, and their future son, John (who appears only in name in the first film), for instance, constitute the white nuclear family who fight against the foreign (computer) invasion represented by the relentless android Terminator. Sarah's role as mother of the savior of humanity identifies her fight as protecting children (her own unborn child) and thereby the future of the world. Most importantly, Cameron's choice of the same actor, Michael Biehn, to portray the heroic "nice guy" of both *The Terminator* and *Aliens* engaged the interest of the male audience of action films, who otherwise could have been put off by a female protagonist.

In the action genre, Cameron cowrote the screenplay for the box-office hit sequel to *Rambo: First Blood, Part 2*, a "gun and muscle" rescue film whose plot prefigures *Aliens*: a single human with special know-how is recruited by a sneaky bureaucratic Machiavelli (who will later betray the protagonist) to go back into enemy territory to save "our people" from "a fate worse than death" at the hands of the communist enemy. The parallels between both films did not go unnoticed by reviewers: while David Edelstein of *Rolling Stone* extols *Aliens'* Ripley for *not* being a "killing machine" like "Sly or Clint or Chuck,"[4] Harvey R. Greenberg entitled his article on *Aliens* "Fembo."[5]

Cameron wrote his follow-up to *Alien* based on Ripley, assuming that the character would be played by Sigourney Weaver, only to find that not everyone at the studio was convinced Weaver was necessary to the budding franchise. Weaver had by now starred in *The Year of Living Dangerously* (1982), *Deal of the Century* (1983), and *Ghostbusters* (1984), so her salary had to be substantially higher than what she had been paid for *Alien*. To his credit, Cameron fought to have Weaver back as Ripley.[6]

Cameron's next challenge was to reenvision a character that had already been established as a spunky, levelheaded, and resourceful female survivor. He decided to use the formula that had made a success of *Rambo*: to send Ripley back to the planet where her crew had discovered the Alien ship with the sole intention of destroying the Aliens, effectively remaking the character into a full-fledged "hero" in the traditional, conservative, American sense of the word.

Thus, if the purpose of *Alien* was to scare, the purpose of *Aliens* was to embolden, to instill the audience with the ethics of the Reagan era American hero. Rather than running from the beast, real American heroes face it, root it out, and destroy it as an act of "war." The protagonists of these conservative narratives—the disabused Vietnam veterans (who must be redeemed), the weathered cop facing an unjust system, the unprotected wife and mother—all follow a higher law, a higher moral code. Red tape is not their forte—*justice* is.

In *Hard Bodies: Hollywood Masculinity in the Reagan Era*, Susan Jeffords discusses the evolving film popularizations of the masculine "hard body" during the Reagan administration. Emanating from the "cowboy politics" of the Reagan years and bolstering public opinion in its favor, the hard-body hero became a Hollywood favorite, his lonely struggle against insurmountable odds generating sequel after sequel: three films for John J. Rambo (*First Blood*, 1982), four for Martin Riggs (*Lethal Weapon*, 1987), and three for John McClane (*Die Hard*, 1988). Following the lead of vigilante cop Harry Callahan (*Dirty Harry*, 1971), these Reagan era heroes are rugged, working-class individualists who defend the "American way of life" because they have a "higher" sense of ethics and morality than those enforced by the system.[7] With *The Terminator*, Cameron opens the door for the genre to include a female lead, even if Sarah Connor is a Reagan era hero in the making, depending on her lover/protector Kyle Reese's know-how to survive the onslaught of the Terminator for most of the film. Only much later, in *Terminator 2: Judgment Day* (1991) will Sarah possess a hard body that permits her to destroy the new, improved Terminator model bent on killing her son, John. Most interestingly, with the introduction of a female lead, the genre's narrative is modified to include the reintegration into society of the otherwise isolated male hard body (as exemplified by Rambo in *First Blood*), via the nuclear family. Later, as Jeffords explains, these hard-body heroes redeemed by the family will take over the traditional nurturing role of the mother, becoming the "super dads" of the 1990s.[8]

Fittingly, *Aliens*, as written and filmed by Cameron, begins by giving Ripley a family—a daughter we never knew she had—then stripping her of it.* Her career, too, is lost. She has traumatic flashback nightmares and apparently suffers from a futuristic version of posttraumatic stress syndrome. She is treated like a hysteric by the Company and the government. She is perched on the precipice whose long wall falls into madness and, eventually, a friendless, nameless death. Ripley's only salvation is through a commitment to the values embodied in the nuclear family, even if she cannot have such a family herself while she is busy fighting the Alien.[9]

In light of the Reagan era narratives of protecting home, hearth, and the nuclear family at all cost, the determined, career-oriented Lieutenant Ripley of *Alien* is shown to be a fake, a failed mother who in reality abandoned her young daughter to an orphan's life. For this, she is punished with horrible nightmares of the Alien bursting through her chest: a monstrous, destructive child replacing her own natural child. She becomes a shadow of her former self, "working the docks"

---

*As we discussed in "Can't Live with Them, Can't Kill Them," these scenes were cut to shorten the run time of the film. We will argue that Cameron's intent to make Ripley a mother and the maternal themes remain in the film regardless of the cuts.

because that is the only job she can get. But Ripley can be redeemed. There are more children out there, and men to be fathers. Thus, even while positing Ripley as the hard-bodied hero of the Rambo variety, *Aliens* effectively draws the New Woman back into the fold of the patriarchal structure where she will protect traditional WASP morality, the nuclear family, John Wayne masculinity, and, perhaps most importantly, the sacred cow of motherhood.

Aliens and *Aliens: Special Edition* Comparative Plot Summary

The following summary includes scenes deleted from the original cinematic release but reintegrated into *Aliens: Special Edition* (director's cut). Scenes cut for the cinematic release are indicated with brackets.

A salvage team discovers the shuttle *Narcissus* in deep space, and inside, the still hibernating bodies of Ripley (Sigourney Weaver) and the cat Jones. Ripley awakes in the infirmary of Gateway Space Station, a facility circling Earth. She is soon visited by Burke (Paul Reiser), who brings Jones with him. He informs her that she was lost in space for fifty-seven years, and the shock causes Ripley to suffer the first of a series of nightmares in which an Alien bursts from her chest. [Later, while waiting for her formal inquest, Ripley learns from Burke that her daughter, Amanda Ripley, died childless two years before.] Ripley enters her formal inquest to defend the destruction of the *Nostromo* to representatives from the Company (now identified as Weyland-Yutani), the Interstellar Commerce Commission (ICC), and "insurance guys." The panel, headed by Van Leuwen (Paul Maxwell), disbelieves her story of the Alien. [Her flight status is suspended, but criminal charges are waived in place of "psychometric probation."] When Ripley demands that Van Leuwen send people to check the planet where her crew found the Alien ship (here christened LV-426), he tells her that they do not have to check LV-426, as families of terra-formers have been on the planet unharmed for over twenty years. Ripley is understandably shaken. [Later, on LV-426, a family of wildcatters (the Jordens) is dispatched by some "head honcho" to "coordinates on a map," where they discover the derelict alien ship. The parents venture inside, leaving their two children in the salvage vehicle. The mother (Holly De Jong) returns in a panic and radios for help as her husband (Jay Benedict) lies on the ground, a Facehugger wrapped around his head.]

Burke and Lieutenant Gorman (William Hope) of the Colonial Marines visit Ripley in her small working-class apartment in an apparently rundown section of the station. They inform Ripley that communications have been lost with the colony on LV-426, "Hadley's Hope." Burke will accompany the Marines on the reconnaissance mission and would like Ripley to go along as an adviser. Additionally, the Company will reinstate her as a flight officer if she goes. She refuses, and Burke then points out the despairing state of her current life: she is clearly depressed and can only find work running loaders in the station's cargo docks. By going back she would be giving herself a second chance. He leaves his card. That night, Ripley wakes from yet another nightmare and calls Burke to tell him she will go, after confirming that their mission is "to wipe out" (not to study or bring back) the Aliens.

Aboard the Colonial Marine starship *Sulaco*, Ripley wakes from hypersleep in the company of Burke and the thirteen-member crew: Lieutenant Gorman, Bishop (Lance Henriksen), Sergeant Apone (Al Matthews), Corporal Hicks (Michael Biehn), Private Hudson (Bill Paxton), Private Vasquez (Jenette Goldstein), Private Drake (Mark Rolston), Private Frost (Ricco Ross), Private Wierzbowski (Kevin Steedman), Private Crowe (Tip Tipping), the medic Private First Class Dietrich (Cynthia Scott), and the shuttle flight crew Corporal Ferro (Collete Hiller) and Private First Class Spunkmeyer (Daniel Kash). During the meal, Ripley discovers that Bishop is a "synthetic person" after he cuts himself with a knife while demonstrating his manual dexterity at the expense of another crew member. Reminded of the treacherous android Ash (from *Alien*), Ripley demands that Bishop stay away from her. At the briefing, Ripley begins to break down while describing the Alien. The enlisted soldiers are dismissive of the mission, calling it a "bug hunt," and Ripley loses her temper. Afterwards, Ripley gains the respect of Apone and Hicks by helping load the landing craft using a heavy powerloader, a skill she learned while working the cargo docks on Gateway Station.

The entire crew of the *Sulaco* boards the lander (called the "Bug Stomper") and drop to the planet surface. [On the way down, Hudson regales Ripley with an impromptu list of how their "badass" weaponry makes them the "ultimate badasses."] The colony is apparently deserted, and the Marines enter the main colony complex to search for survivors while Gorman, Burke, Ripley, and Bishop wait in the armored personnel carrier (APC). Inside they find evidence of a battle as well as the telltale acid burn marks left by Alien blood. The complex is apparently empty, so the rest of the team enters.

In the laboratory, they find Facehuggers in storage tanks. Two are still alive, and one tries to attack Burke through the glass. Bishop begins to review the lab records while the team searches the rest of the complex. They soon detect movement on their motion sensors and almost shoot a little girl, Rebecca Jordan, or "Newt" (Carrie Henn), who has been hiding in the complex's ventilation shafts. Following the signals from the colonists' implanted locators, the Marines (all but Bishop, who stays behind) take the APC and enter the processing station. Gorman, Burke, Ripley, and Newt watch as the squad penetrates the center of the power plant. As they near the locator signals, they encounter Alien-looking, biomechanical modifications to the decks and walls.

In the APC, Ripley warns Gorman that the Marines' armor-piercing rounds could cause a thermonuclear explosion if they hit the station's cooling tower. After Burke confirms her fear, Gorman orders Apone to collect magazines; however, Vasquez and Drake secretly reload, and Hicks pulls a shotgun from his pack. The Marines discover dead and unconscious colonists along the walls encased in semiclear, weblike constructions. One of the colonists hatches a Chestburster, and the Marines burn it (and the colonist) with a flamethrower. The Aliens then attack, and several Marines are killed (some by "friendly fire"), while Gorman ineffectually calls for a cease-fire and tries to organize the group. Faced with Gorman's loss of control after the loss of Apone, Ripley tells the Marines to retreat and barrels the APC down into the processing station to save them. Of the squad, only Hicks, Vasquez, and Hudson survive the attack. Gorman is hit on the head by a canister and knocked unconscious as Ripley forcefully drives the APC out of the station, stripping its transmission in the process. They abandon the APC and call the lander for pickup. However, the flight crew, Spunkmeyer and Ferro, are killed by an Alien that had secreted itself aboard. The lander crashes into the APC (forcing the survivors to make a run for it) and then into the processing station.

The survivors salvage what they can from the wreckage and return to the main complex, where they survey their remaining equipment and barricade as many entrances as they can, protecting each of the two most obvious corridors with two pairs of armed robot sentries. Meanwhile, Ripley takes Newt to the infirmary for a nap. Before the girl goes to sleep, they have an earnest talk about the reality of monsters. [Ripley tells Newt about her daughter.] To assuage Newt's fears, Ripley gives the girl a wrist locator given to her earlier by Hicks. Back in the lab, Ripley and Bishop hypothesize about the nature of the Aliens. Hudson suggests that the Aliens must be like ants, with "one female that runs the whole show." Ripley then discovers from Bishop that Burke is trying to take the two Facehuggers back and, after checking the colony's records, that Burke sent the order to investigate the coordinates of the derelict Alien ship. Ripley confronts Burke with these facts, and he tries to bribe her. Indignant, she turns down the offer, promising to turn him in when they get back to Earth.

[The Aliens attack in the tunnel connecting the processing plant with the main complex in such numbers that one of the robot sentries exhausts its rounds. The Aliens, however, are stopped at the pressure door.] To add hardship to misery, Bishop discovers that the processing plant was damaged and will self-destruct in four hours. He volunteers to navigate a small tunnel to the satellite dish in order to bring the second lander down from the *Sulaco* by remote control. [The Aliens attack from a different corridor and are barely stopped by the two other robot sentries.] Hicks then teaches Ripley to handle a pulse rifle/grenade launcher, after which she returns to the infirmary to find that Newt has fallen asleep under the bunk, so she lies down with her. Ripley wakes to discover the specimen tubes containing the live Facehuggers have been turned over. Her weapon is gone, and the door is locked. Ripley uses a lighter to set off the fire alarm, thus drawing the attention of the Marines, who shoot through the safety glass just in time to save Ripley and Newt from the Facehuggers. Ripley confronts Burke and tells the Marines that he planned to smuggle the Aliens back by infecting her and Newt and that he probably would have sabotaged the Marines' cryo-tubes to avoid witnesses.

Just as Hicks pulls Burke up from his chair, ready to "waste" him, the power suddenly goes out. Hudson and Vasquez go out to check the perimeter and, using the motion sensors, find that the Aliens are inside the complex in spite of the barricades being intact. Everyone goes back to the operations center, and Vasquez welds the door shut. When the motion sensors indicate that the Aliens are still approaching, however, Hicks checks the ceiling and finds that they are approaching through a crawl space. Hicks begins shooting, and the Aliens drop through the ceiling and attack. Burke exits through a back door and locks it behind him, trapping everyone else inside with the Aliens. He is attacked by an Alien as he tries to escape. Vasquez manages to open the door, and they pass through; Hudson, however, is killed as he holds up the rear.

Following Newt's direction, they enter the ventilation shafts, trying to get to the landing pad. Vasquez, who is in the rear, is severely burned on the leg when she shoots an Alien at point-blank range with a pistol. Gorman returns to save her, but they are surrounded and sacrifice themselves by exploding a grenade as the Aliens close in. The concussive blast barrels down the air shaft, causing Newt to fall through a ventilation fan to a lower level. She is captured by the Aliens as Ripley and Hicks try to save her. Ripley and Hicks then make a run for the lander. As they enter, an Alien tries to wedge through the closing door, and Hicks shoots it in the head, accidentally splattering acid over his face, chest, and arms. Hicks is incapacitated from the pain.

Ripley decides to rescue Newt using her locator and commands Bishop to drop her off at the processing plant and wait. Armed with a pulse rifle/grenade launcher combo and a flamethrower taped together, Ripley infiltrates the nest and saves the ensnared Newt just before the girl is attacked by a Facehugger. On the way back, they take a wrong turn and wind up in the nest's hatchery, surrounded by eggs and facing the massive, towering Alien Queen. Ripley threatens the eggs with the flamethrower, and the Alien Queen calls off her looming Warrior Aliens. Ripley then torches the eggs, shoots the Warriors and the burning eggs, and shoots grenades into the Alien Queen's ovipositor. She runs with Newt as the Alien Queen pursues in a rage. Ripley and Newt board the lander and escape just before the complex blows.

Back on the *Sulaco*, the Alien Queen, who secreted herself in the landing gear housing, impales Bishop with her barbed tail and rips him in half. As the Alien Queen pursues Newt, Ripley climbs into a powerloader and attacks. While they fight, Ripley opens a massive air lock and attempts to throw the Queen in; both, however, fall. As Ripley attempts to climb out, the Queen grabs her foot. Ripley then opens the outer door, consigning the Alien Queen to the depths of space, and barely manages to close the door before she, Newt, and Bishop are pulled out. As the ship heads home, the four survivors enter hypersleep.

Rewriting Ripley:
The *Aliens* Threat and Reagan Era Politics

> What we need is Star Peace and not Star Wars.
>
> —Mikhail S. Gorbachev, Soviet premier, to the Indian Parliament, New Delhi, November 28, 1986

Cast in the fairy-tale tradition of "Snow White and the Seven Dwarfs" and "Sleeping Beauty," the opening of *Aliens* focuses on the beautiful,

unconscious figure of Ripley nestled quietly in the safety of her cryo-
tube. What will happen to this woman now? Left with the female protagonist from *Alien*, we can imagine writer-director James Cameron
asking precisely the same question as he set out to outline the *Aliens*
plot. Cameron's background in science fiction and action left him with
understandably little experience in writing for a female protagonist,
and his early work with horror would not help, since the slasher's
running and screaming Final Girl was de rigueur. His *Terminator*, for
example, features a cute waitress as the future mother of mankind's
savior against the machine who spends the majority of the film being
dragged around by her lover/protector to save her from the cyborg
Terminator. Even though Sarah Connor (Linda Hamilton) finally figures out how to destroy the cyborg—by accident—it would be inappropriate to compare her character to *Alien*'s Lieutenant Ripley.
Ripley was in no need of rescuing. The biggest challenge to Cameron's skills, therefore, was deciding what to do with this female hero
from *Alien* who did not even have a first name.

Cameron tackled the problem of what to do with Ripley as one of
"motivation."[10] Ripley will "go back" like a Vietnam War veteran
returning to the terrain of terror, however unwillingly. But unlike Colonel Braddock and Rambo, Ripley is a woman, and women, especially
in the Reagan years, just did not pick up guns, grenades, and missile
launchers and start blowing things to hell. Not without a real reason—
and that reason had to be different from a man's, since women in
action films rarely are the originators of the action. In fact, before
Alien there were only a few authorized reasons for a woman to enter
willingly into danger, and all usually depended on the woman's position as a past, present, or, as in the case of Cameron's own *Terminator*,
future mother. Of course, the most obvious and enduring reason for
women to spring into action is the unchecked threat to children, husband, and family when all male authority has failed. This is the basis
for Cameron's Ripley and the end result even in the cinematic release.
However, as we will see, another covert, less authorized, motive for
Ripley's actions slips through as well. Following the intrusive body
narrative of *Alien*, *Aliens* opens the possibility that Ripley's motivation

is not simply facing her inner demons, but rather avenging a rape, albeit a symbolic one.

The film's establishing shots place the story within the science-fiction patriarchal tradition: we watch as the frozen crystalline structure of Ripley's shuttle is engulfed by a larger ship in a shot clearly reminiscent of the Empire ship's engulfment of Princess Leia's spaceship in *Star Wars*. Dominated and incorporated into the masculine sphere, the smaller female space is penetrated by force (a laser cuts through the door in both cases). A robotic arm enters like a gigantic amnio-needle—or, worse, abortion forceps—searching the interior for signs of life. Satisfied that the shuttle is clear of contagion, the robotic arm moves back, and the humans move in, wearing suits to protect them. Clearly, this is alien territory. Ripley is revealed as one rescuer clears the ice away from her cryo-tube. She is young and beautiful, although we later learn she has been asleep for fifty-seven years. A man's voice expresses both surprise and disappointment, perhaps even derision, as he says, "Bio-readouts are all in the green. Looks like she is alive." The apparent leader of the group removes his mask, and says, "Well, there goes our salvage, guys," revealing that Ripley is no princess, and the pursuit of happiness in *Aliens* is the pursuit of capital. Already, and once again, Ripley has found herself in the way of male profit. The close-up of her face dissolves slowly into a view of Earth. She is finally going home . . . or is she?

We enter Gateway Space Station and its industrial infirmary reminiscent of the womb-obsessive *2001: A Space Odyssey*. Ripley's question, "Where am I?" elicits the black nurse's response, "You're safe." Cameron has begun her journey back into the fold by sending her back into the hands of the Company. Her nightmare is apparently over, and she is surrounded by the comforting sterility of the hospital that echoes the pristine white of the cryo-tube bay on the *Nostromo*.

The film then enters a dream sequence without a conventional introduction (such as a dissolve or a shot of Ripley closing her eyes). Rather, Ripley's dream is set up as a visit from Burke, a Company man who has the difficult task of informing Ripley that she has been in hypersleep for fifty-seven years. The shock seems to send Ripley into a panic, and the sound of her heartbeat dominates the soundtrack. She looks confused and sick as she presses her fingers to her sternum. Jones, who had been relaxing on the bed, suddenly hisses at Ripley and escapes to the floor. His hiss heralds the worst: an Alien is near. Ripley grabs her chest and contorts wildly, flailing about and knocking over a water glass, her IV drip, and other items. Knowing she has an Alien inside, she begs to be killed. She pulls up her gown. A dark, phallic protrusion pushes outward against the inside of her skin, distending her stomach outward.

Ripley screams, "No!" and wakes in the hospital room alone. She clutches her chest, grunting in fear and emotional pain. We do not know at what point Burke's visit ended and the nightmare began or if it all was a dream. This misdirection both heightens the horror of the nightmare sequence by adding to its verisimilitude and suggests the depth of Ripley's psychological trauma as reality and nightmare meld—this is a disturbed, unstable woman, and not the resolute, calm Ripley of *Alien*.

The subject matter of Ripley's nightmare further sets up the themes Cameron will explore in the film. First and foremost is the fear of biological motherhood. As Ripley is in a hospital, surrounded by hospital staff and instruments, her birthing scene is visually more closely tied to normal human labor than Kane's, which happens over a meal. Prefiguring the monstrous Alien Queen, this image of monstrous birth equates the anatomy of the human female with that of the Alien female.[11] The scene also draws on the symbolism of the vagina dentata, as not only do Jones's open mouth and teeth represent the Alien's castrating jaws, but they also visually stand in for Ripley's vagina as he is nestled in her crotch at the beginning of the scene. Ripley's body is a dangerous place. As her dream indicates, she hides a monstrous creature inside of her—which may be variously read as suggesting hysteria (she is subject to a womb illness and thereby dreams of birthing) or the phallic woman (she hides a lethal phallus inside). Lastly, the nightmare of monstrous birth suggests Ripley's anxiety about the fate of her own biological child, as the next scene makes clear.

The next scene has Ripley waiting in an artificial arboretum. Burke enters with the news that her daughter, Amanda, died childless two years before. The effect of this information is complex, for while it adds depth to Ripley's character and makes her a tragic figure, it also reinterprets the Ripley of *Alien* as a single (no husband is mentioned) working mother who left her child alone at home. Ripley is clearly now more concerned about her daughter than her career, as she brushes aside Burke's warnings about the meeting with "the Fed, Interstellar Commerce Commission, Colonial Commission, and insurance guys." She scans the image of the smiling old woman who was her daughter, Amanda Ripley McClaren, age sixty-six at the time of her death, two years before her rescue. Reconciliation with her daughter is not an option and Amy, as Ripley calls her, died childless. Furthermore, we learn of Ripley's broken promise to be home for her birthday. She dissolves into tears, the failed mother mourning the lost daughter. What this short scene does for Ripley's character is to rewrite her as a mother, and a bad one at that, an example of the "soft" Carter era women misled by feminists and the idea of the New Woman into a career that led directly to her failure to keep her parental promise. To this we must add the fact that her nightmares have already established Ripley as severely traumatized. The strong, confident woman who killed the Alien and saved herself is shown to be a victim of her choices. As punishment, she will be haunted by nightmarish images of rape, pregnancy, and death. This moment of personal failure is echoed in the next scene, when she is confronted with her professional failure.

Ripley's failure as warrant officer comes in the form of the faces of her dead crewmates as they appear on a screen behind her. The bureaucratic suits solidly disbelieve her story. The one female suit trusts Ripley's story the least: she is the self-serving, power-hungry professional who has abandoned her womanhood completely in favor of masculine forms of power (as well as wardrobe), and, therefore, she is the most derisive of Ripley, the working woman.[12] Chairman Van Leuwen, on the other hand, clearly believes that Ripley is unbalanced, as he later waives criminal charges in favor of a six-month psychometric evaluation. Incapable of making the impassive board members understand the danger the Aliens pose to humans, Ripley erupts in anger at their indifferent attitudes, waving and tossing aside the papers symbolizing corporate red tape. As a result of the inquest, her Interstellar Commerce Commission license as a flight pilot is revoked. We are left with a Ripley punished by the loss of both daughter and career. She is dismissed as insane, or, as David Edelstein puts it, "like the rape victim who can't convince the jury that *she* wasn't somehow to blame."[13] From now on, as a modern Cassandra, her warnings will be ignored by the authorities until it is almost too late. As the scene closes, Ripley insists that Van Leuwen send someone to check the planet, now baptized LV-426. He dismissively responds that he does not need to because some sixty or seventy families have been living on LV-426 for over twenty years, terra-forming it. The last shots show Ripley's shocked face as she digests the news: "Families . . . Jesus," she mouths, and closes her eyes, summarizing for the audience *Aliens'* most important underlining theme: the clear and present threat to the all-American nuclear family by foreign agents.[14]

Cut to Hadley's Hope, home to the families of LV-426. Children drive their big-wheeled Weyland-Yutani tricycles in restricted areas of the main complex. (A bit later, we also learn that the children regularly play in the air ducts of the station when Newt and her brother, Timmy, argue about "who's the best" at hiding in them.) Al, the beer-bellied manager, first complains about the children, then about "some honcho in a cushy office" who has ordered them to check an unexplored part of the planet. The ordinariness of the scene is discomfiting: the colonists have obviously succumbed to the illusion that they are safe in Hadley's Hope. We, on the other hand, know better: a long tradition originating in western films codes frontier towns as inherently dangerous. This is the landscape of penetration, domination, and, eventually, the shootout. Likewise, in science-fiction narratives, space colonies tend to be wild, barely tamed places where the first law is survival. As in *Star Wars*, the fringe town is where weird, outlaw species consort, many of them looking for a fight. To survive, the hero must learn to shoot, or at least get tough. The only place more dangerous than a sci-fi frontier town is the fragile ship hurling through space that got the colonists there in the first place— and they slept through most of that. In any case, space, as *Star Trek* has expounded, is the "New Frontier," and, like any frontier, it exists on the border between Us and Them.

In the next scene, Cameron introduces the "mom and pop" prospecting family, the Jordens, as they drive through the desolate landscape. When the father spots the derelict ship, he eagerly announces, "Folks, we have scored big this time." For him, the ship represents a claim, and therefore an increase in the shares he gets from the Company. His greed makes him dismiss the security measures his wife proposes; to her careful "Shouldn't we call in?" he responds, "Let's wait till we know what to call it in as," a decision that will require both parents to enter the ship. As we watch their two children wait for them in the prospecting vehicle for such a long time that Timmy, the little boy, falls asleep, we wonder what kind of parents would leave their children unprotected in such a place. Timmy wakes, and just as he comforts his sister with a bit on male savvy ("It'll be OK—Dad knows what he's doing"), the vehicle door opens, and the hysterical mother grabs the radio microphone to call in for help as the father lies on the ground, immobilized, his face covered by an Alien Facehugger. In a repeat of the original film, the Alien has assaulted a male, pointing to male adventurousness and greed as the site of trouble. In *Aliens*, however, the trouble also extends to the man's family and through them to Hadley's Hope, threatening throughout the remainder of the film to expand to Earth. For the second time in the narrative, the Alien species breaks up a family. It has become more than a predator; it has become a home wrecker, in this scene literally embracing and appropriating the father. Like a lover, most horrific in its cross-gendered nature (as a phallic placenta), it clings to his face in a fatal, and family-destroying, kiss.

As discussed in the previous chapter, this mating also destroys gendered individuality: it erases the face and feminizes the male by making him a subject of unwanted penetration and pregnancy. As

Aliens shows us later, once the male is raped and castrated, the being originating from his body will be under the control of the hive. The hive is a common science-fiction metaphor for communism, and communism is a threat that in American science-fiction film is more often than not connected with the threat of the monstrous-feminine. A film that undoubtedly inspired *Aliens*, the big-bug film *Them!* (1954), for example, features the fear of the collective in the form of mutated giant ants that seize humans to take to their nest for later consumption; as humans fight back, it becomes clear that the only way to annihilate the monstrous ants is to kill their queen. Then there is the paranoia of Senator Joseph McCarthy's "witch-hunts," as seen in *Invasion of the Body Snatchers* (1956), in which pods from outer space grow replications of humans that later replace their originals (the 1978 remake made the extraterrestrial threat explicitly feminine, as the pods blossomed and "gave birth" to the replicated humans). After *Aliens*, the Borg collective of the *Star Trek: The Next Generation* television series (1987–1994) and its film spin-off, *Star Trek: First Contact* (1996), constitutes an important example of how the fear of incorporation of free individual bodies into a collective (the television series) translates into the fear of the feminine (*First Contact*), as the meaning of the Borg's tag line, "Resistance is futile. You will be assimilated," acquired an added sexual connotation when rephrased by the attractive, if sinister, Borg Queen.

By the Reagan era, political fears in the United States had shifted from incorporation into the collective—the country had moved well beyond any real worries of a communist revolution—to elimination by the collective. Thus, Ripley gives voice to the Reagan stance on communism by constantly warning everyone that it would only take one of the Aliens getting to Earth (via LV-426) to bring about Armageddon. In this sense, the individual Aliens can be read as so many nuclear missiles let loose by the enemy to attack the American way of life. As we will see, in the true spirit of the American science-fiction film, Cameron will manage to connect his metaphor for the communist threat to one uncanny and dangerous female.

Ripley Revisited: The Forced Hero

> A woman is like a tea bag—you can't tell
> how strong she is until you put her in hot
> water.
>
> —Nancy Reagan

When the Company loses contact with LV-426 and the Colonial Marines are dispatched to investigate, Burke tries to convince Ripley to return to the planet by assuring her that the Colonial Marines are "tough hombres" who can handle anything and, according to Gorman, have "been trained to deal with situations like this." To her credit, Ripley immediately suspects that Burke's motives for going to LV-426 are other than safeguarding the colonists; when he drivels about the Company cofinancing the colony and his stake in "building better worlds," she cuts him short with a tired "Yeah, yeah, I saw the commercial." Burke then changes strategies by pointing out that all she has is a dead-end job "working the docks," meaning, literally, that Ripley runs forklifts and powerloaders at the station's cargo docks. The connotation, however, compounded with the dejected feeling of the scene and Burke's somewhat demeaning manner, is that she is, if not prostituting herself, then at least working far below her station. Indeed, Cameron's camera has already shown Gorman and Burke appraising the filthy corridor outside Ripley's apartment to establish that Ripley is becoming a cigarette-smoking, white-trash loser. Unfazed by her reluctance, Burke throws in an added bonus: if she goes, she gets her career as a flight pilot back. It is her "second chance," he says: a second chance at her career but also to die or wipe out the species entirely. Even more, it is her second chance to be *the woman she should have been.* Burke latches onto Ripley's "failure" to construct himself not as a "Company man," but as her "caseworker" who insists that she better herself.

At the same time, Burke subtly reminds Ripley that he has the power of information access: he has "seen her psyche evals" and knows about her nightmares and their subject matter. This willful disclosure of his penetrating and authorized knowledge of her most intimate, subconscious thoughts demonstrates his (and the Company's) desire to control her. Ripley may not like the fact that he brings up her evaluations, but she never questions his right to do so because Burke, unlike Ripley, has "access." *He* can see *her* files when *she* cannot. She still resists: "I said no, and I mean it," words that echo the slogan "No means no" used by activists against date rape. Her phrase has the effect of recasting Burke's pushing and pleading as forcing, especially as the subsequent scene has Ripley waking from her recurrent nightmare of the Alien bursting from her chest. Only Gorman's somewhat nervous presence dissolves the tension caused by Burke's constant quid pro quo. In the end, Burke will get his way. But why does Ripley accept the offer to go back to LV-426?

In an interview with Don Shay, Cameron explains that he conceived of a Ripley who survived the original Alien only to fixate on the "high-stress situation" of her escape and to "re-live it over and over."[15] What Cameron is describing, of course, is posttraumatic stress disorder, commonly associated with Vietnam War veterans (redefined from the "shell shock" of previous wars) and popularized through films such as *The Deer Hunter* (1978) and *First Blood*. Psychologist and *Aliens* critic Harvey R. Greenberg describes the disorder:

> Post-traumatic stress disorder [PTSD] occurs in hostages, war veterans, and other survivors of ungovernable trauma. Through some misplaced thrust toward mastery, these unfortunates are compelled to undergo eternal rehearsal of their torment both in waking and sleeping life. Innocent reality for others is for them booby-trapped with horrible signifiers: unlikely sights and sounds that trigger off unbearable flashbacks.[16]

What is telling here is the fact that Ripley's disorder, though clearly definable as a form of PTSD, cannot be relieved by medicine—even the "psychometric" assistance of the future. The film clearly posits that this type of help is ultimately useless, a common sentiment of the Reagan White House. She, like Rambo in *Rambo: First Blood, Part 2*, must "go back" and face her fears. Thus, her "emotional reason" for going back lies on getting back her sanity, or, as Cameron puts it, to get "out of the woods."[17] The "going back" plot as described by Cameron is far from new in Hollywood; many traditionally male stories such as westerns and action movies rest on a staple "forcing the hero to go back" scene that involves some form of incentive, coercion, or blackmail. Ripley's trauma and motives to "go back," though based on clear references to battle-induced PTSD, also draw upon a rape-revenge subtext (rape also being a cause of PTSD). One of the film's tag lines directly addresses this threat of rape: "There are some places in the universe you don't go alone." The accompanying poster image depicts the armed Ripley saving Newt from "a fate worse than death." In this context, Ripley's getting "out of the woods," though directly referring to her distancing herself from the traumatic nightmares and her clearly precarious psychological condition (a patient is "out of the woods" when she is no longer "critical"), also draws upon rape imagery, where "the woods" becomes the site where women have traditionally been raped. One has to look little further than the fairy tale "Little Red Riding Hood" to see what a dangerous place "the woods" can be for a woman.

In *Men, Women, and Chainsaws*, Carol J. Clover describes the staple rape-revenge film as apparently inspired by feminist definitions of rape, because it assumes that women live in a "rape culture" where rape is a social and political act for which all males are collectively responsible. Nevertheless, in rape-revenge film narratives, it is a woman's responsibility to save herself and other women from rape, and, if she cannot prevent the act of rape, to avenge the rape. Because this "most quintessentially feminine of experiences, the limit case of powerlessness and degradation," happens to soft (and therefore open) bodies, whether they be female or male—as in the case of *Deliverance* (1972), where the largest and "softest" (effeminate) of the male group is raped in the woods—to get even, a woman must transform herself

"There are some places in the universe you don't go alone":
Ripley and Newt "in the woods."

into a hard body, a tough, masculine woman, in most cases becoming as vicious as her attacker, and achieve a "calculated, lengthy, and violent revenge of the sort that would make Rambo proud."[18] In the rape-revenge film *I Spit on Your Grave* (1978), for example, the female protagonist retaliates against her four attackers by castrating one, hanging another, axing a third, and running over the last with a boat. Unlike the female protagonist of slasher films who runs right up to the end, the rape-revenge heroine (who is not always the victim herself) turns on the attackers and relentlessly pursues *them*.

The scene that follows Burke's attempted manipulation of Ripley fully reveals the rape-revenge subtext that motivates Ripley to go back to LV-426. She wakes up drenched in sweat from one of the chest-bursting nightmares, washes her face with some water, and looks at herself in the mirror—clearly a defining moment. She takes Burke's video-call card and calls him at home, although it is clearly the middle of the night. Without a hello, she demands: "Just tell me one thing, Burke. We're going out there to destroy them. Not to study, not to bring back, but *to wipe them out.*" This is clearly a call for genocide, but it is obscured by Ripley's need for closure. The audience should worry that Burke instantly agrees with her. "That's the plan," he says, looking at her with wide, seemingly innocent eyes. Ripley has a few seconds to decide whether she believes him or not, but that does not matter anymore; she must get rid of her nightmares, so she is in.

Because Ripley cannot refuse Burke's offer, the possibility that she may be violated by the Alien and abused once again by the Company becomes the background of the action. However, Ripley's nightmares already locate her as a victim of rape: betrayed by the Company, almost killed by the robot Ash, traumatized by her encounter with the Alien, marooned in time as she had been in space, unjustly deprived of her job, and cut off forever from her daughter, Ripley is, most of all, a woman raped by the system. And what is the solution *Aliens* offers for such a victim? "Get back on the horse," suggests Burke, backed by the film's clear portrayal of Ripley as flawed, if understandable, in her fear. What she needs is a chance to be a "born again" hero, to come in out of the dark night of the liberal '70s and back into the conservative fold.

Hard-Bodied Heroes

> Ginger Rogers did everything that Fred Astaire did. She just did it backwards and in high heels.
>
> —Ann Richards, in her keynote address to the Democratic National Convention, July 18, 1988

From the moment Ripley accepts the mission to LV-426, *Aliens* follows the transformation of Ripley from a soft body to a full-fledged hard-body hero. To that end, the film first introduces models and foils of the being she will become in the form of the already hardened Colonial Marines. Our impression of them begins with an exterior shot of their starship, the *Sulaco*, as it sweeps by a star system, its elongated, sleek, black-blue body echoing the very weapons the Marines will use against the Aliens. The long establishing shot of the *Sulaco*'s interior, however, reveals something amiss in this pristine, controlled environment: an unsecured locker door adorned with a girly pinup belies the contained rows of shiny guns and phallic, glossy white nukes.

The camera scans the rigid, metallic cryo-tubes perfectly lined in formation and angled up as if at attention: gone is the unified circle of sterile white tubes of *Alien*, replaced by a inflexible, authoritarian order. The first out of his tube, Apone is the stereotypical, gung-ho, cigar-smoking black NCO (a familiar figure from films such as the military love story *An Officer and a Gentleman*, 1982), while the grunts are relaxed if dismissive. This is clearly "just a job" for most of them. The sergeant espouses the military with phrases like "I love the Corps," a statement overtly referencing the Marine Corps and at the same time covertly drawing attention to the Marines' massive display of musculature (by punning on "body") as they exercise in various stages of undress. What we see on display are not natural bodies, but "techno-bodies," bodies that are a product of technique or technology (bodybuilding), that can be enhanced by formfitting machines (mostly guns, but also plated body armor, cameras, microphones, and infrared lenses), resulting in cyborg soldiers. The most obvious techno-body is that of the female gunner, Vasquez, because one cannot imagine a female body "naturally" looking as pumped up as hers.[19]

The almost narcissistic interest the soldiers have in their bodies (Vasquez obviously enjoys watching her biceps at work while she does her morning chin-ups) codes them as penetrable: their firmness of body is clearly a constructed state acquired through discipline, and their belief in the hard body's ability to protect them from harm a delusion. Because their bodies seem impenetrable, it will be horrific to see these, the hardest of national bodies, opened by the enemy. Here the codes of war and horror films clash: in a war film, the showing of bodies prefaces wounding but does not necessarily indicate the impending death for all the soldiers. Likewise, bravado—a commonplace in the war film—does not lead to punishment. In a horror film, however, a display of desirable bodies prefaces their slaughter, and the verbal banter of the characters betrays the sins for which they will be punished. The frank admiration, perhaps even envy, that some of the Marines display for Vasquez's body may signal her masculinization, but it even more significantly indicates their feminization: to admire that which is inherently open, no matter how closed and solid it may appear, is to become open.

Before boarding the transport that will take them down to LV-426, Vasquez and Drake practice moving with their weapons in a type of dance. As the scene rolls, Vasquez initiates the dance, foregrounded in the frame, her hard body rippling with the weight of her weapon. Moments later, Drake joins her, taking a stand right and farther back; Cameron's mise-en-scène is such that Vasquez seems the same size and height as the much larger Drake. While he shadows her deft movements, Drake covertly gazes over his shoulder at her, and his eyes meet the audience's on her hard body. For a moment, we are accomplices in his examination of her: we admire her firm musculature and skill, but we also look for the telltale signs of weakness, her inevitable lack.

Because all the Marines have hard bodies, the film becomes preoccupied with pinpointing masculinity and femininity through sexual banter. Eyeing Ripley, Vasquez asks Ferro (another female), "*Mira!* Who's Snow White?" Ferro belittles Ripley by referring to her as a "consultant" who apparently "saw an Alien once." Hudson (a male), who has been following the exchange, remarks sarcastically, "Whoopee-fuckin'-do! Hey, I'm impressed." By putting Ripley down, the Marines show themselves to be "macho," as opposed to Ripley, the feminine "Snow White." The exchange has the added effect of associating Hudson with the "gossipy" female soldiers who talk "man talk," but are not "real" men—a fact confirmed later when Hudson,

Phallus envy: Drake admires the tough-as-nails body of Vasquez.

who has been the biggest braggart of the bunch, is the first to lose his cool on LV-426. The women's derision of Ripley also connects them to the corporate female "suit" at the ICC inquest; these are women who have betrayed their sex to join the male circle.

During most of the locker-room scene, the camera lingers on Vasquez as an exceptional woman, "the best" of the Marines. She is already flexing her muscles while the rest struggle to get dressed. As a heavy gunner, she must always walk in front of her squad, and her expertise is taken for granted by Drake, the other gunner, who admires her cool, tough attitude. Her prowess at the chin-up bars demonstrates that she can outdo men physically—a fact that causes Hudson some anxiety, which he disguises in the form of a nasty joke: as Vasquez is doing her chin-ups, Hudson asks her if she has ever been mistaken for a man, to which she replies, coolly throwing the joke back at him: "No. Have *you?*" This verbal match tellingly reveals that in a military where women pass for men, men can become like women. It also implies that if a woman is the best of the Marines, then the rest of them must be "pussies," no matter how good the woman may be. Based on the old myth of the military weakened by the presence of women (who were even considered "bad luck" aboard planes and ships), this view regained vigor during the Reagan administration, particularly as it concerned two related topics: women in combat and gays in the military. Both concerns express worry about the castrating or submission of the male body. If women were to be in the infantry, traditional logic argues that the men would worry about them (protecting them, mourning them if they died) more than they would about other men. The otherwise tough soldier would become "soft." Furthermore, the supposed "weaknesses" of the female, such as her burdensome breasts and bras, menstruation, lack of upper body strength, lack of bladder control, and lack of emotional control, all would conspire to undermine the toughness of the men.

The worry over homosexuality in the ranks is of a similar vein: men, "real men," do not willingly place themselves in the passive positions of fellatio or anal sex, nor should they worry that one of their buddies wants to make them passive. Although in *Aliens* Cameron quickly dispels one of these fears (female lack of strength) by focusing on Vasquez's macho prowess, he simultaneously evokes two of the others: Drake, despite his machismo, seems to dote on Vasquez, despite her machismo, while Hudson is clearly overcompensating for some lack. He is, in effect, a "pussy" who masks his inherent weakness (lack of backbone) just as Vasquez and Ferro mask theirs (lack of a penis). In contrast to Vasquez's and Hudson's transgressive (bordering on comical) characterizations, Dietrich, as a medic, has a role more "appropriate" to a woman rather than an infantry soldier or combat pilot, and she behaves in a suitably reserved manner.

During the breakfast scene, the sexual banter becomes specifically masculine, and again borders on rape imagery when the sergeant describes the mission as "rescuing juicy colonists' daughters from their virginity." This type of macho bravado seems oddly out of place in this future "egalitarian" world (unless the female soldiers are lesbians). In response to this inappropriate "boys will be boys" camaraderie, the Marines will all be "raped" by the Aliens.[20] In essence, what they think is funny will stop being funny when it is done to them.

The sexual banter becomes sexual confusion when Frost (who is black) teases Hudson about getting some "Arcturian poontang,"[21] which, according to Spunkmeyer, might have been male. Frost jokingly responds that it "doesn't matter when it's Arcturian." That a black Marine begins the sex talk, as the Hispanic Vasquez did earlier by attracting attention to Ripley's body with "*Qué bonita*, huh?" typecasts minorities as sexual aggressors. (Similarly, in *Alien*, Parker's talk of cunnilingus at the dinner table disgusts Lambert.) This impression is reinforced when, a few moments later, the knife demonstration by Bishop on Hudson is coded as a rape: Drake holds Hudson's spread out hand forcibly in place underneath Bishop's, while Bishop moves the phallic knife with inhuman speed between both sets of fingers and Hudson yells wide-eyed. Bishop starts his demonstration by asking the scared, unwilling Hudson to "trust" him and ends with a soft "thank you." In spite of his apparent skill, a drop of semen-like fluid dribbles from his finger, the detritus of a minor mistake, exposing him as an android and conjuring up the specter of Ash. Like Ash's attack on Ripley, Bishop's knife demonstration echoes the Facehugger's attack. Not only is the image of Bishop's hand covering Hudson's hand reminiscent of the Facehugger's form (particularly when combined with the knife), but the nature of his performance takes on a clear sexual connotation: Hudson is forcibly held down, he is threatened with a phallic weapon, and he screams. That Bishop ends his performance with a soft "thank you" and then later sucks the dribbling white fluid that serves him as blood from his finger suggests a perverse sexuality—his finger acting as a stand-in for the penis, and the act of sucking it referencing fellatio and perhaps also autoeroticism. Like Ash, Bishop is a male-gendered "third sex," and, as Ash had already proven, members of the third sex can be aggressive.

Bishop's aggressiveness, however, is downplayed by his soft demeanor and his preference for the politically correct name "artificial person" rather than "synthetic," all of which, when combined with the knife show and Ripley's distress at learning of his robotic "nature," clearly exploits sterotypical views, and fears, of the homosexual male. Not surprisingly, he declares himself "shocked" when he learns the reasons for Ripley's robophobia, and is quick to reassure her that his "behavioral inhibitors" make him quite harmless.[22] Seemingly considerate, agreeable, and polite, Bishop typifies the accommodating android later epitomized by Commander Data of *Star Trek: The Next Generation*. However, Bishop's connection to the duplicitous Ash makes him a source of mistrust for Ripley, and the audience; so much so, that he will be brought back in *Alien³* as both his "good" self from *Aliens* and his "evil" human creator—the face behind a new Company conspiracy to obtain the Alien for itself. Moreover, no matter what Bishop says about his "behavioral inhibitors," he does actively engage in the "harming" of a human being. Not only is Hudson visibly scared by the knife show, but the potential for real harm is verified by the fact that Bishop managed to hurt himself: even though Bishop covers Hudson's hand with his own, he could just as easily have made a mistake and cut Hudson instead. There is, therefore, an undercurrent of homophobia centered on Bishop, who claims that he is incapable of allowing or causing harm to anyone when, in fact, he can. As in Scott's portrayal of the android Ash, the unnatural "lifestyle" of the robot—whether in or out of the closet—is potentially dangerous.

During the mission briefing, both the loud-mouthed Hudson and the macho Vasquez smart off: Hudson asks Gorman if the mission is "a stand-up fight" or just "another bug hunt," while Vasquez impatiently interrupts Ripley to inform her that all *she* cares to know about the Aliens is "where they are" so she can "kick ass." Their overly confident comments and disrespectful behavior confirm that the soldier's believe that Ripley is a hysterical woman with an overblown story. Blinded by their own techno-bodies and posturing nonsense, the Marines believe they can easily defeat this new enemy. Before long, the "real" men and women among them will have to bow to the truth of Ripley's words.

Such a man is Corporal Hicks: the guy is so cool, he sleeps like a baby through the drop to LV-426. In obvious contrast, Lieutenant Gorman reacts to the drop by breaking into a nervous sweat, which is explained when he confesses this is only his second combat drop. Also meant as a contrast to Hicks, Hudson counters his anxiety by bragging endlessly to Ripley about his squad being the "ultimate badasses." Interestingly, his tirade focuses almost entirely on the "state-of-the-badass-art" technology the Marines bring with them ("independently targeting particle beam phalanx, tactical smart missiles, phase-plasma pulse rifles, nukes, knives, . . ."), not on their training, intelligence, wile, or courage. Unlike John Rambo, who fights enemies almost as effectively with a stick as with a machine gun, these Marines are just cyborgs who would be (and will be) fundamentally crippled without their armor and weapons.

Although Burke and Gorman specifically asked Ripley to come to LV-426 (Burke even bullied her), once on the ground, they foolishly ignore her concerns and suggestions. Gorman, against Ripley's warnings, declares the colony's main complex secure after the briefest of reconnaissances. As they survey the medlab, Burke likewise ignores Ripley's word of caution and leans in for a close look at a Facehugger kept in a tube. The Facehugger, still very much alive, attacks the glass in an attempt to shove its phallic protuberance (and subsequently a Chestburster) down Burke's throat. Hicks jokes that the Facehugger's attempted attack "looks like love at first sight," unwittingly revealing the Alien as Burke's object of desire and hinting at the covert grotesqueness of the Company man.

Shortly after, Hicks's heroic qualities are underscored when he keeps Newt from being killed by friendly fire. Knocking Drake's gun up and out of the way as the gunner fires at a blur of movement, Hicks—who is not cocky, nervous, greedy, or perverse—sees a little girl where others see an Alien. That he calls Ripley to him seems a natural move: two heroes, a man and a woman, conspiring together to save the blond, blue-eyed, female child. Hicks even smiles.

Ripley follows the child through the ventilation ducts into the small, cluttered space where she has been hiding from the Aliens. Newt's "nest" is a collection of garbage—boxes of food, random pieces of clothing, toys, jewelry, and beads—fragments of a society destroyed like herself. Ripley forces her way in and catches her in an embrace. The girl goes limp, her eyes staring. Clearly traumatized by whatever she has seen (and only Ripley can guess at how bad it might have been), Newt is not particularly forthcoming with information about her parents. Gorman, mistaking her for a soldier or an adult in the same way that Drake mistook her for the enemy, declares her "brain locked" and talking to her "useless." He would not like her answers anyway, as Ripley soon finds out. Now in full maternal mode, Ripley feeds Newt some hot chocolate, cleans her face with a towel, and talks to the stolid little girl, complimenting her on her bravery, her survivability, her looks. Finally, she gets to the question adults in these narratives always seem obligated to ask the lone child, even when they know the answer: Where are your parents? Newt's response is angry and blunt: "They're dead, all right? Can I go now?" Mortified, Ripley tries to assure her that she is safe with the soldiers, but Newt does not think their uniforms and guns will make any difference in an encounter with the Aliens. As grumpy as Newt acts, the relationship between her and Ripley is established as a daughter/mother-surrogate pair, both survivors of the Aliens and mirrors of one another. Soon, Hicks will call Newt "Honey," and we have the basis for a family.

Because there is no sign of the colonists, Hudson tracks them using the signals from their personal data transmitters (PDTs): they are apparently huddled under one of the main cooling towers of the colony's processing plant. The squad proceeds to look for them and quickly discovers that the Aliens have changed the human environment to fit their own bodies and needs. Sublevel 3 of the plant is now a black biomechanical structure with viscous walls shaped like vertebrae, tendons, and vaginal orifices that form a vast maze-like dungeon of claustrophobic, misty caves containing an amalgamation of gooey secretions, dead Facehuggers, cocooned human hosts, and nestled Aliens.

Because the nest is also an extension of the Alien Queen's body, as Ripley will discover later, the soldiers are, in essence, entering a monstrous "womb" (as in *Alien*, a labyrinth) in which the colonists have been entombed with arms extended to allow the Chestbursters to freely come out from their bodies. During the reconnaissance, Dietrich finds a female colonist who is still alive but pleads to be killed. The Marines try to get her out of her cocoon, but she begins to convulse and dies as the Chestburster rips its way through her rib cage. Back in the APC, Ripley watches the scene live through the soldiers'

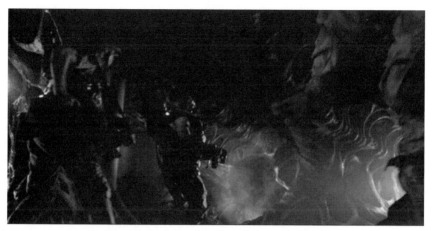

The Marines in the Alien labyrinth-body.

cameras, clutching her chest and groaning, evidently experiencing a moment of female empathy with the colonist, as if the Chestburster were forcing itself out of her body. In contrast to *Alien*, where the Chestburster trauma focuses on the male body—and in particular, Kane—Cameron clearly associates the Chestburster imagery primarily with the female body. That we never see a male "give birth" in this film refocuses the horror from the feminization of males and the desexing of the human body to the more traditional image of a female body being subjected to a violent birth.

The Marines torch the Chestburster, and the cleansing fire causes the Warrior Aliens around them to attack, exposing the soldiers as inept in the face of this enemy.[23] Hurt by Alien acid blood and helped by Hicks out of the nest, Hudson proves that a hard body does not a hero make by asserting that he "did not sign up for this." In *Hard Bodies*, Jeffords explains what the Hudson-type of hard bodies lack with an example from *Lethal Weapon*: here, the hard-body Special Forces vets turned heroin runners are defeated by the cop Riggs (who had their same military training) because Riggs has allied himself with his partner's family (which represents the Reagan focus on family values), whereas the vets are allied only temporarily until they achieve the common goal of profit.[24] In the context of "fake" and "real" hard bodies, Hudson represents the "soft" military man who has the hard body and the training but "signed up" for something other than hard combat and potential death in the name of national defense, as he reveals during one of his many whines. He is "short"—not career military and about to cycle out—and therefore feels cheated of his postmilitary life. In the end, his massive body and loud banter only hide a "computer geek" who has no backbone, no commitment to the purpose, to the nation. This anti-Rambo, who has both the body and the brains, lacks the correct focus to be a Reagan era hero, and so is fated to die. Hudson's overzealous defense during their last stand (which contrasts sharply with his earlier whining) may recuperate him as a "real man" for the audience, but nonetheless demonstrates his excessive and foolhardy nature: unlike John J. Rambo, Hudson does not know when to run.

Similarly, Lieutenant Gorman fails to be a true leader and falls apart at crucial moments during the incursion into the Alien nest. He too seems unable to handle the thought of death for one's country, and is especially troubled by the death of Sergeant Apone, who represents the true military man, following the orders of his superiors without question. But unflinching observance of the rules is not a characteristic of the Reagan era hero (and smacks of the fears of his generation: Nazism and communism). Quite the contrary, as Jeffords states of *Lethal Weapon*'s Riggs, "Like his mentors, Richard Nixon, Rambo, Dirty Harry, and Ronald Reagan, Riggs believes that breaking laws in the process of achieving a larger good—stopping drug dealers, protecting the presidency, rescuing POWs, or maintaining a contra supply route—is not only permissible but necessary."[25] Apone chooses simple obedience to authority rather than the safety of his troops, becoming a hard body that denies the wile required of a Rambo, Riggs, or Dirty Harry. He leaves the thinking, in effect, to the ineffective Gorman, who, in turn, is at the mercy of the ultimate bureaucrat, Burke. During the squad's incursion into the Alien nest, for instance, both Ripley and Burke loom over Gorman like his angel and devil, each giving advice, but Gorman trusts Burke the most, giving Apone the order to collect the soldiers' armor-piercing ammunition only after Burke confirms that Ripley's advice is right: they cannot afford to have the soldiers rupture the nuclear reactor's cooling tanks. In contrast to Apone, Vasquez and Drake show their ability to "think like a Rambo" by disobeying orders and secretly reloading their weapons, while Hicks, always prepared, like a wise little Boy Scout, pulls a shotgun from his pack. We are aware, of course, that Vasquez's and Drake's disobedience could result in the nuclear reactor exploding (information they do not have), but the explosion of the reactor would still reach the "official" desired result: the destruction of the Aliens.

As the Warrior Aliens dispatch the Marines (with a little incidental help from the female Marines),[26] Gorman sits stupefied in his command chair, incapable of giving a coherent order or making a move to save his squad. Unable to endure his indecision, Ripley takes control of the APC and proves herself to be the heroic Ripley of *Alien* by driving it to the sublevel and ramming it into the Alien nest to save whoever is left. Hicks helps Hudson into the APC, then drags Vasquez away as she is trying to save Drake, who has been seriously injured by an Alien's acid blood. As Ripley drives the APC out of the compound, an Alien gets on its roof and tries to get her through the windshield. Ripley slams the brakes, causing the Alien to fall forward, then runs over it. She then speeds away so rapidly over rough terrain that she strips the transmission, and Hicks has to tell her to "ease down." Ripley lacks the coolness of men like Hicks in the face of danger (although she clearly demonstrated such coolness right up to the end of *Alien*). Instead, she acts like a panicky female whose first impulse is to run as fast as she can.

With Gorman knocked out cold during their exit run and Apone probably dead, the survivors argue about what to do next. Vasquez wants to shoot the nest with nerve gas, but Ripley wants to make sure they get rid of all the Aliens, so she proposes to "nuke the entire site" from the *Sulaco*. Burke's opposition to her plan, based on the facility's cost, shows that he thinks the Company commands this mission, not the Marines. In response, Hicks, the archetypal unwilling hero, explicitly allies himself with Ripley by agreeing with her plan. In the face of Burke's evident desire to save a facility that has "a substantial dollar value attached to it," they stand up to the corrupt system in the name of a higher code.

At this point, the narrative engages in a covering maneuver that belies Edelstein's assertion that women "call the shots" in *Aliens*.[27] Although it appears that Ripley has gotten the upper hand in the argument, she has appealed to male authority by eliciting Hicks's support as a member of the hierarchical military structure. She gets her desired acquiescence, but the manner she uses to get it indicates her deference to masculine authority. Ripley does not, in effect, appeal to Burke's reason, but to Hicks's authority, and in doing so she plays the men off one another to get what she wants. Furthermore, Hicks agrees with Ripley only after Burke calls him "only a grunt," making it appear as if his backing of Ripley may be based on something other than the rationale of her position. Burke belittles Hicks's position and authority, so he decides to nuke the complex.

Thus, we see that Ripley is not quite ready to take up the role of action hero. Until her death, Vasquez is the "Rambette" of the film—and an extremely popular character with male audiences, who were not yet accustomed to seeing muscular women in mainstream films. Everything about her, except her sex, is a clear allusion to the epitome of the hypermasculine Reagan era hero. Her one-on-one fight with an Alien in the ventilation shafts as she keeps rear guard is one of the most exhilarating action scenes in the film and a foreshadowing of Ripley's own fight against the Alien Queen. Even the way Vasquez dresses in muscle shirt, fatigue pants, and red headband identifies her with the machine gun–toting Rambo (especially of *Rambo: First Blood, Part 2* and *Rambo III*). She is from the beginning what Ripley will become in the final scenes by incorporating similar dress and weaponry, if not the supermuscular body. Her image alone will inspire a plethora of Amazonian soldiers, from *G.I. Jane* (1997) to *The Matrix Revolutions* (2003). So why, if she is such a heroic figure, must Vasquez die? These days it is a bit easy to overlook what would have been obvious to many viewers when the film came out. Vasquez is a woman in the infantry, and, still in the new millennium, women are as yet not allowed in the infantry. Not only that, she is a macho woman and is clearly coded from the beginning as a potential lesbian when she checks out Ripley's body even more lingeringly than the men and engages in light locker-room talk with them.

In essence, Vasquez would be a Rambo but for the fact of her sex. She has chosen the same life Rambo did as a young man, she belongs to a similar type of unit, and she carries the future equivalent of his machine gun, but for all that she is a woman, and women should not choose that lifestyle. Her transgression of the heroic ideal of the period is simple biology. Thus, by the end of *Aliens*, the hypermasculine Vasquez and the effeminate Gorman are made to join forces so they can redeem their flaws in a heterosexual death clench: as Vasquez and Gorman are surrounded by Aliens, he brings out a grenade, shows it to her, then activates it. They overlap hands around the grenade, opting to die rather than throw it. Gorman dies heroically (taking the enemy with him), and Vasquez can be reconciled with the weakness of her superior, becoming in their mutual death the heroes the Reagan era could not allow them to be in life. Leaving no time for mourning, the film relocates their heroism onto Ripley, who, by the time of their deaths, has become the mission leader and has learned to fire a pulse rifle/grenade launcher, successfully incorporating the hard body and aggressive thinking of Vasquez, but with a different goal in mind: to save the child. Ripley's focus on family as ideologically "appropriate" will allow her to express aggression and strength and survive, making her the first Reagan era female hero and a model for those to come.

Female Trouble

Grown-ups never understand anything by themselves, and it is tiresome for children to be always and forever explaining things to them.

—Antoine de Saint Exupéry, *The Little Prince*

Before fighting for the family, however, Ripley must first exorcise her inner demon: she must externalize her fear so that she can face it head on and defeat it. In the director's cut, Ripley's nightmare, which at first pointed to fears of contamination, is also related to her failure as a mother, expressed as an "empty nest" syndrome, where Newt will fill the place left by Ripley's biological daughter, Amy. In the cinematic release, the nightmare expresses another type of maternal lack: Ripley's childlessness, which makes Newt her chance at a child without pregnancy. In either case, Ripley's dream of giving birth to an Alien represents her own potential for a monstrous motherhood. LV-426 becomes the symbolic representation of her own internal wasteland, the battleground where she must negotiate her fears and come to terms with the "specter of biological birth" with the help of the child Newt.[28]

Perhaps conceived originally as a surrogate for Jones the cat,[29] Newt grew into a composite of child characters from films as diverse as *Them!*, *The Road Warrior* (1981), *Poltergeist* (1982), and *Dune* (1984). On the one hand, she is small, vulnerable, soft, and open: the abused child who must be rescued, the threatened female who must be protected, the blond child abandoned to a loose, liberal social system. Because she behaves like an animal, the soldiers easily confuse her with "the enemy," and Drake almost kills her. Ripley rescues Newt from the garbage, but, as the girl's scruffy hair and filthy face indicate, it will take time, patience, and love to turn her back into the smiling, civilized "citizen" Rebecca Jorden depicted in her old photos. No doubt suffering from her own form of PTSD, she clings to the head of her doll and calls it Casey, as if by doing so she could retain her sanity, or at least feel somewhat safe—the doll is a talismanic remnant of her self as an innocent, doll-playing child that at the same time points to her broken childhood (the narrative of *Them!* uses the same device to indicate the danger its giant ants pose to innocence). Reduced to just a pretty face and a hole, the disembodied doll head iterates the broken and shattered female body and psyche, and visually represents the threat of rape, of bodily rupture and monstrous birth, that has driven both Ripley and Newt into the land of nightmares.

On the other hand, Newt is wise, inscrutable, feral, and hardened: the epitome of the weird child archetype. Forms of this uncanny, if not abominable, child character include the undeluded innocent against whom all other characters must measure themselves (as in the fairy tale "The Emperor's New Clothes"), the survivor of terrors (as in the feral child of *The Road Warrior*), and the adult soul in a child's body whose understanding goes beyond that of adults (as in *Dune*). As a weird child, Newt operates as the "other voice" that ruptures the text of *Aliens* and produces a polyphony of countertexts that other characters (particularly Ripley) must negotiate and, in some cases, try to suppress. Early in the action, Newt knows she is not safe with the soldiers and says so, but Ripley cannot bring herself to believe her, for if Newt is not safe, neither is Ripley. Later, when Ripley reminds the terrified Hudson that Newt has survived the Aliens with "no weapons and no training," he scoffs at the girl's abilities by desperately responding, "Why don't you put *her* in charge?" Ironically, he says this to another woman who also survived the Alien onslaught without weapons or training.

The only two survivors of an Alien attack, Newt and Ripley operate, as Robin Roberts suggests, as mirrors of one another, and, for that reason, they are often shot with their heads at the same level.[30] A heart-to-heart conversation in the medlab further blurs the rhetorical boundary that separates adult and child. At first, their roles seem set: Ripley tucks Newt into bed for a nap, and the girl tells her she does not want to sleep because she worries she will have scary dreams. Ripley treats Newt's fear of nightmares very much like the Company has treated her PTSD: she picks up Casey's head, checks inside of it for scary dreams, and, finding none, suggests that Newt should emulate her doll. Showing wisdom beyond her years, Newt corrects her by responding solemnly: "Ripley, she doesn't have bad dreams because she's just a piece of plastic." One can surmise that Newt has witnessed the same types of horrors as Ripley, and, therefore, Ripley's attempt to minimize them through a logic usually reserved for young children not only belittles Newt's experience but suggests Ripley's own state of denial. Because Newt is not a "normal" child, Ripley's coddling comes across as an insult.

Newt then cuts right to the chase of the fairy tale adults create for children: "My mommy always said there were no monsters, no real ones, but there are. . . . Why do they tell little kids that?" Ripley's response is both literal-minded and simplistic: "Most of the time it's true." The viewer must then wonder to what "time" Ripley refers. Contrary to her statement, when has the narrative of either *Alien* or *Aliens* not dwelled on the monstrous? Rather than answer Newt's question, Ripley's simplified, conservative rhetoric that a world without "monsters" is possible "most of the time" reveals the depth of "the effacement practiced by Cameron upon Scott's script" on the question of the Company's monstrosity.[31] Rather, Cameron has Ripley simplify the truth about monsters by reducing it to an "us versus them" proposition.

While Ripley has repressed the issue of monstrousness (in the Company, in human society as a whole), Newt apparently has been worrying about the possible correlations between the human and the Alien. When she seriously asks Ripley if "Alien babies" are like "people's babies," Ripley denies the similarity, despite the fact that she has been having nightmares of "giving birth" to an Alien. On one level, Ripley is simply behaving like a responsible adult by diverting a child's fear from issues too complex for her to understand. On another level, however, Newt is operating as Ripley's "inner child," as she gives voice to all the fears and uncertainties Ripley is feeling herself. That Ripley still dismisses these fears with adult logic proves she is not yet ready to face her inner demons.

Newt then asks Ripley if she has a daughter, and becomes somber when she learns Ripley's daughter is dead. Unhappy that the conversation has reminded Newt of her own mortality, Ripley takes off her tracking wristwatch and gives it to Newt "for luck," reminding us of her mantra in *Alien* ("You are my lucky star"). Newt is now the "lucky star" that will save Ripley from the Alien. This tracking wristwatch, given to Ripley by Hicks, symbolically confirms the connection between the three of them. Ripley then assures Newt that she will never leave her, invoking the solemn playground promise of "Cross my heart." Ripley, however, does not complete the binding of the vow, so Newt admonishingly asks, "And hope to die?" Ripley, thoughtful, responds firmly: "And hope to die." This childhood pact incorporates both the binding blood symbol (the crossed heart) and the curse (hope to die) should the promise be broken, and reminds the viewer that fifty-seven years ago, Ripley made a similar promise without seriously considering the consequences of failure.

Having nevertheless calmed Newt's fears somewhat, Ripley leaves the room so the girl can rest. She then discovers from Bishop that Burke intends to take the Facehuggers back to Earth and, furious, confronts Burke. He tries to bribe her, disclosing his motivation as pure, unbridled greed. The indignant Ripley promises to turn him in when they get back to Earth, for she has learned from the colony's logs that Burke was the administrator who sent the colonists to check the derelict alien ship without any warning of what they could find there.

That Ripley then willingly turns her back on Burke, a known liar responsible for the death of the colonists, is solid proof of her refusal to see the monstrous in the human. Surely, urgent things happen that should take her mind off Burke for a while (the Aliens attack in one of the corridors, and Bishop announces that the nuclear reactor has been damaged and there are only four hours to a complete meltdown), but the bottom line is that Ripley behaves as if Burke were incapable of betrayal, leaving herself and Newt at his mercy. Instead of telling everyone what she has learned about the Company man, for instance, she goes back to the medlab and lies down to sleep with Newt (who in her infinite wisdom has hid herself under the bed), leaving her weapon on the mattress.

What should we expect from the Machiavellian Burke? Ripley wakes to brutal facts: two Facehuggers are loose in the room, her gun is gone, the door is locked, and the surveillance camera is not operating. Working together, Newt and Ripley then fend off the Facehuggers' attack until Ripley has the presence of mind to set off the fire alarm. The Marines finally arrive at the very last minute and save them both, and Burke is finally exposed for the treacherous monster he is. The Company man, Ripley surmises, put together a scheme to loose the Facehuggers to shut her up and also to use her body and Newt's to smuggle larval Aliens past ICC quarantine. In Burke's mind at least, the two females constitute "natural" wombs and thereby are open to the Alien, himself, and the Company.

Just as Ash did in *Alien*, Burke both represents and covers up for the Company. As a Company man, he is presented as a clear product of a corporate culture that worries more about shares than human lives. To all intents and purposes, he represents the Company's interests in LV-426. However, Burke's duplicity acquits the Company from all blame in the mayhem that constitutes *Aliens'* main narrative. For how could a corporation whose explicit goal is to "build better worlds" be responsible for the death of its own colonists and the destruction of Hadley's Hope? The corporate rape of humanity presented in *Alien* is therefore re-presented here by one ambitious, greedy, immoral, and stupid individual who is willing to hurt the blond, blue-eyed all-American child, Newt, for personal gain. Big Business, Capitalism, Colonialism, and Imperialism are not at fault—bad people are at fault for taking advantage of the bureaucratic red tape of an overbloated administration. Whereas in *Alien* Ash (and Mother) were simply following orders, Burke, the self-serving bureaucrat, pursues only his interests with no consideration for law, morality, or common human decency. In a way, he is worse than Ash, for unlike the android, who was obviously programmed to be scientifically curious (as is Bishop), Burke displays no respect for, or aesthetic interest in, the Alien. He does not even acknowledge its danger; for him, the Alien is just a commodity to be traded for profit. He is so monstrous that he makes Ripley finally take up Newt's challenge and question whether humans are any different from the Aliens: "I don't know which species is worse. You don't see them fucking each other over for a god-damn percentage." Newt is right: monsters exist, and Burke is living proof that not all are extraterrestrial. The only larger enemy, perhaps, is the covert "weapons division" (roughly analogous to weapons dealers or corrupt CIA agents) to which Burke was planning to sell the Aliens.

Burke's intentions to smuggle the Aliens back to Earth metaphorically connects the film with the United States' "war on drugs": while the U.S. government (in Colombia and elsewhere) destroys the "crop," crafty bureaucrats funnel drugs and make money on the sidelines. Burke's plan also alludes to the "cavity search" performed on suspected drug smugglers who may hide substances in their anuses to avoid detection. Furthermore, we see resonances with related smuggling operations of illegal aliens across the Mexican border (implied earlier in a joke Hudson makes about Vasquez's "illegal alien" status). It is no surprise, then, that Ripley's new ally, the heroic Hicks, shows no hesitation about whether to "waste" such a man, putting his gun to the service of morality rather than law (and no one asks for evidence any further than Ripley's say-so). Unlike so many rape victims in an overly forgiving judicial system, Ripley will not only be heard, she will be believed beyond reproach. This is, however, simply rhetoric, for Burke will not be killed by Hicks or any of the Marines or even imprisoned, though no one comes up with a good reason *not* to kill him. Instead, in an act of poetic justice, he will be "terminated" by an Alien during the group's last stand.

With Vasquez's and Gorman's deaths, only the nuclear family of Hicks, Ripley, and Newt are left to meet the faithful servant, Bishop, at the lander. The explosion of Gorman's suicidal grenade, however, causes Newt to loose her footing and fall through a ventilation fan, down a shaft, and into the waiting arms of an Alien in the water below. Ripley, now true to her promise, refuses to leave Newt, and as Hicks is critically wounded in the escape to the drop ship, she must go it alone. With little time for the rescue before the nuclear reactor explodes, Ripley arms herself for battle and warns Bishop not to leave without her.

In the Alien lair, she will meet her dark twin, the Alien Queen, Ripley's last obstacle in the pursuit of her happiness, and also, in the eyes of the film, the nastiest "bitch" of all: she is the black, horrifying mother of all rapists, a creator as well as a killer, the sole ruler of a matriarchal, collective world. Her grotesque nest, a literal prolongation of her body that traps her in the role of perpetual procreator, is meant to cause horror and revulsion; her colossal insectoid body negates the human (as do the "The Bugs" in *Starship Troopers,* 1997). As we will see in the next section, it is this last trapped female who will crystallize all the fears of patriarchy by becoming the villain of both the war and the rape-revenge narratives.

The Alien Body: Weapons and the War on the Female

> Fear of the archaic mother turns out to be essentially fear of her generative power. It is this power, a dreaded one, that patriarchal filiation has the burden of subduing.
>
> —Julia Kristeva, *Powers of Horror*

The *Aliens* trailer advertised the film's narrative as "war": clips of the lean, mean Marines, their warship and battle gear, give way to shots of the claustrophobic lair of the "enemy" containing the dead civilians of Hadley's Hope. Explosions fill the screen, and then darkness, followed by Hudson's terrified cry, "How could they cut the power, man? They're animals!" As the soldiers' motion detectors indicate that the Aliens are getting closer and closer, the music swells, and we see a pair of skeletal black legs descending from the drop ship. The two last shots contrast Ripley cocking her head and the screeching Alien Queen. The title for the film appears and we hear "*Aliens*: This time it's war."

Aliens obviously wants to distance itself from *Alien: this* time we are not running, but retaliating. The affirmation of manpower is confirmed by the images of the armed Marines, the armored vehicles and planes, and the explosions: *this* time, the humans have powerful weapons, not just cattle prods and flamethrowers. The war rhetoric redefines the Marines' raid as a national response to a foreign threat. Because the United States has apparently conquered the universe (the Marines wear U.S. flags on their uniforms), America is obviously one side, the Aliens, barely covering for the Soviet Union, the other. The

Marines, then, are dispatched to deal with a threat that quickly becomes the danger of a nuclear disaster, as the Aliens are nestled in the nuclear reactor of the colony's processing plant. The Marines' option, to "nuke [the Aliens] from space," then, is a clear allusion to Reagan's proposed Star Wars technology.

A thoughtful review of the film, however, seriously undermines the trailer's claim that *Aliens* is a war narrative, for the humans' acknowledged objective is not to win,[32] but, as Ripley declares grimly in close-up, "to wipe them out." But if *Aliens* is not a true war narrative, then what is it? How do we describe a situation where one species professes a desire to eliminate another entire species while at the same time concealing the desire to use the other species as a weapon and a commodity? How do we label an enemy that is itself constructed as a weapon, leaving no separate body to wound?[33] In spite of their given name, the Warrior Aliens are not soldiers. Rather, like the Borg drones of *Star Trek: The Next Generation*, they are weapon-bodies that cannot be made to surrender, but only destroyed completely, or, as Burke hopes, perhaps reprogrammed to fight for the other side like a rifle picked up off the ground. In essence, Cameron rewrites the vampiric Alien of the first film (a subject in its own right) as a minion-weapon: not the enemy per se, but a danger visited upon us by the enemy.

The truth is that the war rhetoric disguises the rape-revenge that must be visited on the originator of the Alien: the Alien Queen. A second look at the trailer shows her as the climactic figure (the music swells on the appearance of her feminine legs from the drop ship) and as Ripley's contender (her open, threatening maw juxtaposed to a close-up of Ripley cocking her head). Her monstrous womb is behind the word *alien:* when the title ALIENS appears, its *I* widens, forming a vaginal shape that flashes bright blue-white light in a subtle modification of the cracking egg of the *Alien* trailer.

Conceived by Cameron as a "new form beyond" Giger's Alien that helps reveal how the Alien's "social organization works,"[34] the Alien Queen, then, displaces the individual Alien as the agent of difference. In essence, Cameron's response to the question "Where do Alien eggs

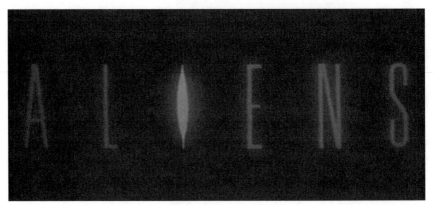

"This time it's war":
The title for Aliens *features the vaginal opening of the* I.

come from?" is radically different from Ridley Scott's. Whereas in Scott's concept human bodies are morphed into Alien eggs (human becomes Alien), Cameron's revision shifts the focus entirely onto an irreconcilable Other, a female (she is not us). The Alien Queen also solves the problem of how to wound the Alien body, since she is its origin as well as its supreme embodiment; hypothetically, the hive is under her command alone. *She* is revealed as the real danger, the Alien drones merely unwitting minions to female power.

Although the humans theorize about her existence, indicating a de facto assumption that a female must be at the heart of all this pain and suffering, the Alien Queen appears in only two sequences at the end of *Aliens*, both devised to compare her figure to Ripley. The first posits the Queen as the creature in the labyrinth. This is Cameron's take on Grendel's Mother from *Beowulf*—the female that is the monstrous form beyond Grendel, and the real source of terror, as she, unlike Grendel, could give birth to more beasts.

Armed to the teeth, Ripley goes into the Alien nest and rescues Newt from a Facehugger in the nick of time. As she tries to negotiate the passages, Ripley makes a false turn that takes them to the very center of the maze, the Alien Queen's hatchery. Ripley knows she is in deep trouble when she sees the eggs of monstrous life. She slowly turns around to find a way out of there but hears a visceral squishing sound, then sees the protrusion of the Alien Queen's ovipositor laying a slime-covered egg. This obvious comparison between Alien reproduction and defecation leaves no doubt that the Alien Queen is meant to represent the abject archaic mother, a colossal and repulsive reproductive body.[35] At last, Ripley has met her Shadow, the grotesque dark mother of monsters that externalizes and gives solid shape to Ripley's fears of giving birth to a destroying Alien.

The Alien Queen's heavy Darth Vader–like breathing punctuates Ripley's guiding gaze as it pans left, following the Queen's enormous ovipositor full of translucent eggs, upwards to her shiny, spiderlike erect body. The effect the Queen has is aptly conveyed by David Edelstein: "[Ripley] watches in awe as the Queen Mama uncovers herself, one black arm after another peeling away from the giant trunk, and there's a hush, as if this really were a sacred place; the womb of the universe."[36] The "Queen Mama" is also armed and dangerous: she hisses, showing Ripley rows and rows of razor-sharp, crystalline teeth, and her hiss is answered by the Warrior Aliens lurking nearby.

Ripley sets Newt down carefully on her feet and attempts a rudimentary form of communication with the Queen—namely, firing her flamethrower into the air, then pointing it at the Alien Queen's eggs. Apparently displeased at Ripley's show of power, the Alien Queen screeches but dismisses the Warrior Aliens because Ripley is holding her eggs hostage. As Ripley and Newt carefully back away, an egg opens, revealing the Facehuggers as yet another weapon of the Queen. This re-vision of the Facehugger from an apparently mindless creature whose only quest was to implant an embryo to an apparent minion of the Queen's controlling mind transforms the whole hatchery into an armory. Ripley realizes that they will not be allowed to get out of there so easily. She cocks her head, as if sizing up her opponent, and opts to flame all the eggs around her. The Queen screeches in rage. When the Warrior Aliens attack, Ripley blasts away with her pulse rifle. Seized by an uncontrollable rage, she then sweeps her rifle back and forth, firing round after round at everything in sight until she runs out of ammunition. She then pumps several grenades at the Alien Queen's egg sac, exploding it with all its contents. As Ripley exits the hatchery, carrying Newt with her, she flings the ammunition belt filled with grenades into it.

Reproduction, then, is shown as the real threat in *Aliens*: a common Reagan era fear that the control of reproduction and reproductive mechanisms (abortion, birth control, homosexuality, and even abstinence) could become a weapon, particularly against the traditional, nuclear family. Thus, the opposition of these two females has, as Amy Taubin has noted, "a historically specific, political meaning. If Ripley is the prototypical, upper-middle-class WASP, the alien queen bears a suspicious resemblance to a favorite scapegoat of the Reagan/Bush era—the black welfare mother—that parasite of the economy whose uncurbed reproductive drive reduced hard-working taxpayers to bankruptcy."[37] What in another time would have been the evil witch (Medea, for example) here becomes a crazed Welfare Queen, living off the state and producing hordes of illegitimate children, who rampage about destroying human (white) society. The worst conservative fears here come true: the womb has become a weapon wielded by a husbandless, inhuman "bitch." Ripley acts on behalf of the conservative interest, and within conservative rhetoric, when she attacks, not the Alien Queen, but her egg sac, in a gross sterilization. She exacts retribution on the womb for what it has done to her, to Newt, to the Marines, to the crew of the *Nostromo*, to humanity.

Getting Even: Ripley's face as she shoots the Alien Queen's ovipositor.

As Ripley and Newt make a run for the waiting drop ship, the Alien Queen tears herself free from the constraining and death-dealing womb to follow Ripley and exact her revenge. Ripley does not stop to fight, and she and Newt make it to the ship safely and escape to space just before the station explodes.

Back on the *Sulaco*, Ripley finally acknowledges Bishop with a subdued but affable, "You did all right." Bishop has redeemed the specter of Ash, the taint of insidiousness and betrayal that made Ripley suspect the android in the first place. Most importantly, through his heroic actions, he has appropriated masculinity: Pinocchio has finally attained its goal of becoming a boy. Their brief moment of connection is shattered, however, when Bishop goes into a violent paroxysm that seems a particularly nasty combination of Kane's and Ash's deaths. His body—convulsing and spurting white liquid—is the image of the betrayal Ripley always expected: somehow the android has managed to sequester an Alien inside himself. But, rather than the Chestburster we dread (would it be an android hybrid?), a long spike surfaces from his chest. It is the Queen's barbed tail. The Alien Queen, who had been hiding in the drop ship's landing gear, lifts Bishop to her and violently rips him in half with her inner arms, dropping the two parts away like garbage. His upper torso lies gasping, disgusting and worthless on the flight deck.

What the Alien Queen is interested in is Ripley and Newt. Ripley gestures Newt to run while she attracts the gaze of the Queen. Once Newt has found a hiding place in an open floor grate, Ripley runs for a cargo dock, pursued by the Alien Queen, who is stopped by the dock's sliding door. Like a fairy-tale witch, the Alien Queen then busies herself trying to trap Newt with her long claws, but stops when she hears the cargo dock's door open. Ripley comes out in a power-loader and commands the Alien Queen to leave Newt alone with the now famous line, "Get away from her, you bitch!" This appropriation of Ripley's line to describe the Alien Queen is yet another covering move to absolve the patriarchal Company of any residual blame from *Alien*. The misplaced anger Ripley felt toward the "bitch" computer MU/TH/UR is here recast as legitimate rage at the real "bitch" whose monstrous brood caused the death of the *Nostromo*'s crew. This time, Ripley knows where evil *really* lies, and she will stomp it out.

Thus, this final confrontation between the Alien Queen and Ripley, aptly dubbed "the Battle of the Big Mamas,"[38] implies that it takes a female to take out a female, a very common sign of patriarchal ideology, as Margaret Atwood shows in *The Handmaid's Tale*. The mechanoid, yet undeniably female bodies clashing in mortal combat is an argument for the proper sexual order. This battle, *Aliens* seems to be saying, is the way things should be: not female soldiers in combat, not grown men shooting at little girls or blabbering in fear, not corporate thieves sacrificing all for profit, but real men standing up and fighting the enemy for the family until they cannot fight anymore and real women standing up and fighting for the future of their children against the ever-present shadow of monstrous motherhood. Condemning the welfare mother, the woman who has an abortion, the depressed woman who kills her own children, this confrontation between Ripley and the Alien Queen is the purview of women, for the monstrous mother is an expression of every woman's sin.

We have come full circle from the trailer. The woman faces the "bitch" who is really herself. The difference is only one of degree.

As a mother, Ripley is now fully authorized to utilize the skills of the Reagan era hero. She goes "mano a mano," using the best weapon the hero has: ingenuity. During an interview, Cameron explained his expectations for this final encounter between Ripley and the Alien Queen:

> I wanted to have the final confrontation with the alien as a hand-to-hand fight. To be a very intense, personal thing, not done with guns, which are a remote way of killing. Also, *guns carry a lot of other connotations as well*. But to really go one on one with the creature was my goal. It made sense that Ripley could win if she could equalize the odds.[39] (emphasis ours)

Denied the phallic connotation given to Vasquez by her guns, Ripley, the Final Mom must transform herself into a cyborg to wrestle the

Alien Queen. In an allusion to the final scene in *Alien*, Ripley once again dons armor to make up for her lack. The powerloader, earlier a symbol of her fallen status as a "dock worker," then of her usefulness when moving storage boxes for the Marines, here augments her body to counteract the physically larger Alien Queen. But, as Tim Blackmore notes, "the power loader, impressive though it may be, traps Ripley. Her fall in the loader nearly kills her: only by abandoning the machine and relying on her own strength does Ripley survive."[40] Thus, in the end, like the female knight Britomart of Spenser's *The Faerie Queene*, Ripley must ultimately disarm to return to home and family. Accordingly, Newt welcomes Ripley back from the fight with the proclamation, "Mommy!"

Cyborg Ripley defends Newt from the Queen: "Get away from her, you bitch!"

In the end, *Aliens* has the force of inevitability that permeates *Apocalypse Now* (1979): the insanity of war rages around the protagonist, but released from its common variety of death (even immune to it), the hero moves inexorably toward the inevitable encounter at the heart of darkness. The soldier on the edge will meet the soldier who has gone beyond the pale. Their eyes will meet in a moment of recognition, and the hero will know, finally, that the horror of madness and death lies at the heart of darkness. So, too, in this female version, a woman on the edge (a survivor of the horrendous terror of the borderlands) will move through the desolate landscape toward her inevitable encounter with the monstrous mother. Even though for a moment they understood each other, Ripley bitch-slaps the Alien into space as the audience cheers and sings, "Ding dong, the witch is dead, the wicked witch is dead."

Conclusion: A Few Good Men (and Women)

> We're an ideal political family, as
> accessible as Disneyland.
> —Maureen Reagan

Ripley was not only a bad mother who left her daughter alone while she gallivanted around space, she was also one of the worst fears of the Reagan era—the single mother with a career.[41] Starting as a soft, open body, Ripley is portrayed as feminine (in obvious makeup and fluffy hairstyle) and vulnerable, even if with a certain resolve. Later, she is given a first name, Ellen. Thus, *Aliens* wants us to believe that its feminine, rouge-cheeked female is the "real" Ripley and the War- rant Officer Ripley of *Alien* an "at work" performance. In this context, Ripley's initial encounter with the original Alien is recast as a sym- bolic run into the perils that "loose" women face (AIDS, sexually transmitted diseases, unwanted pregnancy) that explains why her nightmares consist of being infected/impregnated and giving birth to a monstrosity. The theme of infection also serves to enhance the "soft body" image of *Alien*, recasting the crew of the *Nostromo* as weak and vulnerable. In other words, if the Marines of *Aliens* can kill hundreds of Warrior Aliens, and Ripley can kill their Queen, the original Alien could not have been that bad. Sure, Ripley thwarted the Company's self-destructive impulse, but at what cost? Not only that, but, as Ju- dith Newton has posited, she has stupidly returned to the very Com- pany that betrayed her.[42] James Cameron's Company, though, is hardly Ridley Scott's, the one that considered the crew of the *Nos- tromo* "expendable." In this context, Ripley, the hero of *Alien*, is ini- tially recast by *Aliens* as a useless, hysterical woman going to waste,

ruin, and insanity. Going after the Aliens and destroying them becomes the way to destroy her nightmares, fear, and guilt, and also to
refashion herself as a successful woman, a hard body capable of
single-handedly taking on the Alien Queen. Just as Rambo's body
created a national desire for hard bodies like his,[43] *Aliens* rebuilds the
broken woman Ellen Ripley into a hard-bodied mother who confronts
the Alien "bitch" to protect her young and the human race. Ripley
becomes the national mother, forced to protect her young against the
foreign threat. In *Aliens*, at least, her goals remain clearly aligned with
national ideals. In the end, this Ripley has not "busted loose."

At the same time that *Aliens* transforms Ripley into the first female
Reagan era action hero, the film disavows both the possibility of a solo
female hero, or a lesbian female hero by constructing Hicks as her
ideal heterosexual partner. In the rape-revenge narrative, Hicks
stands for the "missing guy," the nice one who would have stopped
the killing or rapes with his love. He never takes part in the squad's
sexual or racist banter, and he takes Ripley seriously even at the
briefing, when she is at her most nervous. As the true hero of the
action narrative, the strong, quiet Hicks remains cool and collected
while everyone else, including Ripley and Vasquez, have to be "eased
down," establishing that in the future men continue being the rational
side of humanity and an indispensable part of the system. Clearly
posed as Ripley's equal, a man who admires her courage, respects her
opinions, and follows her wishes, Hicks represents the different
"other" male who is not intimidated or dismissive of the heroine's
strength and is capable of being her partner, as opposed to the rest of
the males in the film, who commit identifiable mistakes. Thus, Hicks
is the only man fit to live and the character the male audience would
most like to be. As Cameron would have it, Hicks does his absolute
best, but in the end loses his armor and is seriously wounded, and so
Ripley steps in. Now is the moment of authorized aggression—we
have no fear that anyone could confuse the message and believe that
Ripley is an argument for women in the military.

The Carter era soldiers, especially the weak Lieutenant Gorman,
have no good reason to fight. Ripley, however, has found the reason

in the child Newt. The nation must protect its women and children. Like the heroes of many 1980s action films who fight, at least in part, to get a child, wife, or lover back, Ripley fights to recover her lost daughter, and, most importantly, binds a male to her quest, creating an impromptu family, even tucking her new child into bed in the film's happy ending. One gets the sense that Ripley is, in Reagan era terms, "fulfilling her inner destiny" as mother, protector, and destroyer of Aliens. Thus, as Greenberg asserts, we easily overlook the fact that "the Queen fights with equal bravery to ensure that her children not yet born will be spared the fate of those Ripley has just incinerated."[44] Not only do we overlook it, we *do not care*. And we do not care because Cameron has constructed a film where, ideologically, it is *her* or *us*. As both the cinematic release and the *Special Edition* show, Ellen Ripley stands for the redeemed Reaganite, who has returned to family and the hard-body politics of right and wrong, good and evil, Us and Them. She is in her place, a woman fighting women's battles. She has a new daughter, a prospective mate, and is heading home to the good old Earth.

CHAPTER 3

"The Bitch Is Back": The Iconoclastic Body in *Alien³*

All I would like in my life, what I wish for very much, is to someday have the strength and be free of the resentment and anger that I carry around with me like Linus' blanket for just long enough to become one of those people who is better than the worst thing that ever happens to her. How I would love to be that woman.

—Elizabeth Wurtzel, *Bitch: In Praise of Difficult Women*

Occult Bodies

To say that *Alien³* was not what fans of *Alien* and *Aliens* expected would be a gross understatement. The cause of the confusion is understandable: although *Alien³* was advertised as "3 times the suspense, 3 times the horror, 3 times the action," it is not a suspense film, nor a war film, nor even properly a horror film; there are no guns, no soldiers, no nukes, and no ravaging hordes of Aliens attacking cute little girls. *Alien³* is, in effect, the very opposite of *Aliens*. Unfortunately, according to most reviewers, it was not very good either: *Time* gave it a grade of C for its "glum, distancing story" and its "lack of the conjurer's touch," while *Newsweek*'s David Ansen called it "the least scary, least emotional, and the least cathartic of the series."[1] Put off by the film's bleak story, some reviewers condemned the film as a downer that reduced Ripley's heroism in *Aliens*, while others bemoaned the lack of individuation of the supposedly "motley crew" of convicts and the remake of the Alien into a creature that was, according to *Commonweal* critic Richard Alleva, "no more frightening than Barney the Dinosaur."[2]

What all of the charges against the film share in common is a recognition that *Alien³* seems to operate as a response to, or rejection of, *Aliens*. Where *Aliens* is exhilarating and explosive, *Alien³* is introspective. Whereas the former emphasizes individual choice and action, the latter emphasizes collaboration and the collective mediation of responsibility and suffering. *Alien³*'s hysterical inmates and the androgynous, shorn Ripley, armed only with fire and ingenuity, counteract *Aliens*' hard-bodied, heavily armed Marines and womanly Ripley. Most importantly, *Alien³* rejects the maternal impulse of *Aliens*' quest to place Ripley back in "home and happy family"; thus, Ripley's apotheosis in *Alien³* erases the traditional happy ending of *Aliens*, leaving us with the image of a radically different, defiant type of hero. As Stephen Mulhall writes in *On Film*, "[Director David] Fincher presents his film as awakening Ripley from Cameron's dream, his fantasy of what constitutes a fulfilled existence for his protagonist, and his fantasy of human life as something that with the right degree of effort on our part can be made to come out right."[3] Instead, Fincher's film presents life as a generally ugly affair where heroism means making the best of the worst.

Surely one problem with the reception of *Alien³* was the fact that the writers and director make little effort to cater to the burgeoning *Alien* fandom. Its closed ending, for example, in which Ripley and the "last" of the Alien species die, did not correspond to the external, popular narratives engendered by *Alien* and *Aliens*. By 1992, the series had become a franchise, complete with action figures, trading cards, novelizations, and spin-off novels (some featuring Ripley), an *Aliens* comic series, including the *Alien vs. Predator* crossover, and numerous video games. This mass of secondary narratives invented for Ripley and the Aliens helped create the widespread impression that its protagonist existed outside the film trilogy; confronted with her death in *Alien³*, the spin-off novelization *The Female Wars*, for example, brings Ripley back as an android to fight Momma Alien on the Alien home planet.[4]

Alien³ also threw audiences off by positing Ripley as the center of the narrative arc and her death as the end of the series. The writers correctly surmised the emotional impact of the ending of the film: Ripley's death *would* matter to the audiences. But by making the film essentially her story, her nightmare, they sacrificed what heretofore had been the driving force of the narrative: the Alien creature itself and its threat to all of humanity. Many, of course, would see this move as a flat-out cinematic error even though it adds an emotional depth to Ripley's character that James Cameron could not imagine. We would argue that this narrative shift is the least of the film's problems, particularly considering the mayhem surrounding its production. For, as David Thompson bluntly asserts, the twisted making of *Alien³* could be an excellent illustration of how *not* to make a movie. First, producers Giler and Hill hired William Gibson—the progenitor of cyberpunk fiction and, indeed, the coiner of the term *cyberspace*—to revamp the series, but his script was not to their satisfaction. The second writer, Eric Red, of *The Hitcher* (1986) and *Near Dark* (1987) fame, invented a new protagonist that worked for Special Services and introduced a shape-shifting Alien. His script was also scrapped. The third writer, David Twohy, known for *Warlock* (1984), envisioned a prison planet as the setting for the film. Seriously displeased with the writing process, Renny Harlin resigned his post as director. Giler and Hill then hired Vincent Ward (*The Navigator: A Mediaeval Odyssey*, 1988) as director and John Fasano to write the script yet again. For their plot, Ward and Fasano reversed the concept of *The Navigator*: Ripley lands on a planet inhabited by monks still living as if in the Middle Ages, where she battles the Alien with the aid of an abbot. Ward was subsequently released from the project, and newcomer David Fincher was hired as director with orders to simplify Ward's script with the aid of Larry Ferguson, although Giler and Hill ended up rewriting much of the script, even changing the monastery back into a prison.[5]

Fincher came to *Alien³* following a blazing success as a director for television commercials and Music Television videos for such stars as Michael Jackson, Billy Idol, Paula Abdul, Don Henley, Steve Winwood, and, perhaps most importantly, Madonna, all of which had earned him the title "the king of MTV." As director of the Madonna videos *Oh Father* (1989), *Express Yourself* (1989), and *Vogue* (1990) and codirector of *Madonna: The Immaculate Collection* (1990), Fincher helped create the image that made Madonna into a pop icon. What better collaborator than Fincher to help Sigourney Weaver propel Ripley off the screen and into iconography?

By *Alien³*, Sigourney Weaver had established herself as an outstanding actor. She had received a nomination for a Golden Globe and an Academy Award for her portrayal of Ripley in *Aliens*. Two years later, both her leading role in *Gorillas in the Mist* (1988) and her supporting role in *Working Girl* (1988) were again honored with Globe and Oscar nominations—this time she won Golden Globes for both. Her success had earned her the right to negotiate for a producer's position, and she proved to be as highly opinionated and strong willed as her character. After all, no one could say he or she knew Ripley better than Weaver. The time was ripe for her, like Ripley, to be in control of her destiny.

Given the many distinct views that permeated the production of *Alien³*, it would be misleading to attribute all the film's flaws to Fincher. Rather, Fincher took what he was given and made it into a workable, if not brilliant, film that evidences the Fincher style that emerges later in *Se7en* (1995), *The Game* (1997), *Fight Club* (1999), and *Panic Room* (2002). Still, the film's "schizophrenic" feel has left critics with the impulse to tease out one narrative or symbolic thread and ignore deeper inconsistencies. It is possible, for example, to read *Alien³* as referencing the AIDS epidemic[6] or, more predictably, as a Christian fable,[7] but no matter how keen these readings are, they simply overlook the complexity of the overall film. Therefore, rather than pursue one single critical reading to make sense of the film, we examine the different "voices" evidenced in the text and how they play off one another to different effects. In order to make at least some attempt at clarity, we will discuss the film as a network of three separate but concurrent accounts: the Christian allegory, more a background than an actual story; the biological narrative, which functions as an interrogation of the sexed body; and, finally, the impact these intertwined narratives have on the construction of gender.

Many critics have hinted at the Christian narrative of *Alien³*— mostly to point out similarities to the 1928 *La Passion de Jeanne d'Arc* by Carl Theodore Dreyer—but only Kathleen Murphy has elaborated a coherent critical study she fittingly entitled "The Last Temptation of Sigourney Weaver." In her article, Murphy points out how the main theme of *Alien* and *Aliens* is the disruption of the flesh; thus, it was only a matter of time before someone turned an *Alien* film into a narrative of the battle between the flesh and the spirit in the vein of Martin Scorsese's version of Nikos Kazantzakis's novel *The Last Temptation of Christ* (1988). In fact, *Alien³* continues the trend of genre bending begun with *Alien* by borrowing themes from apocalyptic, occult, and possession films (as well as prison films) and re-presenting them as science fiction. Furthermore, as the film intended to close the series, *Alien³* chronicles the last battle of Lieutenant Ripley and the Alien, and so it seems fitting that its writers would construct it as an apocalyptic narrative. To up the odds, this time Ripley has been infected with an Alien Queen, so that her image reminds us simultaneously of the innocent female carrier of the Antichrist (as in *Rosemary's Baby*, 1968) and the male exorcist with "a demon in his chest" (via *The Exorcist*, 1973).

We need not move to the fiery finale of the film to infer Ripley's hellish nature in regards to the patriarchy. In essence, we quickly realize, Ripley has landed in feminist Hell. Fiorina 161 is a maximum-security work facility for double-Y chromosome (the so-called hypermale) rapists and murderers. The specific reference to DNA-based sex, as well as the extreme genetic-based masculinity of double-Y chromosome males, rapidly links biological imperatives with the inmates' fundamentalist religion. Whether religion itself serves as a way to transcend essential biology or as a justification for masculine biological narratives remains to be seen; what is clear is Fincher's conflation of the traditionally competing models of religion and biology: the inmates literally embody biological deterministic narratives supported by evolution while professing to embody Christ.

Although the Judeo-Christian tradition and biological narratives evidence ample material for interpretation, *Alien³* also presents a narrative seemingly independent of, and often at odds with, the Christian symbolism and biological determinism. This intersecting narrative draws upon the previous *Alien* films in its presentation of the human body as open, penetrable, and thereby feminized. In *Alien³* the fear shifts, however, from the penetration and specularization (an opening up for examination) of the body to a realization that the pristine body, on which we base so much of our individuality, never was. The döppelganger-contagion fear of *Alien* and *Aliens* shifts to a viral fear where the human body is the battleground of a war with oneself. Thus, as if Ripley has not been through enough already, she now must confront both the literal creature without (the doglike Alien) and the literal creature within (the larval Alien Queen), as well as the social monster without (the misogynistic men) and the personal monster within (her own fear of death).

The advertisement campaign for *Alien³* introduces the gendered narrative and dark tone of the film: constructed variously in trailers and posters, the ads worked around the tag line "The bitch is back," as they showed a close-up image of Ripley's head turned toward the camera with an Alien menacing her on the left. Obviously seeking to attract viewers by implying that the "bitch" Alien Queen from *Aliens* would be a part of this film, the phrase nevertheless evidences multiple meanings when we realize the Alien next to Ripley is not a Queen. The "bitch" who is "back" must then be Ripley. We learn later that the Alien Queen lurks in fetal form inside Ripley, and, as the film progresses, we will witness the Alien bitch inside conflate with the human female outside.

"The bitch is back":
But which bitch is which, as the one on the left is not the Queen?

By collapsing the dichotomy between Ripley and the Alien, *Alien³*
is the first of the *Alien* films to openly address the abject status of
women covertly posited in *Alien* and *Aliens*. As we have argued, Cameron's film in particular portrays the female neatly categorized into
two types of "bitches": the bad bitches, as symbolized by the Alien
Queen, emasculate men and bend them to their evil will. The good
bitches (such as Cameron's Ripley and Vasquez) fight the bad bitches
and their broodish, subservient males, who are little more than pussy-
whipped brutes. In *Alien³*, however, Ripley is constructed as a liminal
body, both the whore-destroyer and the good woman savior of humanity, and as such embodies abjection as Julia Kristeva describes it in
Powers of Horror: "What does not respect borders, positions, rules.
The in-between, the ambiguous, the composite."[8]

As the film progresses, Ripley's "bitchiness" is first reinterpreted
as defiance to excessive and misplaced male authority, then defiance
of male sexual aggression, and finally defiance of the patriarchal Company itself. But perhaps a more important fact is that the male aggression toward her is shown so overtly. Here, the film seems to tell us, is
what men *really* think of Ripley, never mind what *Alien* and *Aliens*
tried to sell before. Like the female address videos of Cindy Lauper
and Madonna[9] and the female buddy picture *Thelma and Louise*
(1991), *Alien³* shows the male world through the woman's eyes: a
world filled with machos, patriarchal authoritarians, rapists, murderers, and idiots who want to keep the woman locked up and "safe,"

most often from themselves. We are indeed overwhelmed by the uni-lateral misogynistic oppression of Ripley from the moment she awakes on Fiorina. Less obvious is Fincher's use of fetish at every turn to undermine the very misogyny the narrative sets up.

This displacement of the body exposes how the Judeo-Christian religious narrative, particularly of the Fall of Man, and the biological narrative, specifically biological determinism, walk hand in hand to support misogyny and patriarchal dominance. Fincher, we would argue, directly assaults both by first setting up the religious narrative and deconstructing it to reveal the biological narrative lurking beneath. Both narratives meet in the final exposing image of a female Christ figure caught in the act of a glorious immolation-abortion. Ripley's letting go is not only a slap in the face of the Company and the patriarchy, but also a slap in the face of all who wanted her to continue as the perpetual victim-savior Final Girl of the *Alien* series. No wonder the fans were pissed off.

Religion, Fetishism, and the Displacement of Sex

> Christianity gave eroticism its savor of sin and legend when it endowed the human female with a soul.
>
> —Simone de Beauvoir, referring to when the Council of Nicea, by a single vote, declared women to be "human"

Alien³ begins by deconstructing the triumphant music that accompanies the 20th Century Fox logo: its final chord is held, then built into a booming discord, which abruptly cuts. Eerie tones accompany the vastness of space. Images come in quick flashes, fading in and out, suggesting a drifting in and out of consciousness. We see Ripley's and Newt's faces in their cryo-tubes, the side of the ship *Sulaco*, and . . . an open Alien egg. A sweet voice sings in Latin: *Agnus Dei, qui tollis peccata mundi* (Lamb of God, who taketh away the sins of the earth).

The fingers of the spidery Facehugger appear behind Newt's cryo-tube. We hear the crack of glass and witness green Alien blood dripping onto the floor and burning. The Alien blood is mirrored by the spread of human blood slowly staining a thin, white, cotton material, a sign of the corruption of the original seamless, white, and spotless being. The iconic opening—the bodies displayed like heroic saints, backed by the angelic music of the Ordinary Mass—evokes the perfect, incorrupt body of Christ. Thus, Cameron's Sleeping Beauty preserved in ice has become Fincher's saint in her glass reliquary.

Saint Bernadette of Lourdes and "Saint Ripley": the incorrupt body.

In fact, Fincher has remade the war vessel *Sulaco* into a holy site where the iconic bodies of a fetishistic religion lie in state: this is the Ripley who twice before faced the Alien and survived, these are the hands that saved the child Newt and killed the Alien Queen, this is the heart that cannot be defeated.

Evil, however, has erupted in the holy place. The acid blood has started a fire in the cryogenic compartment, causing the ship's alarms to sound. A video image shows the Facehugger attached to one of the sleepers (which one, it is not clear). The fire rages. The *Sulaco*'s computer forces the cryo-tubes to the emergency evacuation vehicle (EEV) and hurls it into outer space, where it is attracted by a nearby planet. The film's titles inform us that this is Fiorina "Fury" 161, an "outer veil mineral ore refinery and double Y chromosome work correctional facility." As if an afterthought, another title appears: "Maximum Security." The EEV plummets into the planet's ocean like a blazing meteor, presaging disaster and alluding to Satan's fall, for "Fury" 161 is a hell planet with fires perennially burning from its core and rubbish and filth for its landscape. We could also consider the crash landing an ironic allusion to the science-fiction classic *Planet of the Apes* (1968), since Ripley, like astronaut Charlton Heston, will find herself lost in a world of veritable apes who think of her as an inferior species. And while in *Planet of the Apes* "the new Eve" dies during the space journey, in Fincher's film, Ripley as the new Eve is about to create havoc in the all-male population of Fiorina 161.

The birth imagery of *Alien* and *Aliens*, where the astronauts were awakened from a deep sleep by the ship's central computer, is in *Alien³* replaced by images of death and contamination. The *Sulaco* aborts the EEV, which, unlike Ripley's shuttle in *Aliens*, will prove dangerously contagious. When Fiorina 161's inmates peer into the bloody, muddy, messy womb/tomb of the EEV, site of rebirth for Ripley and death for Newt and Hicks, they cannot know it contains a monstrous life that brings death. As night falls, Spike the dog barks at the figure of a Facehugger creeping slowly toward him, but his warnings go unheeded.

Only Ripley has survived the crash. We see her being placed on a metallic table. She is damp and filthy with mud.[10] In a perverse association, Fincher intersperses shots of her displayed body with information about her dead companions and glimpses of their remains—the spark that made them likable characters in *Aliens* gone, dead, irretrievable. Covered with grime and juxtaposed with grotesque images of death, Ripley's body, which in the previous two movies had been an object of desire, has lost its virgin sheen and appears unclean, corrupt, fallen.

Our formal introduction to the world of Fiorina 161 comes as a low-angle close-up of Superintendent Andrews (Brian Glover). He is holding a "rumor control" meeting in a large multilevel room with the apocalyptic feel of *Mad Max Beyond Thunderdome* (1985). We see the back of a convict's shaved head: it carries a bar code, presumably his identification number. The inmates listen in silence until Andrews tells them that the only survivor of the crash—he pauses for effect—is a *woman*. The inmates hoot, holler, and make clanking noises. A woman. Andrews looks ill at ease as their chatter becomes menacing: "Is she pretty?" The threat of rape hangs in the air.

Other inmates are apparently mortified because communing with a woman is against their religious principles. As convict Morse (Danny Webb) angrily points out, the potential presence of Ripley "freely intermingling with the inmates and the rest of the staff" offends those that, like him, have taken a vow of celibacy. Their Malcolm X-like religious leader, Dillon (Charles S. Dutton), worries that the presence of a woman will translate into a disruption of the convicts' "spiritual unity." And Dillon could not be more correct: Ripley/ Eve has brought with her the serpent that will destroy the men's carefully preserved Eden. Andrews assures the convicts that a rescue team is under way (to rescue them from her?), then cautions his assistant, Mr. Aaron (Ralph Brown), and Dr. Clemens (Charles Dance) about allowing "the woman" outside the infirmary. Against the general tension, one convict utters a warning: "Better get here soon, or there won't be much left." Without even waking up, Ripley, "the woman," already spells trouble for Andrews.

Cut to the prison infirmary. Ripley wakes from hypersleep, dizzy, confused, and feeling terrible. Dr. Clemens is beside her bed, ready to give her a shot. The aggressive impulse of the bald, phallic, double-Y chromosome males is counterpointed by Clemens' spurting needle, which Ripley allows him to insert into her arm: an intimate act that prefigures the actual sexual encounter that happens between them later. Fincher's extreme close-up of the needle insertion is erotically charged and highly fetishized: close-ups of her face and arms stand in for the "lack" that makes her a woman. She inquires about Newt and Hicks. Clemens tells her they are dead. She gets up in a hurry, stark naked, with the full intention to investigate the EEV. Although Clemens has obviously seen her undressed (he later tells her he knows her name because it was stenciled on the back of her underwear), he reacts in shock to the display of her willfully exposed body. Interestingly, the audience does not have a referent for his reaction, for Fincher's camera looks away from Ripley's difference, displacing it onto her head and feet.[11]

This first displacement of sex is followed by Ripley's request to examine Newt's body. Although we understand with her that Newt's death by drowning may mask an Alien invasion, symbolically Ripley's interest in Newt alone demonstrates the film's early concern with gender and the penetrability of the female. The contrast to *Aliens*, where no one suspected Newt of being infected, is striking: in this film, everyone, including Ripley herself, is concerned with the "damage" the female body might do.

Left alone with the cadaver, Ripley first attempts to investigate its interior from the surface: closing Newt's eyes, she feels the girl's throat and chest. She then opens the corpse's mouth and attempts to peer inside. She is interrupted, however, by the inquisitive Clemens, who is slightly disconcerted by her inspection. Ripley asks for an autopsy, claiming a risk of "contagion," but cannot bring herself to tell Clemens what kind, so she says it could be cholera. Clemens is skeptical, so Ripley begs him with one soft "please" that communicates her intense need to know and her deep fear of what she could find inside the girl.

The autopsy is a contrived and violent study of depths. At first glance, Clemens is opening up Newt's body, but what he is really interrogating is Ripley's psyche—uncovering Ripley's secret. Although we do not see the cutting up of the body, the action is symbolized by a blood spill coursing down the drain and the bloody gloves Clemens cleans on his apron. At Ripley's insistence, he takes a saw— "Careful," she whispers, revealing to the audience that she fears an Alien will be set loose—and he breaks through the corpse's chest while Ripley looks on in pure agony. The moment reminds the viewer of Ripley's empathetic reaction to the female colonist who hatched a Chestburster in *Aliens*. Once again, Ripley's nightmare is being played out on another female body, only this time she is the one requesting that the body that stands in for her be opened. She must, in effect, deconstruct the text of the girl's body to deconstruct her own fear.

Clemens pries open Newt's rib cage. Terrified of what she will see, Ripley closes her eyes for a moment . . . but the girl's body is clear.

Unlike in *Alien*, where Kane's convulsions and bodily eruption were photographed in gory detail and witnessed by the whole shocked crew of the *Nostromo*, in this film the body being violated is already dead, we never see the opening, Ripley looks away, the girl's blood runs down a drain, and there is no Alien inside. Ironically, the sight of Newt's virginal interior does not lead Ripley to the logical conclusion, even though her earlier empathetic behavior insinuates that the Alien is in her own chest. By transferring her fears of contamination onto the body of Newt, and by opening that body, Ripley feels cleansed, and once again denies the ever-present reality of the monster, thereby enabling its birth and growth.[12]

Surreptitiously, however, the religious narrative has intruded once again and met with the body narrative. The autopsy was not simply a medical examination that ensures there will be no virgin births on Fiorina, but a ritual enactment that recasts Newt as a sacrificial offering whose open body and blood signal the new life to come, for Spike the dog is about to give birth to a new type of Alien.

Superintendent Andrews is livid when he discovers that, contrary to his orders, Ripley has been "parading in front of the prisoners," that at her request Clemens has performed an unauthorized autopsy on Newt, and that, to top it all off, Ripley claims there is a risk of a cholera epidemic if they do not cremate the bodies of Newt and Hicks. Eyeing Ripley, he takes his patriarchal wrath out on her:

ANDREWS: We have twenty-five prisoners in this facility, all double-Y chromos, all thieves, rapists, murderers, child molesters, all scum. Just because they've taken on religion doesn't make them any less dangerous. I try not to offend their convictions [meaning Ripley's presence does]. I don't want to upset the order. I don't want ripples in the water and I don't want a woman walking around giving them ideas.

RIPLEY: [Answering sarcastically] I see. For my own personal safety.

ANDREWS: That's right.

Andrews' wonderful pun on Ripley's name as the effect that she has on his "smoothly run facility" shows that, like his men, he thinks of women only as trouble. His attitude explains why Clemens did not ask permission for the autopsy. It also explains why Ripley is unwilling to tell anyone about the Alien—Andrews would dismiss her as hysterical (which he does later).

The setting for Newt's and Hicks' funeral is the cavernous furnace room. Warden Andrews' procedural reading from some future version of the *Book of Common Prayer* (that tried and true all-purpose reader of British imperialism) is almost laughingly typical, as bad or worse, in its own way, than the lack of words at Kane's funeral in *Alien*. His alteration of the actual text ("Earth to earth, ashes to ashes, dust to dust; in sure and certain hope of the Resurrection")[13] commits the bodies of Hicks and Newt to "the void" without any hint of resurrection. Dillon's intrusion at the end of Andrews' reading comes as an unexpected rupture in the text. Unlike Andrews, Dillon improvises, and his oration describes a worldview where pain, suffering, and death are all part of life. As he speaks, Fincher punctuates his lines with shots of Spike's delivery of the Alien:

Why? Why are the innocent punished?
[Dog shakes and whimpers.]
Why the sacrifice? Why the pain?
[Dog flops onto side.]
There aren't any promises. Nothing is certain.
[Dog convulses violently.]
Only that some get called, some get saved.
[A tear slides down Ripley's cheek.]
She won't ever know the hardship and grief for those left behind.
[Dog's chest convulses, sprays blood.]
We commit these bodies to the void with a glad heart.
[Shrouded bodies fall into the furnace. Dog convulses violently and growls.]
For within each seed, there is a promise of a flower.
[The Alien erupts bloodily from dog's chest.]

And within each death, no matter how small
[Ripley's nose bleeds]
there is always a new life,
[blood-covered Alien "coos" on floor]
a new beginning.
[Alien stands.]
Amen.
[Dillon holds up his fist in the "black power" salute. The Alien
    stretches its jaws and extends a toothed tongue.]

Although the wrapped up bodies of Hicks and Newt remind us visually of Kane's contained body, there is an emotional tone to the scene
foreign to *Alien*. As the bodies fall into the furnace, they are superimposed over a close-up of Ripley's sorrowful face. These were people
she deeply cared for, and now they are gone. But she is not alone: a
new Alien has been born to fill the gap left by the deaths of Newt and
Hicks. The shot of the inmates' echoing "Amen" and close-fisted salute stands as a visual welcome to the Alien, who shivers and then
skitters away growling. At the same time, the conjunction of Dillon's
oratory and the images of the Alien's birth is ironic, for the bloody
newborn Alien does not look like the "promise of a flower." Rather,
its birth from a black dog suggests a monstrous birth, a demon, a
mockery of the Lord's creation.[14]
    Ripley's nosebleed further connects her body with that of the dog,
indicating, in fact, her status as contaminated "bitch." It is a red flag
that indicates "something is going on inside the body,"[15] a sign of the
interior life/self that points to the stained innocence in the film's opening shots. The blood that indicated contamination now indicates her
difference, her monstrosity. The fact that the blood erupts from Ripley's nose and not her vagina in no way diminishes the importance of
the symbolic bleeding, for the face (specifically the mouth) is how the
Alien enters the human body. Furthermore, the nosebleed represents
the confluence of the microcosm and macrocosm—what is happening
in the outside world is happening inside Ripley. She has become that
which indicates the future and that which protects against it. She is

the omen, the harbinger of evil, the totem, the protector, the Madonna: she has been revealed as the fetish. Her transformation is complete as, with hair shorn like Jeanne d'Arc, she showers just meters away from the inmates—how can we not think of Marion in *Psycho*?

The Female Man

> A woman shall not wear a man's apparel, nor shall a man put on a woman's garment; for whoever does such things is abhorrent to the LORD your God.
>
> —Deuteronomy 22:5

This is the body the studio advertised: shorn and sullied, Ripley stands squared in the frame in dark undershirt, pants, bulky jacket, and gloves. The shaved head and borrowed clothes make her look masculine, or perhaps androgynous, but definitively not attractive— and yet this image was supposed to *sell* the film. The poster's tag line reads, "In 1979 it came from within. In 1985 it was gone forever. In 1992 our worst fears have come true. It's back." Like the trailer's proclamation that "The bitch is back," these lines create an odd context for the pronoun reference *it*. Could the poster be referring to Ripley as an "it," like the ambiguously gendered Pat from *Saturday Night Live*?

Well, of course not. As any fool can tell, the "it" is the monster that comes from within. Yet "it" also refers to Ripley, as her androgynous image suggests. Here we have a woman, alone, dressed like a man, defiant, clench-jawed, standing in place of the monster of the title. This is not Lieutenant Ripley, not "Mommy," and certainly not "Ellen." This—this "it"—is a woman shorn and bereft of all traces of womanhood, a mother bereft of man and child, an officer without rank or uniform, a beast hunter without a flamethrower/machine gun/ grenade launcher combo. Her appropriation of the prisoner's look— right down to the gloved hands, the shaved head, and dirt—indicates a blatant transgression of the sex/gender barrier.

130

Shorn and sullied: the abject woman.

But then, Fincher was no stranger to transgender performance. While Ripley's poster image may seem a far cry from Madonna, it may be instructive to remember Madonna simulating the male in *Express Yourself* by wearing a double-breasted suit and a monocle, only to throw the coat's top open, flashing her lacy brassiere. As she dances, she grabs her crotch in a parody of Michael Jackson's trademark dance move, her demeanor implying not cross-dressing, but appropriation. Madonna makes no attempt to fool our perception, to *become* male. Rather, the symbols of power (the suit, the monocle) are appropriated by her body and thereby take on a new (if culturally ambiguous) meaning. Similarly, Ripley's shaved head, masculine dress, and self-assured demeanor blurs the gender boundary, if in a less playful way.

Weaver's shaved head draws simultaneously upon several intersecting, if conflicting, cultural referents: images of monks and nuns mingle with that of prisoners—particularly those from World War II concentration camps[16]—and with military maniacs and skinheads. But in Ripley's image the rejection of traditional femininity à la Sinèad O'Connor also meets the fetish image of the mesmerizing Lieutenant Ilia from *Star Trek: The Motion Picture*. For, as Ros Jennings notes,

> The use of close-ups, and specifically head shots, to represent Ripley, also seem to create her as a fetish. In these shots she is calling on a whole certain "look" which has been encoded within the Hollywood cinema. Ripley's "look" is not only reminiscent of Maria Falconetti's classic image of Joan of Arc, but also—given the beautiful way in which her close-ups are lit—they conjure up parallels with the likes of [Greta] Garbo and [Marlena] Dietrich, who were two stars who specialized in the head-fetish shot.[17]

However, while Weaver's shorn head and Fincher's camera work fetishize Ripley, Jennings (crediting Weaver's role as producer) also sees a shift in her presentation from passive object of desire to the active subject of desire. As the photos of Falconetti and Weaver below indicate, while their physical appearance is strikingly similar, they convey quite different embodiments. The contrast is arresting: Falconetti's Joan is transcendent, her body a mere shell for the purified spirit about to take flight, her eyes vacant, turned inward. Weaver's Ripley, on the other hand, is actively engaged with her surroundings, her eyes casting a penetrating gaze. She is, to borrow a phrase from Elaine Scarry, radically embodied—all there and all aware.

Ripley, blatantly disobeying Superintendent Andrews' orders, crosses the gender boundary by deciding to eat breakfast with the inmates in the mess hall. In a take on the prison film cafeteria scene, which usually involves a tête-à-tête between the protagonist and the cell-block leader, she moves softly around the cafeteria, while the inmates follow her moves nervously (one even crossing himself, as if to guard himself from evil) and takes her tray to the table where the spiritual leader, Dillon, is seated. He looks away, refusing eye con-

Falconetti embracing God. Weaver defying the sinful Dillon.

tact. When she attempts to thank him for his homily during the cremation of her friends, he interrupts her with a warning that he hopes will send her packing: "You don't wanna know me, lady. I'm a rapist and murderer of women." Ripley, not flinching in the least, answers softly, "Well, I guess I must make you nervous." The men at Dillon's table are flabbergasted at her response, and she seizes the opportunity to take a seat, adding insult to injury by invading the men's personal space (the convicts have left an empty place between them to avoid physical contact).

We are struck by how masculine she looks, especially compared to Junior (Holt McCallany), the convict she sits beside. Head down, Junior focuses on looking at the table, unspeakably angry at her transgression and we are aware of his telltale teardrop tattoo marking him as a murderer.[18] Dillon takes off his glasses, apparently giving up on scaring Ripley away.

DILLON: Do you have any faith, sister?
RIPLEY: Not much.
DILLON: We've got a lot of faith here. [Junior looks at Dillon.]
    Enough even for you.
RIPLEY: I thought women weren't allowed.
DILLON: Well, we've never had any before, but we tolerate any
    body, even [with determination] the intolerable.
RIPLEY: [softly] Thank you.
DILLON: That's just a statement of principle, nothing personal.
    [Ripley lowers her head in acknowledgment.] You see, we've

got a good place to wait here. And until now [he smiles] no
temptation.

Dillon's "You don't wanna know me, lady" implies more than it
seems, for "know" can be taken in the sense of "to understand" but
also in the biblical sense of "to have sex with." Dillon's second pronouncement, "I'm a rapist and murderer of women," indicates that
his being, "I am," is dependent upon his sin: he is "a rapist and
murderer of women." He does not say "I was" or "I have committed
rape and murder." He is his sin, and his pronouncement implies that
we all are our sins. Ripley's sin is to be a "lady," not in the sense of
the Virgin Mary, "Our Lady," but in the sense of "the intolerable."
Though Dillon's "the intolerable" could refer to all of sinful, degraded
humanity (including the prisoners themselves),[19] its most obvious reference is Ripley as "woman" in all its negative connotations, but
particularly as "temptation." Ripley's responses, on the other hand,
show that she is resolved to be accepted on her own terms. She stares
unflinchingly into the eyes of Dillon, "a rapist and murderer of
women," and suggests that *she* makes *him* nervous. She exudes feminine power at its height. She not only does not seem afraid of these
men, she is not afraid of these men because she has seen much, much
worse. Although her boldness initiates a precarious (and precocious)
bond with Dillon, her composure inevitably challenges the "less enlightened" convicts. Led by the tear-sporting Junior, some of them
will later attempt to rape her.

Following this intrusion into the male space and psyche, Ripley
commits the daring (and surprising) act of proposing sex to Dr. Clemens. As Ripley and Clemens are having a few shots of an obviously
"homemade" alcohol, she questions him for background information
on Fiorina. At one point, Clemens inquires whether she likes her new
haircut. Ripley smiles a bit and touches her head, which sets her to
thinking (about her looks?). Clemens looks at her, and she looks at
him looking at her, so he moves away and tries to steer the conversation away from them. He asks what she was looking for in Newt during
the autopsy. Ripley does not acknowledge his question, instead asking

if he is attracted to her. Playing dumb, Clemens asks her what she means: "In what way?" "In that way," she responds, indicating that she means sexually with a modest movement of the head. Clemens marvels at her direct approach, and she explains, simply, "I've been out here a long time."

This is an unusual scene for a science-fiction film, where sexual desire is normally repressed,[20] and it is certainly most unusual in its representation of female desire as natural. As a rule, Hollywood films depict female sexuality as permissible only in terms of romantic, heterosexual relationships; any other manifestation of desire suggests a monstrous sexuality. In *Ghostbusters* (1984), for example, Weaver plays Dana Barret, a nice girl who becomes possessed by a demon. The possession makes her, among other things, sexually aggressive in a way that strikingly contrasts with Ripley's desire in *Alien³*: "Do you want this body?" Dana purrs at Ghostbuster Dr. Peter Venkman. *Alien³*, however, negates both impulses: Ripley may feel affection for the good doctor, but she definitely is not in love with him, nor is she a sex fiend. Rather, Ripley, an astronaut who has been in outer space a really long time, is simply asking for sexual relief.[21] That her rather mundane request for sex seems transgressive is as much a commentary on Hollywood as on the previous *Alien* movies. After all the surviving and killing and flame-throwing, Ripley turns out to be a normal woman with normal desires, not a virginal superchick.

In spite of *Alien³*'s R rating, the viewer never gets to see the sexual act. Rather, Ripley and Clemens' encounter is framed around the scene of convict Murphy's death at the hands of the Alien while he cleans a ventilation shaft. Murphy finds what appears to be a shed skin. Then, thinking he sees Spike in a small side shaft, he leans in to inspect it. The Alien strikes him on the head, making him fall back into the shaft's large fan that slices him to pieces. Thus, the attack on Murphy operates as a stand-in for the sex act itself (as exploding fireworks do in more conventional films). Most interesting, if disturbing, is the comparison between the vagina and the filthy and lethal ventilation shaft, for it insinuates Ripley's contamination and also alerts the viewer to her status as a deadly woman.

The postcoital scene begins with a shot of the fetishized, almost identical heads of Ripley and Clemens. Then we see from Ripley's point of view that Clemens, like Fiorina's convicts, has a bar code tattooed onto the back of the head. Significantly, Ripley is behind Clemens in the traditional male position as if she has, could have, taken him from behind. Again, there is a break with traditional film depictions of heterosexual encounters, since the female holding a male from behind most often indicates a failed sexual encounter, impotence, and, by association, a "feminized" male. As their dialogue reveals, this was not the case for Ripley and Clemens. Certainly, as Jennings points out, this postcoital scene plays with ironic simultaneous gay and lesbian references: the similitude between Ripley and Clemens' heads, faces, and clothing is emphasized with alternating close-ups. Fincher's substitution of head shots for the rest of the body, moreover, continually dares us to imagine the difference between Clemens and Ripley while taunting us with the similarity of their looks. We must assume the male body and the female body that we are not shown, which obviously leaves a window of interpretation open within the text of the film for gay and lesbian readings.[22] The impression of similitude is enhanced by the fact that we do not see Clemens behave in the traditional male role of active or aggressive lover. In fact, he is the one who is cuddled, and he seems apprehensive and possibly even nervous during the postcoital interchange; he even softly says "Thank you" for sex in a way that ironically echoes Bishop's "Thank you" to Hudson for being the unwilling subject of his knife trick in *Aliens*.

In spite of their recent physical intimacy—and perhaps one could even say they have a certain level of empathetic intimacy as well—both Ripley and Clemens are still harboring potentially damaging secrets. That Ripley cannot tell Clemens about the Alien and that he does not disclose the reasons why he has been in prison is further evidence that their relationship is "casual" without the romantic undertones present from the beginning between Ripley and Hicks in *Aliens*. Whereas Ripley and Hicks come together to protect the child Newt and form an essentially chaste nuclear family, Ripley and Clemens engage in unauthorized carnal activities revolving around shooting up, death, and sex, and we should remember that one of their major bonding scenes is performed over the open, bloody body of the child Newt. By comparison, Ripley's interaction with Dillon seemed infinitely more open and honest.

Clemens' bonding with Ripley, however cursory, gets him absolutely nowhere with Warden Andrews. Immediately following their sexual encounter, he is summoned to the site of Murphy's death, a death that Andrews quickly blames on Ripley: this is what happens to men, he states, when they walk around with an erection. Ironically, Clemens also finds some basis to suspect Ripley as well—the telltale burn mark in the tunnel and the fact that Murphy "fell into" a fan, which was actually blowing his way, makes the doctor wonder what she may know or be hiding. Even worse, back in Andrews' office Clemens is dressed down for betraying the boy's club and allowing Ripley to wander about freely. Andrews, tired of being disobeyed and clearly agitated by the apparent erosion of his authority due to the woman, stoops to blackmail and threatens to tell Ripley about Clemens' dirty past. Essentially, the woman—a clear threat to patriarchal authority—must be made to obey at any cost.

Rape, Death, and Abjection

> Rape fattens on the fantasies of the normal male
> like a maggot in garbage.
> —Marge Piercy, "Rape Poem"

Ripley's treatment goes beyond the objectification and attempted control of a woman. The sheer depth of the mistrust, fear, and loathing surrounding her, without any apparent redeeming qualities for anyone other than Clemens, labels Ripley as the lowest of the low. The film thus appropriately sends her to the trash heap in search of her former savior and friend from *Aliens*, the android Bishop. Logically, of course, it makes no sense at all that Bishop's remains would be discarded, as the Company would want what is left of him since his "brain" is a computer that could easily be made to divulge all the information acquired on LV-426. But the scene does serve to reinforce the level of abjection in the film by sending Ripley looking for a former "friend" who has literally become "garbage." Like a scavenging leper, she sifts through the detritus of the fallen men. Not only is she at the "rat's ass end of space," as the convicts describe Fiorina 161, she is searching through the filth. It is at this very moment, when she apparently could not do any worse, that she is cornered by four prisoners, who attempt to rape her.

Three interrelated narratives coalesce in the rape scene. First, rape is posited as a biological imperative that is only kept barely in check by patriarchal authority. Thanks to Andrews' constant reminders that these men are all "filth," combined with the fact that they are genetically "abnormal," we are invited to see the attempted rape as a product of their biological imperatives. Surely Andrews would see it that way. These men cannot help themselves. As such, it makes sense that their misogynistic religion is just another symptom of their biology.

Second, rape is posited as failure of the spirit to control the needs of the body. Dillon specifically codes the actions of the men as "a lapse in faith" that overturns their vows of celibacy. (Morse's earlier comment that this vow "also includes women" clearly implies that, before Ripley's arrival, same-sex couplings were the primary temptation on Fiorina.) Dillon, therefore, prevents the rape and delivers a fitting "reeducation" of his brothers by beating them with a steel pipe.

However, these traditional views on men, women, and rape are undermined in the way Fincher shoots the scene. In this third narrative, rape is portrayed solely as an act of power. This is emphasized in the lack of flesh exposed: Ripley's pants are not breached, nor is her top ripped off to expose her breasts. A knife becomes the visual stand-in for the penis. Junior's victory scream at having Ripley at his mercy further indicates the power and gender dynamics at play in rape: this is Man defining himself through Woman.[23] Thus, although the convicts' actions reflect a world of essential biology (Ripley is female, they are male), the film deconstructs their impulse by refusing to show Ripley as the feminine. The scene is not about lust or reproduction: it is about defining masculine power through the subjection of the female body. Junior's use of sunglasses to hide his eyes and his intention to take Ripley from behind demonstrates an obsession with anonymous penetration and suggests, not vaginal sex, but sodomy. That Ripley's baggy attire hides her "female parts" further emphasizes she is not "asking for it." At the end of *Alien*, the male audience could understand why the Alien approaches Ripley dripping K-Y jelly, but nothing whatsoever in *Alien³* justifies Ripley's body as a traditional object of desire. In fact, the attackers show no curiosity about her body at all. It is almost as if she were a new male in the prison about to be "initiated."

Furthermore, we must consider that Ripley is not safe because she has been publicly labeled as the intolerable Other by Superintendent Andrews, who places himself in the position of "protecting" Ripley from the men as well as the men from Ripley: a position based on his presumed ability to control the movement of bodies about the facility. We quickly learn that he is incapable of controlling anyone. Ripley, like her attackers, wanders freely about the facility. She is just as disdainful of Andrews' orders as they are. We must wonder, then, if Ripley is really in any more danger due to her sex than any other outsider. What led us to this notion in the first place besides Andrews' own warnings and behavior? Her sex, clearly, is a danger to his authority; but, at the same time, her sex is only a word: something said of her and about her, but never actually visually correlated with her body. We realize that "woman" in *Alien³* is a patriarchal construction of mythical proportions.

There is, however, something in the complex more dangerous than woman, and the film quickly moves to the unveiling of that demon. For the Alien is the supreme rapist and murderer of this narrative, as its attack on convicts Boggs (Leon Herbert), Rains (Christopher J. Fields), and Golic (Paul McGann) in the labyrinthine tunnels of the facility proves. If we accept the biological deterministic narrative that rape is a function of double-Y chromosome males, that they cannot help themselves, then we must further accept the argument that the Alien is, likewise, a product of its biology and is simply conforming to genetically transferred instinctual behaviors. This possibility is informed and supported by the altered form of the Alien from humanoid to canine. Cujo aside, we are more likely to think of a doglike creature as behaving on instinct than with true malice. However, the religious context also supports the reading that the Alien's attack is somehow a punishment for the attempted rape of Ripley. It makes no difference that the exact prisoners are not punished; rather, their fate is a collective one as evidenced by their lack of individuality in appearance and dress. Thus, divine punishment is not particular (as Dillon's is) but collective. Likewise, minor details in the scene support a divine retribution reading: in a sort of hidden joke, the prisoners who are killed have just been discussing which curse words God does and does not allow while, of course, mentioning the words themselves.

As if nothing had happened, as if she had not been the victim of an attempted gang rape just moments before, Ripley prepares to activate the remains of Bishop (Lance Henriksen). And a gruesome affair it is. His head has been broken open, one eye is milky white from severe damage, and his skin is slick with grime and goo. Ripley peels back a large flap of skin from Bishop's skull and shoves an electrical probe deep into his ear and another into his skull. Hotwired like a car, Bishop comes around. Still the likable android from *Aliens*, at first he sees the inherent humor in their situation: he cannot stop himself from teasing Ripley about her shaved head ("I like your new haircut"), and he jokes to ease Ripley's worry about his pain ("My legs hurt"). Appropriating the feminine voice of the *Sulaco*'s computer, he then replays the ship's flight record, confirming the presence of "an" Alien on board (he never mentions a second one or which cryo-tube was "infected"). Bishop also confirms that the Company, like the omniscient Judeo-Christian deity, "knows everything," giving Ripley good reason to fear that her imminent "rescue" is a Company cover-up to obtain the Alien. In yet another reversal of Cameron's

140

Aliens, Alien³ once again depicts the Company as the true villain of the narrative.

However, the purpose of the scene is not to add to the story, for the audience has already guessed much of the information that Bishop puts forward, but to link Bishop and Ripley in their misery and abjection. Deprived of Newt and Hicks, Ripley now must face the degradation of the agreeable android who had proven himself humane by staying put during hard times on LV-426. The heroic Bishop is now a piece of garbage, a "glorified toaster," as he calls himself. No wonder the android requests to be "disconnected" after he has been of service, as he would rather be "nothing" if he cannot be "top of the line." Like the impregnated female colonist in *Aliens*, Bishop's presence serves the need to place the grotesque body on display, to have that body confess its death drive, then see its life extinguished. Ripley grants Bishop's request, but the issue is not resolved, as she will make a similar request of Dillon when she learns her own body has been breached by the Alien.

Meanwhile, Golic has managed to escape the Alien and is brought into the infirmary covered in blood and babbling about "the dragon." Drawing on the figure of the dragon as a symbol for Satan as well as the hellhound, the Alien could be read as the instrument of God's wrath (and, simultaneously, of God's grace) on the sinners of Fiorina, for they have chosen to play it safe—to hide from the world. If facing Ripley tests the men's faith, facing the Alien will test their mettle, the sense of *who they are as men*. Always true to form, Andrews refuses to believe in mythical creatures and instead automatically assumes that the biological defect of the prisoners has once again won the day: Golic has killed Boggs and Rains himself. Ripley, on the other hand, believes Golic and asks for a private moment with Andrews to tell her story.

In a repeat of *Aliens*, the man in charge dismisses her story as hysterical. Ripley does not care, but wants to know if there are any weapons they can use against the Alien. There are none. "Then we're fucked," Ripley exclaims bitterly. "No," says Andrews. "You are fucked. Confined to the infirmary. Quarantined." Woman, he seems to be saying, is a disease. She looks at him in shock and disbelief, and he takes the opportunity to have Mr. Aaron take her out of the office. He cannot resist one last jibe that inadvertently connects the Alien with the convicts: "I think you'll be safe from any large, nasty beasts while you are there." Obviously, Andrews believes Ripley's story of the Alien masks her fear of Fiorina's men because that is what he expects from women: foolishness and hysteria. His opinion of Ripley contrasts harshly with our own, for we know from *Aliens* the real fools are those who take the Alien as a hallucination.

Ripley returns to the infirmary for a round of needles and confessions with Clemens. His story makes us aware of the perverse nature of his relationship with Ripley, for he uses the same tool, the syringe, with which he doped himself and accidentally killed eleven of his patients. His sin confessed, the Alien comes for him and dispatches him quickly. Ripley attempts to escape but is cornered by it, and she cowers in terror. It moves its head near hers and lets its phallic tongue out slowly, as if considering something, while she looks away, expecting its blow at any second. The close-up of their heads contrasts their images: one shiny black and deliberate, the other white and paralyzed by fear. That it does not kill her is by no means our first clue that she is infected, but it is a striking image: Death has stared her in the face and allowed her to live. To it, she represents its future: the only reason she lives is because she is a surrogate womb. It leaves her dragging the body of her lover up into the ceiling.

Andrews, who has dismissed her story of the Alien as fantastical, almost chokes in bile when she interrupts his second "rumor control" meeting yelling "It's here!" Losing his composure, he spits out: "Stop this nonsense at once! Stop it!" This is his final confrontation with "this foolish woman," for the Alien grabs him from above and kills him with virtually the entire crew as witness. Now there is no doubt that the creature is real and that these rapists and murderers will learn the fear of violation, of death, at the hands of the ultimate predator.

However, if the heavens have sent them the dragon, they have also sent them Saint Ripley (as *Newsweek*'s David Ansen christened her). As the nervous men argue about who will be in charge now that Andrews is dead, the camera isolates and foregrounds Ripley, making the inmates look tiny behind her to contrast her calm deliberation to their panicked state. We know what is coming before it happens: Dillon calls for Ripley to take charge. After all, she has battled the Alien before, and survived. Ripley does not move, though Dillon's request has radically shifted her position in the world of Fiorina. Ripley, now freed of the accusation that she is hysterical, casts off the cloak of Cassandra and becomes, rather, the phallic woman. Her knowledge, her experience, and her training replace her physical lack.

What is truly interesting, however, is that she does not *do* anything different. She does not suddenly pull out a gun or a flamethrower or climb into a powerloader like she did in *Aliens*. Stripped of all the accoutrements shackled to her by Cameron, her motivation is no longer (at least literally) maternal, nor is she required to "man up" (behave like a man) in order to take charge. Though a woman, she has been asked to take charge, a proposition that neither the crew of the *Nostromo* in *Alien* nor the Colonial Marines in *Aliens* ever seem to consider. Dillon, on the other hand, proves to be a man who can yield authority when it is necessary.

Dillon's gesture is not well received by the rest of the convicts. "Forget Shirley Temple," says one inmate, ludicrously pointing to Ripley's lack of Shirley Temple charm and trademark blond curls. They want Dillon to lead, but he flatly refuses: he is not "the officer type," meaning that he cannot make decisions that would imperil his flock. Ripley clears her throat to catch their attention and asks about the facility's weapons status and about surveillance equipment. Frustrated by the men's powerlessness, which is exacerbated by their need for a woman to lead, Morse gets in her face and loudly explains to her the facts of the situation: "We got no entertainment centers, no climate control, no view screens, no surveillance, no freezers, no fuckin' ice cream, no guns, no rubbers, no women; all we got here is *shit*." They are, in effect, powerless, unwanted, broken, abandoned, and forgotten. They are the abject. He rounds up his diatribe by blaming the woman for their condition: "What the hell are we even talking to her for? She's the one that brought the fucker! Why don't we take her head and shove it through the fucking wall!" Ripley, who has just been through an attempted rape, stares at him without even blinking, daring him. Dillon deflates Morse with a very soft "Morse, why don't you shut the fuck up?" He's an idiot: she's their only hope. The men are helpless; the woman must lead. It could not get worse than this . . . or could it?

Ripley's Secret Self

> Your body is a battleground.
> —from a composition by Barbara
> Kruger designed as a poster for the
> massive pro-choice march that took
> place on April 9, 1989, in
> Washington, D.C.

Once the necessary impossibility has occurred—that these men accept this woman as their leader—the film seems to forget that any division between them ever existed. There are no further references to her sex, or to the attempted rape. Rather, their biological imperatives are displaced onto the Alien, which Ripley envisions as a "lion" lurking near its prey. This adroit definition of the Other as a biologically determined (instinctual) creature indicates, by association, that biology is the Other, the enemy that must be defeated. Suddenly, to be human (the opposite of the Other Alien) is to occupy a position in defiance of biological narratives.

Constricted by the lack of weapons, Ripley puts together a feminine trap: they will use fire to chase the Alien into the giant womb-tomb of the unused toxic waste storage room. The plan requires that everyone spread a dangerous flammable substance on the floor of the facility's tunnels. Predictably, the Alien kills an inmate, who drops his lighter stick into the flammable muck below, and the whole place becomes an inferno. Fortunately, the facility's sprinklers still work, but at least ten men die.

As she makes the rounds with Dillon, Ripley feels extremely nauseous. She decides to use the EEV's neuroscanner to check for "blood clots" and "fractures" that would explain her sickness. Fearing for her safety, Mr. Aaron follows her and ends up working the scanner while she lies in a cryo-tube. Perhaps because Mr. Aaron is apprehensively watching for the Alien outside, it takes him a while to identify a blurry dark shadow labeled "foreign tissue" as a larval Alien inside Ripley. Ironically, the penetrable female body denied in *Alien* in the form of Ripley comes full circle: she, now the only conceivable hero of the franchise, has finally fallen prey to the Alien.

The image on the scanner is an ultrasound turned on its head: this is not the happy mother looking at her unborn child and asking "Is it a boy or a girl?" but rather a shocked woman refusing to believe she has a death-dealing infestation. "What does it look like?" she asks Mr. Aaron. "Horrible," he responds. Ripley asks him to freeze the image—she must see to believe. She sits a few seconds with her eyes closed, dreading what she will see. She takes a breath, faces the scanner screen, opens her eyes, and there it is: her worst nightmare in plain black, white, and gray.

Thus, the "us versus them" dichotomy of *Aliens* is internalized, and the battlefield becomes, not the Alien body, but the human body. For the first time, the Alien is openly acknowledged not only as an outside force that threatens to engulf, penetrate, or explode the human body, but as an interior corruption, a "child" that is perceived as a cancerous growth. As Camille Paglia writes in *Sexual Personae*:

Pregnancy demonstrates the deterministic character of woman's sexuality. Every pregnant woman has body and self taken over by a chthonian force beyond her control. In the welcome pregnancy, this is a happy sacrifice. But in the unwanted one, initiated by rape or misadventure, it is a horror. Such unfortunate women look directly into nature's heart of darkness. For a fetus is a benign tumor, a vampire who steals in order to live.[24]

In Ripley's chest, in her heart, lies darkness, the beast, the evil within. The literalness of her infection, however, is the most important issue, for it transforms Ripley's heretofore heroic body into an abject body that is to be discarded when her dark child is born. Ripley's body now belongs in the narrative of demon possession, supernatural pregnancy, and monstrous motherhood: the occult film. In the fashion of Father Karras in *The Exorcist*, for example, Ripley is the exorcist with a demon in her chest. And while Ripley is an innocent vessel of the supernatural, like the impregnated mothers of *Rosemary's Baby* and *The Seventh Sign* (1988), her image also partakes of the female jackal/bitch mother of Damien in *The Omen* (1976).

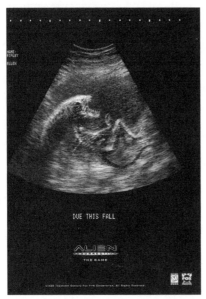 

Monstrous Other or Shadow Self? Contradicting Depictions of the Alien Queen

No longer simply a monstrous creature to be dispatched, the Alien Queen has literally become part of Ripley; so much a part of her, in fact, that her image is almost indiscernible on the EEV's scanner output. Thus, although some advertisements for *Alien³* show the Alien Queen fetus as an independent being—an image reiterated in the *Alien Resurrection* video game poster above—the film emphasizes the interconnectedness of the host and the "foreign tissue" growing inside her. Ripley the Woman, Ripley the Intolerable has become now, by association with the Alien Queen, Ripley the Monstrous. And though she will continue to refer to the fetus as an "it" throughout the film, as we will discuss later, her final actions indicate that she has accepted this monstrous female not only as her own "child" but also as a part of her self.

Significantly the advertising poster for *Alien³* figures the fetal Queen replicating the yin-yang symbol. The image expresses the dynamic interaction between the Alien and Ripley: not separate anymore, but two parts of a whole. Thus, Ripley's externalized shadow self from *Aliens* becomes in Fincher's film her secret self.

Having learned about the Alien inside her, Ripley feels repugnance, vulnerability, and powerlessness. Whereas she could calmly stand being scorned and abused before, what can she say now that her body has betrayed her? She is—has always been—a victim and a monster, polluted since the beginning of the narrative. Now she knows that her pollution will infect the entire planet and, perhaps, Earth. She attempts to warn the rescue ship that Fiorina 161 is "toxic." When Mr. Aaron refuses to send her message (he has a wife and child he would like to go back to), she seeks another venue: death before the Alien Queen bursts through her rib cage.

Ripley sets out to look for the Alien, basing her search on a metaphor: it is somewhere "down there in the basement," she surmises. For the basement, the world below of the unconscious, is the land of nightmares where we all meet what demons we fear most. In *Alien³*, however, Ripley's worst fear is already inside her, and what waits in the basement below can no longer frighten her; rather, Ripley willfully seeks death in the depths.

Ripley's engagement with the Alien is not expressed in terms of defiance as in *Alien* and *Aliens* (where she called her foe "son of a bitch" and "bitch," respectively), but in terms of need. Once down in the basement, Ripley calls to the Alien as if to a lover ("Where are you when I need you?") or a fearful child ("Don't be afraid . . . I'm part of the family"). What she wants from the creature is a simple favor: for it to end the long nightmare she has endured since *Alien*.

Ironically, the very fact that she is "one of the family" keeps the Alien once again from killing her, even though she aggressively provokes it, and so Ripley turns to Dillon for death instead.

Dillon could kill her easily enough—he is, after all a murderer of women—but he needs her to help fight the Alien and save his men. She will get her "quick and painless" death, he promises, but only when the Alien is dead. Besides, the being she carries inside of her makes her, at least for a brief time, impervious to the Alien, and that is just about the best weapon they have. Such are the prerogatives of motherhood.

Madonna or Whore?: The Last Temptation of Ripley

> Better to Rule in Hell than serve in Heaven.
>
> —Satan, from Milton's *Paradise Lost*

> Well-behaved women rarely make history.
>
> —Laurel Thatcher Ulrich

The inmates take their places in the great hall for one last meeting. Dillon, standing on the platform below, tells them it is time for plan B, but the men are scared. Dillon uses the tried-and-true appeal to manhood: "Just sit here on your ass. The rest of you pussies can sit it out, too. Me and her [indicating Ripley] will do all the fighting." If they thought Ripley was intolerable just for being a woman, then a woman fighting while they hide and wait for rescue is an intolerable irony. The new plan—to taunt the Alien into the giant lead mold and drop hot lead over it—requires they use themselves as bait in the facility's labyrinthine corridors. Understandably, the convicts whine. Calmly, seriously, Dillon points out that all they have left is the choice of how to die: "like men" or "on their knees, begging." The moment of their trial and judgment has come.

When asked by Mr. Aaron why not wait it out until the rescue team arrives, Ripley steps in to lay it out for them: the Company is not coming to rescue her, or them. All they want is the Alien, and perhaps everyone on Fiorina will be killed just for having seen it. She tells them, "They think we are crud." The Company is not interested in its prodigal sons. The game, they have to realize, is no longer Men versus Women; the only game is Power, and Power does not recognize sex except as a rhetorical tool of convenience. Thus, while Dillon appeals to their machismo, Ripley appeals to their equally abject status: like her, like the crew of the *Nostromo,* and like the Colonial Marines of *Aliens,* they are nothing. Realizing the truth, admitting they are unwanted and despised, sets them free.

The convicts know there is very little chance they will survive, but they try anyway. Lost in the labyrinth, they struggle to trap the Alien, but for the most part they end up trapped themselves. The Alien, as always, knows the maze better than the humans, but this time it seems to operate more on instinct than intellect. Behaving very much like the lion Ripley takes it to be, it chases the convicts on all fours and, unlike the previous Aliens, it stops to maul its prey. Every now and then we see the running, screaming humans from its point of view, as if Fincher were trying to replicate the attacks of the giant shark in *Jaws* (1975). Outside the labyrinth, Ripley waits for them to flush it out: she is in charge of keeping the Alien inside the piston chamber by blocking its entrance; because it does not want to hurt her, the reasoning goes, it will not try to get out.

But the plan does not work because one panicky convict starts the piston too soon. Dillon convinces the Alien to leave the labyrinth by pretending to threaten Ripley. Incensed, the Alien follows him into the mold, and Dillon chooses to stay with it so Morse can pour the hot lead over both of them. The anguished Ripley reminds him of his promise to kill her, but he knows what he must do and so tells her she is "in God's hands" now. Throwing his ax down and taking his glasses off, Dillon engages in a hand-to-hand combat with the Alien, refusing to budge even when his flesh is torn apart and yelling to it, to himself: "C'mon! Is that all you've got? Fight, motherfucker!" Though his words and actions echo the heroism of Parker and Vasquez, Dillon's macho sacrifice surpasses them both: this is the fight of one who is not afraid to die, of one who understands the symbolic gesture of a rapist and murderer surrendering his life in a struggle to relieve the world of an even worse rapist and murderer. Unlike Vasquez, who battles the Aliens remotely with guns and explosives, Dillon chooses to fight the demon up close and personal and die embracing it.[25]

The hot lead Morse pours over both does not kill the Alien, and it jumps from the bubbling metal. Ripley leaps onto a chain that activates the water sprinklers. The sprinklers douse the Alien: its exoskeleton shatters, then explodes from the internal pressure. One down, one more to go.

In the meantime, the Company's rescue team has arrived, illuminated like a host of angels. It is led by a familiar face: Bishop. For a moment, like Ripley, we are confused. Could it be that Ripley's guardian angel has really come to rescue her? But she knows *her* Bishop is gone, and the team leader reassures her he is not an android, but the human after whom Bishop was modeled. He smiles reassuringly, telling her that the Company wanted her to see a "friendly face," and that he has come to help her by taking the Alien from her and destroying it. When she is understandably suspicious, he tempts her: if she agrees, she will live, perhaps even have children. Interestingly, Bishop's seemingly angelic offer alludes to the devilish temptation of Jesus of Nazareth in Nikos Kazantzakis's novel *The Last Temptation of Christ*: the choice of *not* being the Son of God, *not* going through the painful apotheosis, *not* being the savior of mankind, and becoming instead just a normal man. The implication that Ripley can be saved, cleansed, made anew, made into the old Ripley, returned to the happy motherhood of *Aliens*, lingers for a few moments, tempting us as well as her.

But Ripley knows what she is, what she has always been for the Company, and she also knows there is only one answer: No. For the Company is the nastiest rapist of all, and Bishop's prompt, "You will have to trust me," has been the unmaking of many women before her.

She resolutely closes the mesh gate to stop the Company men from coming onto the gantry where she stands. At this moment she reminds us of Sharon, the protagonist of the apocalyptic film *The Rapture* (1991), who gives up all worldly pleasures to become one of God's chosen—until, that is, she is forced to kill her own starving daughter and starts questioning whether she should love a God that exacts suffering on his people. Thus, when God's rapture happens, Sharon refuses to enter the Kingdom of Heaven, choosing instead to stay alone forever, becoming, in effect, God's adversary. Similarly, Ripley, as the thwarter of the wishes of the godlike Company, proclaims herself as *the* adversary of this narrative. She asks Morse to move the gantry over the main furnace. Standing alone in the brink, sure about what she must do, Ripley takes a leap of faith and defiance: Christ the Lamb meets Milton's Satan.

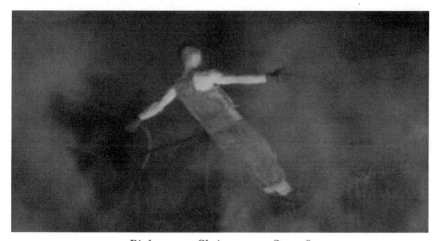

Ripley: new Christ or new Satan?

As Ripley falls, her secret self, her Alien Shadow, her godsend and her escape, bursts out of her chest. The image eerily reminds the viewer of the Immaculate Heart of Mary and the Sacred Heart of Christ, with the Alien Queen-embryo taking the place of the symbolic, exposed heart. As a reproduction of the Virgin of the Immaculate Heart, Ripley's body imperfectly represents the perfect feminine form: immaculate, virtuous, maternal, compassionate—perhaps what is left from her *Aliens* self. As a replication of the Sacred Heart of Jesus, it points to Christ's heart "overflowing with love for men," but at the same time rejected and despised.²⁶ Through the most complete abjection, Ripley has moved beyond evil into love, a love that can even encompass the being that has killed her. Ripley grabs the new-born Queen in a firm but loving embrace: her baby, herself. Her final throes echo those of the female warrior-saint Joan in *The Passion of Joan of Arc*: transfixed, transcendent. As Ripley falls into the purifying fire, her very body becomes the Immaculate Heart and Sacred Heart, with the Alien as the transfixing sword or the perennial crown of thorns. The sun rises on Fiorina as she is delivered into the flames, indicating the ever-revolving interaction between light and darkness.

The Immaculate Heart of the Virgin and Ripley transfixed.

But Ripley is no Joan, for in *Alien³* there is no God but the Company to submit to, and Ripley rejects that option. Neither is she Christ, nor the Virgin, nor, as the men would read her, the intolerable whore. Released from the constraining narrative of biological determinism, which drives the social control of gender imperatives (particularly in the form of religion), Ripley has drawn upon herself all meaning in this falling prison of biology and religiosity. She has become a polyphonic text. No longer the perennial victim of the Company and the Alien, Ripley manages to make her death a victory, her figure fusing with the Alien Queen to give birth to a legendary bitch. Her final discursive act is beyond sacrifice and macho heroism: it is the act of those who know themselves abject. Her immolation is both passive and all-consuming. At least in this respect, *Alien³* manages to transform dystopia and apocalypse into triumph.

152

But what about the audience that has just lost its hero and its Alien? Many viewers identify with the evil Bishop's desperate "Noooo!" when Ripley leaps to her death, for she has thwarted our desire to keep the Alien (and her) with us. Many others, though, understand that hers is the best choice: the patriarchy always desires what the woman has inside of her (her womb or her child) but never the woman herself. [27] Woman is only suffered to live because of her reproductive power. By *Alien³* Ripley understands too well that the Company has never cared for her: it just needs her compliance to have control over the Alien Queen she carries, and if the Alien Queen lives, she will generate thousands more like her, and humanity will be extinguished. In this sense, Ripley's jump is nothing short of an abortion, or as David J. Skal called it, *"Sigourney's Choice."*[28] Like Sophocles' Antigone, who refutes the law of the state when she chooses her own method of death rather than accepting the death sentence assigned to her, Ripley rejects the patriarchy by jumping into the fiery depths, taking her child with her. [29] As a female hero, Ripley speaks the only way a woman can properly "speak," through her body and the products of her body. This is her commentary, her last and final statement to the Company, to us. She leaps both to save humanity and to tell the patriarchy *this body and its products are mine, not yours.*

Ripley, Signing Off: "To Every Woman a Happy Ending"

Whereupon, one day, with a cry of joy, leaving both humanity and intelligence behind, the soul may leap to what it then suddenly recognizes beyond the mask. *Finis tragoedie: incipit comoedia.* The mode of the tragedy dissolves and the myth begins.

—Joseph Campbell, *Primitive Mythology*

By *Alien³*, Ripley has become a familiar figure in popular culture: the *Alien* Woman. Her image instills almost the same fear as the creature itself, for when we see her, we know the Alien must be near. *Alien³*, however, reveals that this woman not only evokes the monster she fights, but that Woman is herself a monster, and like the Alien, an intolerable Other. That a bunch of rapists and murderers finally give voice to this cultural truth only serves to reinforce the legitimacy of the claim: at the "rat's ass end of space," there is no longer a need for genteel illusions. Even Warden Andrews, whom we might expect to make some concessions to her rank, sees only a woman, and a woman means trouble. Thus, where *Alien* displaces female monstrosity onto the Alien and *Aliens* imagines a monstrous, evil Alien Queen, *Alien³* cuts right to the chase—what we are really afraid of is the female in any and every form, whether she be a monster, an officer, a sister, a virgin, a prostitute, or our own mother. For the all-male inhabitants of Fiorina 161, for example, she is the intolerable body that precludes sin and death; for the Company, she is the dangerous antagonist to its desire for the Alien.

Once *Alien³* confesses the covert misogyny of the previous films, we are confronted with a spectacular irony: this woman is an intolerable monster, and she is also the protagonist, the hero, and the best of us all. The defiant Ripley, like her counterparts Thelma and Louise, opens a door for the possibility of another world to exist—the world of *Alien Resurrection*, for example. As Taubin explains about *Alien³* and *Thelma and Louise*: "By choosing to hurl herself over the brink rather than bend to the will of the state, the hero guarantees her transformation from woman to myth."[30] More recently, *Crouching Tiger, Hidden Dragon* (2000) reaffirmed that this is the expected route of all true heroes (female or male)—the leap of faith into the next level of existence. Ripley has become a goddess in her own right. Transformed and mythologized, she becomes the eternal foe, the mother-destroyer of the patriarchal order.

Ripley, like a true hero, "transcends the worst that has ever happened to her"[31] and becomes something new. She and her shadow plunge together into the cleansing fire of eternity and the world beyond. The epitaph on Nikos Kazantzakis's tomb eloquently expresses this divine resolution of the self:

> *I hope for nothing.*
> *I fear nothing.*
> *I am free.*

Fincher cannot resist adding an afterword. With the tone of finality, Fiorina 161's facility shuts down: the massive doors close and lock with a resounding clang, the lights dim, and, finally, the fires of the furnace are extinguished. The rescue team leads Morse away. He turns around to look at what is left of the facility, but one of the Company guards shoves him on. Defiant to the last, Morse spits "Fuck you," for he finally understands who is to blame for the death of his mates and for the creation and the destruction of the hell world he inhabited—the awful power of the Father is that no one else can rule, even in Hell. He marches along with the Company men. The film is concluded, and the series is (apparently) over.

Fincher's camera, however, sneaks us back into the locked facility and wanders to the cryo-tubes in the EEV: that womb, that crystal coffin from which our hero first emerged and to which she returned after the fight was won. We hear the ghost of her voice, scratchy, as if from a long time ago and from far away, speaking the words she spoke when she was the hero of the moment and before she became the grander hero she never wanted to be: her final, hopeful words from *Alien*, now become her epitaph, "This is Ripley, last survivor of the *Nostromo*, signing off."

The film's last image is an indictment of a universe that does not care about the passing of its heroes. The happenings in Fiorina 161 become just a Company memo flashing across the screen: "Weyland-Yutani work prison Fury 161 closed and sealed. Custodial presence terminated. Remaining refining equipment to be sold as scrap. End of transmission." Fincher's ending is a damning condemnation of a technocratic corporate capitalism that desires nothing more than to get its hands on the Alien so it can kill more effectively with less remorse and delusions of morality. The ending is also a bleak lesson that Fincher will reprise in *Fight Club*: you cannot win and you cannot ever get free, but you have to fight them. This is a pessimistic, violent version of "Think globally. Act locally." The real heroes, Fincher seems to be saying, are always the forgotten ones, and, in the end, we all die. It is just a matter, in Dillon's words, of how you check out.

CHAPTER 4

"Who Are You?":
Alien Resurrection and the
Posthuman Subject

> Malcolm: God creates dinosaurs. God
> destroys dinosaurs. God creates
> man. Man destroys God. Man
> creates dinosaurs . . .
> Ellen: . . . Dinosaurs eat man. Woman
> inherits the Earth.
> —*Jurassic Park* (1993)

Buffy the Vampire Slayer Meets *City of Lost Children*

One gets the sense that *Alien Resurrection* is the concoction of a bartender gone mad: a crossbred, cultural cocktail of postmodern reference running in a high-speed blender—with ice. For the fourth installment of the series is, above all, a pastiche that playfully evokes other films (particularly referencing its own ancestors in the *Alien* trilogy), film genre conventions, and contemporary culture in the parodic mode. This should not be surprising, considering that the men in charge of resurrecting the franchise and its female protagonist were screenwriter Joss Whedon, creator of *Buffy the Vampire Slayer* (1992) and writer of *Toy Story* (1995), and French director Jean-Pierre Jeunet, best known in the United States for his fantastical *City of Lost Children* (*La cité des enfants perdus*, 1995).

Whedon's *Buffy the Vampire Slayer*, a clever appropriation of both the vampire and superhero genres, populated with quirky characters that revel in witty repartee, offers a starting point for the odd world of *Alien Resurrection*. In *Buffy*, Whedon takes the typical victim of slasher films, the ditzy blond cheerleader with a fluffy name, and turns her into the hero of his narrative: a tough slayer in spandex who spends her time fending off the local vampire infestation with martial arts, a sack of wooden stakes, and a certain fashion sense between cheerleading practice, classes, and prom night. The television series *Buffy the Vampire Slayer* (1997–2003) shared the oddball humor of *Alien Resurrection*, lending a fresh angle to the burgeoning millennial market that included other television shows such as *Millennium* (1996–1999) and the indomitable *X-Files* (1993–2002). As with the television series *Xena, Warrior Princess* (1995–2001), *Buffy* succeeded in bringing the female superhero out of the sidekick role and into the forefront of public consciousness.

Once again a producer, Sigourney Weaver helped recruit director Jean-Pierre Jeunet, who was already internationally acclaimed for *Delicatessen* (1991), a black comedy that mixes true love and cannibalism, and *The City of Lost Children*, a surrealistic fairy tale starring a crazed inventor who has children kidnapped so he can steal their dreams (both codirected with Marc Caro). Much in *The City of Lost Children* anticipates the themes and characters of *Alien Resurrection*. Both films, for example, are brilliantly conceived and filmed explorations of the monstrous and the freakish, featuring mad scientists, imperfect clones, thick-headed strongmen (in both films played by Ron Perlman), and a cute "little girl" female who is intelligent and strong-willed enough to defy even death. And while *Alien Resurrection* certainly does not have the fairy-tale feel of *City*, both films draw on Terry Gilliam-esque, retro-SF techno-fetish (e.g., *Brazil*, 1985) and

158

distorted perspectives to suggest the decadent, nightmarish quality of their respective worlds.

Reviews for *Alien Resurrection* vary depending on whether the critic enjoyed the strangeness of the film: Janet Maslin in the *New York Times* could not disassociate herself from the film's graphic excesses, dubbing the film "the most freakish and macabre" of the *Alien* franchise to date and charged Jeunet's "ghoulishly fecund imagination" with making the story "so murky that even the screen's toughest woman warrior remains largely stuck in the mud."[1] Brian D. Johnson of *Maclean's* described it as "an orgy of gelatinous ooze and splatter" whose action was as exhilarating as "that old midway nausea machine called The Scrambler," and concluded that the whole was "plain alienating."[2] On the side of those who enjoyed Whedon and Jeunet's new twist on the twenty-year-old franchise was *Time's* Richard Schickel, who pronounced the film's "self-satirizing impulse . . . hip without being campy."[3] Writing for *Rolling Stone*, Peter Travers extolled Whedon's daring script—"In space no one can hear you scream, 'Hey, stupid, ever heard of DNA?'"—and the "visual marvels" Jeunet achieved in the specimen lab and the underwater scene.[4] But it was *Entertainment Weekly's* Lisa Schwarzbaum who put her finger on the importance of the film: "*Alien Resurrection* power-kicks the whole definition of the Horrifying Other into a fresh, deep, exhilaratingly thoughtful, millennium-sensitive direction: We have met the alien, and they is us."[5]

To fully appreciate *Alien Resurrection*, one must be aware that it references an impressive array of film narratives and genres, most obviously those of classic and cult vampire and Frankenstein movies, the thriller *Jurassic Park* (1993), and the disaster-on-the-high-seas oddity *The Poseidon Adventure* (1972). Still, the films *Alien Resurrection* references first and foremost are those of the *Alien* series. Take, for example, one provocative exchange between the pirate Johner and the Ripley clone that made it to the film's trailer: while walking warily down the dark corridors of the spaceship *Auriga*, watching for sudden Alien attacks, Johner, by way of conversation, asks the Ripley clone what she did when she "ran into [the Aliens] before." With a sardonic laugh that alludes to Ripley's choice in *Alien³*, she responds, simply, "I died." Rather than having Weaver's character look back in anger, as both Cameron and Fincher do, Whedon and Jeunet free the Ripley clone to look back with irony.

Because this is pastiche, every statement of fact draws attention to itself, and thus implies a question. In the last example, the clone's tongue-in-cheek answer to Johner's query interrogates where the seat of individuality, identity, and personhood lies by appropriating the name "Ripley" for a creature that is not quite the Ripley of the other three films. While it is true that the Ripley in *Alien³* died as a result of her confrontation with the Aliens, the Ripley clone is not the original, but an imperfect copy with hybrid DNA. At the same time, because the Ripley clone has inherited Ripley's memories, she has access to those memories and can remember a time when "she" died.

Alien Resurrection's tongue-in-cheek dialogue has its equivalent in the mise-en-scène. In one of the film's introductory scenes, for example, two heavily armed guards stand outside a secure hatch looking deadly serious in the dark, narrow passage. The stage is set for a dark military thriller, perhaps along the lines of *Aliens*, but this time on a ship. On closer inspection, however, small details subtly undermine the seriousness of the scene. For one, the guards are both chewing gum. Most importantly, one of the guards is apparently left-handed, while the other is right-handed, which means that their rifles, held at "present arms," are inexplicably aimed at each other's heads—and their fingers are on the triggers. One good bubble pop from one of them and they are both dead.

This subtle absurdity, which many audiences would not notice on a conscious level, sets the stage for a narrative that could be called many things—the words *odd, foreign, disjointed, bizarre,* and *freakish* come to mind—but we would make the case that, though it may be all of these, the tone of Jeunet's film is lovingly parodic, again making us see the referent, in this case, the soldiers of *Aliens*, in a completely unexpected way. The absurdity of the military is confirmed when the commander, the buffoonish General Perez, played by Dan Hedaya, is killed by an Alien as he is saluting soldiers who died "in action" (that

Not a good ad for the NRA: two soldiers of the Auriga *ready for action, and about to be caught in the cross-fire.*

is, trapped in the escape pods as they tried to avoid the Aliens). Cross-eyed from the blow to the back of his head, Perez vulgarly removes a piece of his "mind" from the hole.

The parodic element in *Alien Resurrection* also relies on intertextual references to the actors' previous performances to convey added meaning to the text.[6] As we have shown, Sigourney Weaver, in particular, plays off Ripley in the previous *Alien* trilogy, while Ron Perlman alludes to his performance of One in *The City of Lost Children* and the swash-buckling space pirate from the science-fiction comedy *Ice Pirates* (1984), which even features a joke on *Alien*'s Chestburster in the form of a monstrous "space herpe." Perlman's Johner also references the beast-men roles he played in *The Island of Dr. Moreau* (1996) and the lion-man Vincent in the TV series *Beauty and the Beast* (1987–1990). Winona Ryder gives depth to the humane robot Call by playing off her "coming of age" roles in *Beetlejuice* (1988), *Edward Scissorhands* (1990), and *Bram Stoker's Dracula* (1992), which in turn posit the Ripley clone as a demon, as the Frankenstein creature, and as a vampire.

To complicate matters further, the themes that dominate the tangled web of *Alien Resurrection* come from a wide variety of narratives. The body narrative, which served as the centerpiece of the previous three films, seems to have exploded, encompassing the whole of the film. The introductory scenes for the main titles, for example, offer a golden spectacle of morphing flesh, hair, orifices, bared black teeth, a human eye, before the discombobulated mess dissolves into the staple science-fiction shot of a spaceship traveling through space. The *Auriga* is no average spaceship, though: it is a military research station carrying a team of scientists bent on reconstructing Lieutenant Ellen Ripley and the Alien Queen she has inside her. The exploration of space becomes, in this film, an exploration of the body at its molecular level, the morphing flesh indicating the fusion of the human and the Alien bodies before the story even properly begins. In *Alien Resurrection*, the meeting of the woman and the monster has already happened. They are one. All that remains is for her—and us—to figure out what that means.

In this respect, the one and only protagonist of *Alien Resurrection* is the Ripley clone, despite General Perez's assertion that she is just a mere "meat by-product" from the creation of the real object of desire, the Alien Queen. As the site of the crossing of the species, the Ripley clone is the site of fear: Is she human? Is she Alien? Can we trust her? Is she a new Sil, the monstrous female alien bent on reproduction of *Species* (1995)? Or is she a newborn hero about to discover her calling? As a created being, she alludes to the creature in Mary Shelley's *Frankenstein*, who, abandoned by its maker, struggles to understand what it is, and what it wants. As the liminal body between humanity and the Alien, the Ripley clone becomes the living critique of what constitutes the human and what the monstrous. For monsters of different ilk abound in the film, from body-snatching pirates to Frankenstein medicos to gung-ho milicos to the Ripley clone(s) and the Aliens themselves. Even the determined female robot Call, who, following in Ripley's footsteps, risks herself to stop the Aliens from spreading, is a direct technological descendant of the twitchy Ash from *Alien* and an illegal Second Gen(eration) synthetic being. Earth itself has become monstrous, "a real shit hole," the hypermale Johner assures us. In the topsy-turvy world of *Alien Resurrection*, humans are monstrous, and freaks are humane.

The crisis of identity between subject and object, hero and villain, human and Alien also echoes the tensions that predominate in the narratives of superhero comics. Like other dark heroes in the tradition of Batman and Blade, the Ripley clone is torn between two identities and "fights evil" while being "one of them."[7] In the context of the film, she is superhuman: she has superior strength and speed, lightning reflexes, and heightened senses. Her acid blood burns through metal. She is a freak.[8] But most of all, she is an unknown quantity. No wonder the driving question of the film becomes "Who are you?" She is in the same position as the "mystery man" of superhero narratives who is so often asked "Who are you?" that the very phrase parodies its own meaning. At the same time, the question starts Ripley on a journey of self-discovery, which ends, as Whedon has explained, with her "accepting her own kind of humanity, on her own terms even if she does not necessarily fit the description of 'human.'"[9]

To help her find her way is the android Call. Together, Ripley and Call make up, as Travers would have it, a pair of "Yang and Yin action figures with a common foe."[10] Smartly appropriating the Ripley/Alien Queen dynamic of *Alien³*, this not quite human duo negotiates the labyrinthine space of female relations in a patriarchal universe. From antagonism through maternalism, sisterhood, lesbianism, heterosexuality, feminism, postfeminism, and the posthuman, Ripley and Call finally locate, not only their own reasons to live, but a hope for the future of Woman in the humane.

"She's Perfect"

[Adam] had come forth from the hands of God a perfect creature, happy and prosperous, guarded by the especial care of his Creator; he was allowed to converse with and acquire knowledge from beings of a superior nature: but I was wretched, helpless, and alone. Many times I considered Satan as the fitter emblem of my condition.

—The creature, in Mary Shelley's *Frankenstein*

163

The opening scenes of *Alien Resurrection* leave us with little doubt as to who, or what, is the centerpiece of the film. The heavy guarded door lifts upward as the camera advances, and we see figures dressed in white moving about an upright metal cylinder. Echoing the motion of the door, the metallic casing of the cylinder lifts upward to reveal a frontal view of what looks like the prepubescent body of Lieutenant Ellen Ripley (Sigourney Weaver). Her crossed arms cover her chest vampire-style, while special effects "erase" her apparently hairless groin. As we stare at her, so do the doctors: it is as if the film is admitting that the subject matter of *Alien*, *Aliens*, and *Alien³* has been a creation of males all along.

As the camera zooms in on her seemingly innocent child-body, we hear a voice-over in Weaver's voice: "My mommy always told me there were no monsters. Not any real ones." Since Newt had voiced those exact words in *Aliens*, the clone's body partakes of her image: the unprotected girl child victimized by monsters that should exist only in nightmares.[11] The clone's face then morphs from young to mature, revealing that she has been "aged to perfection"— presumably the age Ripley died on Fiorina 161. The voice-over concludes: "But there are." This assurance that monsters exist would seem to signal the mature clone as the monster, but because the voice-over is Weaver's, the words simultaneously point out the other monsters of this narrative: the gaping scientists admiring the cloned body. One of them, Dr. Gediman (Brad Dourif), whispers in an almost worshipful tone, "She's perfect." The utterance summarizes his position as the Naziesque scientist in the relentless pursuit of the perfect race and conflates Ash's admiration of the Alien in *Alien* with Burke's greedy gaze at the contained Facehuggers in *Aliens*. In one sentence, *Alien Resurrection* has fused woman and Alien, hero and monster.

Like a ritual, the opening of *Alien Resurrection* has presented us with a reenactment or simulacra of birth and, even more, of mythological and legendary births. The Ripley clone is a being conceived by a father alone. She is Athena, Galatea. She is a dark Sleeping Beauty, the perfect female in the crystal case whose presence prefaces chaos, destruction, and death, as did the femme fatales in *Lifeforce* (1985)

"She's perfect": the doctors admire the Ripley clone.

and *Species* (1995). Most of all, the Ripley clone embodies the creatures of Mary Shelley's *Frankenstein*[12] as they have been translated into cultural myth. Like Frankenstein's patchwork creature, the Ripley clone breaks down the boundary between bodies by merging Alien and human DNA. She will also prove to be faster, stronger, and smarter than her purely human creators. Like the creature's mate, who in Shelley's book is not allowed to live, the clone represents a malignant reproductive potential, the progenitor of monsters.

The removal of the Alien Queen embryo from the clone's chest also happens within a sealed surgical tube. On her back this time, the sleeping and now distinctly dark-looking Ripley clone sports an inscrutable Mona Lisa smile as the doctors open her chest cavity and take the Alien fetus out. She, we learn, was not the object of desire at all, but merely relevant as the Queen's host, as a surrogate mother. As a "womb for hire," her presence on the scene after the birth of her "child" is neither expected nor wanted. Only after the larval Queen is safely removed from her chest do the doctors decide to let her live. Gediman's anxious request to Dr. Wren (J. E. Freeman) to "keep her" establishes the power relations between the doctors and also sets up the clone's role as a pet, like a stray dog or cat that Gediman has been allowed to bring into the house.

The next scene takes us down an impossibly deep cylindrical cell onto the body of the clone sealed inside a white diaphanous bag, presumably to help her heal. A guard stops to look down on her body, and his gaze takes us to a close-up of the clone as she wakes up inside the bag. In a series of shots interspersed with darkness (as if she is waking and passing out), she takes her first gasps of air and slowly writhes out of the bag. The effect is that of a chrysalis in a cocoon struggling to get free and, at points, of a body emerging from its death shroud. The protective sack also evokes a garbage bag, since the *Auriga* scientists have taken what they wanted and tossed the clone away.

Once her head and hands emerge from the material, the Ripley clone explores her own body meditatively. She touches the scar on her chest, then her arms, and stops at the digital number 8 tattooed on her left forearm. Like the bar code on the back of the convicts' heads in *Alien³*, the tattoo is a form of forced identification given to those radically subjected to the system. She has been marked as if she were an inventory item.

As the numerical representation of regeneration and the balancing of opposing forces,[13] the number 8 tells us quite a bit about how we are supposed to read the clone: not only has she been regenerated or "resurrected," she supposedly represents the balance between the Alien and the human, as if such a thing were possible. Perhaps even more disturbing, however, is the symbolic implication of the 8 as the symbol of infinity (∞). Not even suicide, it seems, can put an end to Ripley or the Alien. But is she Ripley? The number on her arm apparently denies so. Appropriately, the as yet unnamed clone does not seem to know herself and looks up, as if the answer to her identity lies somewhere above her cell.

During an examination a few days later, her excellent health gets the attention of Dr. Wren, who begins to see her as an unforeseen bonus of the cloning project. Feeling exceedingly satisfied with her test results, Wren announces to the manacled clone that he expects she will make them "very proud." The clone's animal-like posture and inhuman placidity—she does not even seem to blink—suggest that she does not understand what he says; yet, when he places his face close to hers, invading her space, she reacts to the threat by breaking the cable on the manacles and grabbing Wren by the throat. It takes a strong electric blast from a guard's weapon before she will release him. How, we must wonder, can we expect anything good from this woman who, from the moment of her unwanted rebirth, finds herself locked up, alone, and on the cold, hard floor? After this show of strength, the "humanization" of the clone begins. The Ripley clone, confined by manacles and a garment reminiscent of a straitjacket, receives basic language instruction from one of the female scientists (who are never named). Presented with images of cherries and a glove, the Ripley clone responds (with a little prompting from the scientist) with "fruit" and "hand." That her first "lessons" are linguistic, particularly following her attack on Wren, demonstrate the importance of language in control. If they can communicate with her on a level above the basic behavioral modification (stimulus response) of the animal, they can ostensibly control her more fully.[14]

As interesting a subject as she is to the scientists, the Ripley clone is merely a "meat by-product" for the single-minded General Perez, who refuses even to refer to the clone as anything but "it"; what the military wants is full-grown Warrior Aliens, not half-breeds. Still, he seems concerned as he watches the Ripley clone learning how to speak with the help of the female doctors, because her adult language skills are the result of "inherited memories" caused by an accidental genetic crossing with Alien DNA. General Perez's greatest fear, the fear of all totalitarians, is that the Ripley clone will remember,[15] and that, now endowed with superior strength, stamina, speed, and healing capacity, she will try to get rid of the Warrior Aliens they will soon be growing in the *Auriga* labs. As the scene progresses, the clone's radiant white face fills the screen, superimposed over the men's dark faces watching her learning to speak and pondering on how she fits in their plan. As an unknown quantity, she is clearly the threat and the object of desire of the narrative; as such, she replaces the now familiar Alien Queen and her shadow offspring.

Perhaps as a consequence of the "genetic crossing," the Ripley clone seems resistant to her conditioning, as evidenced by the ironic tone her emerging language takes. As she sits, still manacled, with Gediman eating in the mess hall, the clone looks at her fork, for which Gediman, showing her his fork, supplies the word, "Fork." The Ripley clone repeats: "Fuck." Gediman corrects her with certainty, "No, it's 'fork.'" What Gediman cannot understand is that in the overall context the Ripley clone's "fuck" does have meaning: (1) "Fuck, here I am again"—a kind of cosmic and filmic joke on Weaver/Ripley; (2) "We are fucked, the Alien will kill us all"; (3) "Fuck you [the doctors] for doing this to me"; and, perhaps more literally, (4) "I know it's a fork; I'm fucking with you."

When Gediman tells her that the Alien Queen is growing, the Ripley clone responds with the absoluteness of one who has experienced this narrative many times over: "She'll breed. You'll die."[16] Perhaps her hybrid nature helps her to see the vulnerability of humans with unprecedented clarity, or perhaps her extensive knowledge of the pettiness of humans makes her ascribe victory to the Aliens. So far, for example, she has assumed the doctors are hirelings of the Company ostensibly researching the potential of the Aliens as bioweapons, but Wren walks in and sets her right: the Company has been history for quite some time; this is a project of the United Systems Military, with goals beyond the narrow-minded "urban pacification" envisioned by that now defunct corporation.

This is an interesting twist in the series. The Company, arguably Ripley's most consistent and toughest foe, is no more. What this means, then, is that there is no one organization to blame for the evil and degrading acts committed during the narrative (the United Systems Military is too vague an institution to even stick in the viewer's mind). The effect of getting rid of the Company, then, is to diffuse evil among all humanity: humans are not minions of an uncaring corporation, but a monstrous species on its own terms. And nobody proves this better than the self-important Dr. Wren. Like Ash, Wren admires the Alien itself and believes it will prove very useful, once it is tamed. He even looks forward to being the master of a new race, not unlike Victor Frankenstein.[17] The Ripley clone laughs at his arrogance and warns him that the Alien cannot be tamed—it is not a tool but an agent, and it will kill them all. Cruelly, Wren answers that if they can teach Ripley to behave (and she is part Alien), they can teach the Alien to submit as well. But the audience knows he is an arrogant fool to believe so. As a direct product of the indomitable Ripley and the fierce Alien, the clone cannot be controlled any more than the genetically reconstructed female dinosaurs of *Jurassic Park*. And like them, she will soon find a way to freedom.

Getting Kinky in the Twilight Zone

> Give them an alluring woman stronger than themselves to submit to and they'll be proud to be her willing slaves!
>
> —Dr. William Moulton Marston, creator of *Wonder Woman*

Strange things happen on the fringe. Once one leaves the regulated spaces of society, the landscape is populated by the extreme, the freakish, the abnormal. Enter the *Betty* with her motley crew of oddball renegades. The viewer quickly learns as much about them as she will ever know. Captain Elgyn (Michael Wincott) is the slimy, sexpot pirate to a degree that would make Han Solo's mercenary heart of gold shrivel into nothingness. If the audience does not get the hint when he sensually growls his authorization code to the *Auriga* as "E-A, T-M, E," then it surely should as he fixes his female pilot, Hillard (Kim Flowers), with a lusty, appropriative stare and comments that "no matter how many times you see it, just seeing a woman all strapped up into a chair like that . . ." Her less than innocent "What?" lets the viewer know they both understand the bondage reference. Hillard, Elgyn's mate, is little more than a replica of Chalmers, the sexy pilot from *Spacehunter: Adventures in the Forbidden Zone* (1983), and, ultimately, just as disposable. The dreadlock-bedecked Christie (Gary Dourdan) is the cool macho gunslinger. Johner the thug is there mainly to "hurt people," and Vriess (Dominique Pinon), the techno-geek cripple, has a crush on the cute, young, plucky-but-nice-girl mechanic, Call. If this were a boy band, Call would be the sensitive one.

169

The first time we see this strange little "family" together, the scene is constructed like a Backstreet Boys pinup or an X-Men lineup. For a long moment, the camera holds. The group does not move, allowing the tension to build: this is the essence of "cool." Clearly the prototype for the crew of Whedon's feisty, if short lived, "western in space" *Firefly* (2002–2003), the crew of the *Betty* is an off-color, smarmy-sexual nighttime drama waiting to happen. Their posturing, of course, is calculated to throw off the *Auriga*'s guards so that they miss the obvious; namely, that Johner's thermos is a weapon, that they should search Vriess's chair for miscellaneous hidden armament, and that a pair of pistols are strapped to Christie's arms. As in *Aliens*, the setting of *Alien Resurrection* is the final frontier of space, where a pirate's best friend is a smuggled gun. Having been in sticky situations before, the crew of the *Betty* knows what they are about and effortlessly sneak their weapons on board.

The "oh so cool" arrival of the motley crew of the Betty.

In a stock scene from the western film where the outlaw meets with the less-than-respectable lawman in the local jail, Elgin meets Perez in the general's office. They share a whiskey and exchange some rather vulgar comments about Elgyn's new female crew member, Call, by way of homosocial bonding. Elgyn's rude and condescending view of Call as a "little girl playing pirates" who is "extremely fuckable" exposes the male view of any woman as a potential sex object. That the earlier scenes with Call highlight her sensitivity and courage as she defends the paraplegic Vriess against the ape-man Johner only serves to underscore the typical male crudeness of Elgin and Perez. The fact that Call is played by Winona Ryder only intensifies the crass and unbearable truth of the scene. Whedon and Jeunet are clearly exposing the boy's club banter for what it is: typical and despicable.

This is the second time in the film that a woman has been described as an object: whereas Call is a "filly" (a young female horse ready for breeding), Ripley is an "it" and a "meat by-product." Both, it seems, are a piece of flesh available for (at least verbal) trading. The denigration of the female body prefaces the images of Elgyn's cargo: frozen humans kidnapped to serve as hosts for Facehuggers. Both men are, therefore, revealed as excessive and perverse, and their exchange of bodies for cash seems an echo of their verbal exchange of Call.

Finally allowed out of hand and ankle cuffs, the Ripley clone is in the recreation room dunking basketballs with the skill of an NBA professional. Wearing massive boots and a deep brown-red costume fastened at the back, her body shot from below to make her look even taller than she is, the clone looks like a parody of James Whale's overgrown monster in *Frankenstein* (1931). The clasped back and laced-up pants of the Ripley clone's wardrobe indicate discipline, bondage, and confinement, implying, on one hand, that her abilities are still under the control of the sadistic Wren, but also that she is a fetish object. She is "strapped in" to her outfit like Hillard was strapped in to her flight chair. Of course, the real fear surrounding the fetishized, controlled body is that the terrible potential held barely in check could get loose.

Obviously, the clone's power will get loose eventually, but not before the narrative tests her on the freak-o-meter. Johner sees her playing ball, proclaims he likes "the tall ones," and moves in for a crude strike. His advances turn into a power struggle: he tries to grab the basketball from her hands, but she deflects him in amusing ways; he offers to play another type of "indoor sports" with her, but she remains silent. Only when he rudely smells her from behind and orders her to give him the basketball does she get fed up. She bounces the ball between her legs into his crotch, and the implication is clear: *she* balls *him*. In a show of superhuman strength, she then sends him flying across the room with a single blow. When Hillard reacts to the attack on Johner by throwing the basketball, the clone catches it dead-stop in midflight with the palm of one hand. As the situation gets rougher, Christie (clearly not the "turn the other cheek" type of guy) picks up a weight bar and hits the Ripley clone square in the face with it. She barely moves under the impact, but throws him a vaguely surprised look. The only sign of damage is a tiny dribble of blood from her nose. She deflects his second and third hit, whacks him in the head with the basketball, and resumes her game as if she had never been interrupted. If we had any doubt before, and we could not have too much left after her assault on Wren, we now know that the clone is a dangerous freak. She has single-handedly bested three of the *Betty*'s crew.

Wren, who has been watching the whole scene from the doorway with Gediman, decides to, once again, play the master. Applauding her performance loudly, he calls her name—"Ripley"—whistles loudly as if calling a dog, tells her the fun is over, and holds his hand out for the ball. As the clone walks toward Wren, her face blank, the bewildered Johner blurts, "What the hell are you?" He has unwittingly aligned himself with the doctors' view of Ripley—she is an *it*: not a woman, as he originally thought, but something *not human*. Without one look of acknowledgment, the clone responds to both male demands by shooting the basketball backward through the hoop from an impossible distance while walking, causing general amazement (Weaver actually made the over-the-shoulder shot for the scene). As she passes by the doctors on her way out, Gediman declares admiringly, "Something of a predator, isn't she?" Probably an in-joke referencing early plans to make the fourth installment in the *Alien* series an *Alien vs. Predator* film,[18] Gediman's comment nevertheless indicates the difference between the Ripley of the previous films and this Alien woman. Ominously, she wipes some blood from her nose and flings it to the ground, where it sizzles and slowly burns the deck plating. Like the pirates, the Ripley clone is also a body hiding a weapon, and the weapon she hides is the Alien itself.

A long shot of the *Auriga* and the image of the sun disappearing behind the planet it orbits calms the mood of the narrative. In a series of shots chronicling the "after hours" actions of the principal characters, Jeunet builds on classical forms of fetish to comment on one last, decadent form. First comes the foot fetish in the guise of General Perez obsessively shining his boots and Elgyn massaging Hillard's feet while staring at her wriggling buttocks. Vriess embodies the techno-fetish as he guiltily "snags a piece" (a euphemism for sex) of equipment here and there in the *Auriga*'s supply rooms. Fetish consumerism and gun-fetish meet as Johner, Christie, and Call watch incessant infomercials for handguns. But the pièce de résistance comes in the form of Dr. Gediman in the *Auriga*'s lab as he records the behavioral patterns of three grown Warrior Aliens kept in a cell. Clearly fascinated by one of the specimens, he begins to mirror its head movements, even perversely kissing the glass separating them (the logical extension of Burke's fascinated interest in *Aliens*). We get the impression that Gediman was a kid who used to pull the legs off living spiders and follow along behind snakes, who watched all the gory slasher and *Faces of Death* films, had tarantulas and boa constrictors as pets, and thought roadkill was cool not only to look at but to photograph and save for later. His furtive look over his shoulder clearly indicates that what he is doing with the Alien is deliciously dirty; Wren would surely not approve of him indulging himself in such perverse play. His grotesque desire to mimic, to *be* the Alien body, contradicts Wren's earlier assertion that things are different now that the Company is not in charge: men like him and Perez and Gediman, the leaders of humanity, still desire the Alien.

In response to Gediman's adoration, the Alien thrusts out its inter-locking jaw in an attempt to kill him, but the jaw is stopped by the glass. The doctor, displeased with this disrespectful phallic display, blasts it with a freezing gas that clearly causes it pain. The Alien stops, however, its second attack before Gediman's hand strikes the gas release button. Surprised, Gediman comments, "We're a quick learner." His use of the pronoun *we* highlights the similarity between him and the Alien and underscores the fact that it is studying him as well.

Meanwhile, Call has gotten silly drunk (unwisely, considering the company she keeps) and, now ludicrously wearing boxing gloves on her hands, annoys Johner and Christie by spilling her drink all over them. She leaves the TV room presumably to get some air, but once outside she seems remarkably sober and quickly finds her way to the Ripley clone's cell, which she enters with a key ring of atomizers. She draws a knife from her boot and approaches the prone form of the clone, who is resting under a massive metal structure reminiscent of a spider, creating the impression that Ripley is likewise a spider wait-ing for Call, the little busy bee. As Call gets ready to strike the clone with her knife, she sees the scar on the clone's chest and stops, realiz-ing she has arrived too late to impede the birth of the Alien Queen.

The clone, who has only been pretending to be asleep, opens her eyes and asks in a faintly mocking tone, "Well . . . are you going to kill me, or what?" Call responds that there is no use in killing her, since the doctors already have the Alien Queen. Call then wonders, like Perez, what is the purpose of keeping the clone alive now that the doctors have obtained what they wanted. "I'm the latest thing," the clone explains with a smirk. She knows she is a fad, so she lies await-ing the inevitable—the Aliens' escape—to make her getaway. Dis-tracted by a guard walking above, Call looks away. The clone inspects her, looking as if she could eat Call for lunch with some fava beans and a nice Chianti. Call offers to end the clone's pain. In response, the clone impales her own hand on Call's knife, her acid blood burn-ing the blade. They look each other in the eye, both shadows of the heroic Ripley of the previous trilogy, connected by the knife and the wound on the open palm, now in a face-off.

"Who am I?": Call confronts the Ripley clone.

Following *Alien³*, the hand wound would seem to indicate the Ripley clone as a Christ figure, as it clearly evokes the marks of stigmata. Whedon, whose *Buffy* series used the same image to reveal the town mayor's demonic nature, may have had a second referent in mind: the low-budget, lesbian-themed vampire film *The Velvet Vampire* (1971).[19] Even without the cinematic reference, *Alien Resurrection* has effectively created a discursive space for lesbianism between Ripley and Call, as the most obtuse of viewers would recognize that one woman sticking something into another woman carries at least *some* connotation of lesbianism. The clone thereby comes to signify a dangerous sexuality. As her blood burns the blade, one is left to wonder what her kiss might do. Would sex with her burn the penis away? Castrate and cauterize the wound? She now has, as Parker said of the Alien in the first film, "a truly wonderful defense mechanism."

Looking down on her smoking knife, Call asks the Ripley clone, "Who are you?" but when the clone responds, using the identity given to her by the doctors, "Ellen Ripley," Call rejects that identity: Ellen Ripley died a long time ago, on Fiorina 161. Confronting the fact that she apparently is *not* Ellen Ripley confuses the Ripley clone: if she is not Ripley, who is she? Call explains that she is a construct, a body grown for the sole purpose to obtain the fetal Alien Queen. The clone disagrees: she is something else, a new Dr. Jekyll, perhaps, for she can feel the Alien inside her, "behind [her] eyes . . . moving." Call stares at her in horror and disgust, but asks for her help in stopping the Alien. The clone looms over Call and caresses her face as if she were the living image of the little girl Ripley loved and lost. She tells Call that her mission is futile; she will die. Call responds disdainfully that she is not afraid to die. Like death herself, the clone grabs her by the throat and pulls her near, returning Call's offer to end the pain right then and there.

When the Ripley clone grabs Call by the throat and pulls her close, we understand that this is a love scene between the perverse and the innocent.[20] The clone smells Call the way Lecter smells Clarisse in *Silence of the Lambs* (1991) or Van Helsing smells Mina in *Bram Stoker's Dracula* (1992), as if trying to pull her essence inside herself; her action also mirrors Johner's sexual aggressiveness just a few scenes earlier. She then rests her face against Call's in a loving, almost maternal moment, but lets go when she hears noises outside: the soldiers are looking for Call. Call exits the cell immediately, only to be caught by Wren.

And here is where the structures that the film has so steadily been building up begin to crumble. Suspecting that the crew of the *Betty* are conspiring with Call, Wren rounds them up and accuses them of espionage. The pirates fight to escape, distracting Gediman from controlling the Aliens with his punishment button. The Aliens break out of their cell, taking Gediman with them, and triggering the *Auriga* into alert. The Ripley clone, aware that the Aliens could pose a threat to her, uses her acid blood to short circuit a door and makes her getaway. General Perez is killed by an Alien, and the soldiers evacuate the ship, leaving the pirates, Wren, and a soldier named Distephano (Raymond Cruz) to fend on their own. As the group escapes toward the *Betty*, Elgyn wanders off alone down a dark hallway, apparently after a gun. He is pulled halfway through the grating by an Alien that strikes him in the lower back, killing him.

The rest of the crew members rush into the scene, only to confront an Alien. As it advances, Elgyn's body moves, attracting its attention. It lowers its head to inspect Elgyn's body. A shotgun materializes from below and fires, blowing the Alien's head off. Seconds later, the Ripley clone emerges from the hole. Oddly, she has managed to change outfits: instead of the constricting, padded outfit, the clone now wears a shiny, brown-black leather combination. Clearly meant to connect the Ripley clone visually with the Aliens, the outfit also adopts the dominatrix style of notoriously twisted femme fatale characters such as Catwoman in *Batman Returns* (1992)—she is out, she is free, and she is bad.

The obvious implication of this scene is that the normal male lead—set up along stereotypical lines as never before in the *Alien* series—has been usurped by the clone. She is even more cocky and self-sure than the man she replaced, even to the point of mocking her own role as the new hero of the film. "Was it everything you hoped for?" is her first line to Call after emerging from the hole, quickly followed by the startling, "Who do I have to fuck to get off this boat?" The heroic, maternal Ripley of *Aliens* is long gone; she has been replaced by a thing of darkness in leather fetish wear that displays what Elyce Rae Helford describes as the "aggressive individualism and 'projected' sexuality of rock-me/postfeminism," of Tank Girl.[21] This version of Ripley will not hesitate to have sex with or kill whoever is in power—male or female—to make her escape possible.

The Ripley clone further establishes her sexual dominance by ripping off the tongue of the Alien she just killed, and offers it to Call as a "souvenir." This is actually one of the most radical moments of the series, as the interlocking jaw of the Alien has been its supreme weapon and the site of our fears of rape and death for three films. That the Ripley clone can, with a small grunt, seize the symbol of power and offer it as a keepsake is an incredible feat, in terms of both physical power and emotional strength.[22] The toothed tongue, that symbol of the power of penetration and feminization of the human body, in the hands of this formidable castrator becomes a flaccid piece of meat, something disgusting rather than horrific, the fallacy of its awesome power exposed as so much hype.

Ripley's Believe It or Not

> In bio-technology at the *fin-de-millennium*, the womb has gone public, alienated from nature, inscribed by eugenics, bonded to public law, and made fully accessible to the exchange principle.
>
> —Arthur and Marilouise Kroker, *Body Invaders: Panic Sex in America*

The flight through the *Auriga* doubles as a journey of self-discovery for the Ripley clone. The first stop, a storeroom with a door marked 1–7, unveils the clone's monstrous origins. She enters to discover the laboratory where her predecessors are kept. Varied attempts to create a fetus in fetu—that is, an Alien fetus nested in a human fetus—float in large and small tanks.[23] The Ripley clone walks from one to the next in horrified fascination, directing our gaze toward the preserved monstrosities. One has an enlarged head and a tail. A second looks like a human female but has a set of bared Alien teeth coming out of her cheek. Two others have what look like Alien bodies but human skin. The overall display reminds us of the "pickled punks" of carnival side shows, with a twist: these bodies are not of abnormal humans or joined twins,[24] but the result of a union between a human and an extraterrestrial, a mix that cannot exist but in the imagination. Their origin, as well as their hideousness, places them beyond the natural; as such, they have to be seen to be believed.

A shot of the Ripley clone's face from behind one of the specimens connects it to her. It is as if she were looking at herself in one of the distorting mirrors at the fun house and became disturbed by what the image reveals. The moment exemplifies Leslie Fiedler's musings on the secret self in *Freaks*: "Where and when, I am left asking—no longer sure that one body equals one self, and one self one body—

A little shop of horrors: inviable Ripley-Alien hybrids kept on display.

does my own 'I' begin and end?"[25] As covert images of the Ripley clone, the bottled clones exteriorize the dark twin she feels inside her and provide sister images for her self. The Jekyllean doubling so familiar to horror, however, is superseded by images of fusion, as in each bottled clone the human twin and the Alien twin have been unwittingly muddled up by the scientists. Neither human nor Alien, the clones occupy what Elizabeth Grosz calls the impossible middle ground of the freak.[26] We are to understand that the difference between these monstrosities and Ripley is simply one of visibility.

On a bed at the back of the lab lies what we assume is number 7: still alive, her face and part of her torso is human, but the rest of her body is still visually monstrous. Her oversized and grotesque right arm is joined to her body, and she has a surgical scar on her chest, indicating an attempt to remove whatever type of Alien embryo she had inside of her. Number 7 begs to be killed, contradicting the visual representation of her monstrosity with her desire to die, which links her to the humans in the *Alien* series who wish to die as humans rather than live on as monstrosities: Captain Dallas in the unused scene from

Alien, the female colonist in *Aliens*, and, of course, Ripley in *Alien³*. The Ripley clone does not speak to her. After all, what is there to say? She sees what has been done to her, to all of these females. This time, however, the source of the betrayal is crystal clear: unmediated by Alien eggs and Facehuggers and Queens, the monstrous condition leading to the suicide request has been produced, not by an Alien, but by humans. Call, who has followed the Ripley clone into the lab, silently hands her a flamethrower in perfect understanding. In an act of self-erasure and a reinscription of the suicide in *Alien³*, the Ripley clone incinerates number 7, then burns each of the tubes, all the while crying profusely.

As in the *X-Files* episode on which the scene seems to be based,[27] the hybrid clones are products of a vast conspiracy for power and control by the ruling institutions of Earth. In the case of *Alien Resurrection*, the lab scene may be read as a visual representation of feminist views about the construction of woman: men (the patriarchy) create the Other, "woman," as an index of power. As the created Other, therefore, "woman" sees herself (in this case literally) as a hideous creation, good for little more than producing offspring. The use of the flamethrower from previous *Alien* films here turns from destroying Aliens to the destruction of abominable bodies resulting from the medico-military attempt at constructing the woman Ripley.

Notably, Call is the only member of the group who understands the anger and distress Ripley feels, even if she later pleads for Wren's life when Ripley turns toward him in anger, flamethrower in hand. In fact, in confirmation of their earlier bonding in the lab, Call gives Wren a good punch in the face for the clone's pain after Ripley drops the flamethrower at Wren's feet and turns away in contempt. Meantime, the macho Johner looks on the carnage of the lab, shrugs his shoulders, and says to Christie, "Must be a chick thing." His boys' club jest, like Parker's cunnilingus reference in *Alien*, hides his nervousness at the fact that, at least in the *Alien* universe, men can suffer the same abuse and bodily violation as women, as the party discovers in the next site of Alien experimentation.

The second room the group enters is a slaughterhouse filled with the dead bodies of humans used by the scientists as hosts for the Alien Chestbursters. They find one survivor, Purvis, who is infected but has not given "birth" yet. The pirates argue loudly about what to do with him, but no one can look Purvis in the eye and tell him what is going on, so the Ripley clone steps in and coolly notifies Purvis of the facts: the pirates hijacked Purvis' ship and sold his body to a human (Wren), who put a monster in his chest that will eventually kill him. Purvis is predictably stunned by the information, but manages to ask the question de rigueur: "Who are you?" The Ripley clone gives him a big toothy smile and, in the film's culminating irony, she claims, "I'm the monster's mother."

While *Alien³* appropriated the term *bitch* to signify Ripley's new connection with the Alien Queen, the Ripley clone's sardonic appropriation of the title of the monster's mother implies that the Ripley clone is, at one and the same time, the monstrous mother of this narrative and yet, finally, *not responsible for the consequences of her monstrosity*. Her moral obligation to these "humans" is over; and who can blame her? Her memories tell her that she faced the Aliens three times, was betrayed by humans three times, and even died once. What has been done to Purvis has been done to her many times over. As far as she is concerned, he is *their* problem. And for once, the humans show a sense of morals, for the code of the pirates—"No one is left behind"—counts for Purvis also. They take him along in hopes that they can freeze his body when they get to the *Betty*.

In what is clearly set up as a turn on the underwater death and rebirth scene popularized by *The Poseidon Adventure* (1972) and *The Abyss* (1989), the group approaches a section of the ship impassable except by an extended underwater swim. Christie and Vriess, now strapped together (Vriess's chair having been abandoned at a ladder), lead the way into the underwater odyssey through the galley. Hillard, obviously not aware that showing fear and going last are often lethal combinations in horror flicks, has a moment of apprehension before diving into the water after her crewmates. Two Aliens attack, of course, and Hillard is dragged slowly away by one of them. The protagonist is confronted, yet again in the *Alien* series, with the image of a woman suffering the fate that she fears for herself, only in this instance her Medusa-like stare at her "offspring" while they take Hillard indicates that she is no longer empathizing with the victims of the Alien—perhaps Call is right and the clone will turn on the humans when the moment presents itself.

Luckily, Johner kills the other Alien, so the group can continue swimming toward the exit. They find it covered by a heavy, semitransparent membrane that, unbeknownst to them, is surrounded by circles and circles of Alien eggs. They push together through the membrane in a grotesque parody of impregnation. Like *Aliens'* Marines, they are breaking into the monstrous, lethal womb of the Alien body, bursting through the hymen like so many sperm about to meet the egg (which, of course, signals the sperm's death as an "individual" organism). Once they are through the protecting wall, gasping for breath, they become aware of the opening eggs. Revealing its indiscriminate sexual compulsion, one Facehugger jumps the Ripley clone, who is able to dispose of it after some struggle, thanks to her superior strength. Christie fills the room with grenades, allowing the group to enter the now ravaged nest and start climbing the ladder that will take them to the next level. Always trying to get the upper hand, Wren pretends he cannot break the lock for the door, asks Call for her gun, and promptly shoots her in the chest, claiming snidely, "You really are *way* too trusting." She falls, face down and arms spread, into the water below, in a grotesque reversal of Ripley's sacrificial leap in *Alien³*. Unlike the wise Ripley, who willingly goes to her death rather than once again fall into the hands of the Company, Call's "death" is a meaningless result of her innocence: in essence, she fails the test that Ripley passed long ago. Wren exits through the door, asking the ship's computer to lock it behind him as Vriess attempts to shoot him. Meanwhile, the first Alien is back and attacks Christie and Vriess. Christie tries to shoot it, but in a twist reminiscent of *Jurassic Park*, the Alien spits acid into his face, causing him to let go of the ladder. As they fall, Vriess manages to grab a rung. Johner finally kills the Alien, but its body still hangs from Christie's boot, and Christie, knowing that he is dying, cuts the straps that tie him to Vriess and lets himself fall into the water. Christie, true to his name, sacrifices himself for the paraplegic Vriess, leaving only Call and Distephano as the "normal" of the bunch in what has increasingly turned into a parade of physically and psychologically handicapped escapees. Johner's angry blasting of a tiny spider immediately after not only parodies his killing of the Alien, but also serves to highlight the centrality of the "black widow" theme permeating the imagery of the film.

A buzzer warns them the exit Wren secured is about to open. They ready their guns, expecting the worst. The doors unlock, revealing an extremely wet, yet very much alive, Call.

Andro(id)gyny: Simulacra and the Feminine Self

> If you prick me, do I not . . . leak?
> —Data, "The Naked Now," *Star Trek: The Next Generation*

Shocked but happy, the motley crew welcome Call back. The Ripley clone, however, cannot understand how Call survived such a close shot. Smelling a rat, so to speak, she makes a cursory investigation of Call's chest, exposing a hole from which issues a telltale white fluid. The clone is taken aback: Call is an android. This android, though, is not the instrument of a corporation like the menacing Ash or a puppet of the military like the benevolent Bishop. As Distephano explains, Call is a fugitive Auton (from autonomous) robot, a Second Gen(eration) android created by other androids. Second Gens ruined the synthetic industry because they "did not like to be told what to do," causing the government to recall them, though a few (like Call) got away. From this exposition, we can infer that Call's actions are her own, even if the Ripley clone explains the impulse behind her nobility as programming: "I should've known. No human being is *that* humane." Clearly meant as an indictment of humans, present company included, the clone's statement has many other implications. Unlike

Ash, for example, Call typifies those robots that are, in J. P. Telotte's phrasing, "not so much our *replacements* as our *extensions*, not really our *mismeasure* but in some way an *expansion* of the human measure."[28] As an extension of the human, Call is a highly complex tool created to improve the life of its creators; but she is also an expansion of what it means to be human—an embodiment of the "humane" that simultaneously questions where "the human" resides. For as Susan Wolfe argues of *Star Trek*'s Data, the fact that in science-fiction films androids can enact "humanity" flawlessly exposes the human as artifice.[29] Like Data, Call is *performing* a subject position—"the truly humane"—which does not biologically exist, since, as the clone maintains, no human is as humane as Call.

The clone's statement is also a subtle joke on the android's performance of the feminine, perhaps to remind us that Ripley had also been criticized as "too humane" for saving Jones the cat in *Alien* (and, by extension, by saving Newt in *Aliens*, and all humanity in *Alien³*). Indeed, Call is not only performing the human but a human female who is consistently treated by others as "a little girl playing pirates." In effect, Call is not simply a robot impersonating a human female, but a robot impersonating the idea of a human female, which does not exist within the world of the film beyond her own performance.[30]

As if to underscore the constructed nature of gender, the men rapidly fall into stereotypical, macho, boys' club language. They discuss Call as if she were not there, while the camera focuses on her expressions of embarrassment and shame. Distephano begins by referring to her as if she were a cool car: "Wow, a Second Gen!" Purvis dismisses Distephano's enthusiasm by reducing Call to an appliance: "Great. She's a toaster oven." Using double entendre, Johner suggests a way to deal with Call's "wound": "You got a socket wrench? Maybe she just needs an oil change." He then quickly shifts from referring to Call as a "she" to using the objectified "it" to degrade her even further: "To think I almost fucked it." The macho implication that he could have had sex with Call if he had so desired is mixed with sexual revulsion at her robotic body. The "extremely fuckable" Call has stopped being desirable in the eyes of the men. They do not want to mess with her any more than they want to mess with Ripley, if for a different reason.

The choice to make Ryder look boyishly cute by giving her a short haircut and dressing her in a mechanic's blue overall and clunky boots clearly marks her as attempting the masculine performance, if of a less masculine sort than Vasquez; she has certainly been "one of the guys," drinking and watching gun shows for hours up until this moment. Thus, Ripley's earlier gift of the phallus and Call's disgusted reaction to it suggest a lesbian homoeroticism, at least to some degree. That Ripley will later probe Call's exposed "wound" with her fingers certainly opens the text of the film to a queer reading.

Thus, Call's android body indicates a sexual transgression like both Ash and Bishop—she is not really a "sex" at all, but only the sexual performance, or gender. Call's female gender marks her as doubly lacking, as all androids are feminized by their nonhuman status. In other words, as "Woman" is already a societal construction of Otherness, the female-gendered android is twice the minority of the male-gendered android.

Whereas Ash's body served as a symbol of the subjugated worker and Bishop as the site of homophobia (in *Aliens*) and abjection (in *Alien³*), Call's body clearly references the societal construction of "Woman." That Purvis calls her a "toaster oven," referencing Bishop's expression of his abjected state in *Alien³*, further objectifies her as a creation, a possession, little more than a kitchen appliance.

Even more telling is how Call's "outing," like with her predecessors Ash and Bishop, recodes her in the males' eyes as dangerous. Now labeled a "big old psycho" by Johner, Call brings to mind the irrepressible female synthetics of science fiction that evoke patriarchy's fear of the feminine: the unruly Maria in *Metropolis*, the criminal runaways Pris and Zhora in *Blade Runner* (1982), and, most of all, the lethal Eve VIII in *Eve of Destruction* (1991), who has a nuclear bomb in place of a uterus. For all through the film Call has voiced with repeated—and alarming—insistence that they must blow up the *Auriga* to ensure the end of the Aliens, and now that she has been found an android, the viewer and the pirates know that she has the capacity to connect to the ship's computer. The question, then, is the same as with Ripley: will Call turn on the humans to ensure the destruction of the Alien species?

When asked to access Father to open a way through the *Auriga* to the *Betty*, Call confesses she cannot link remotely because she destroyed her modem (a cute anachronism), presumably to avoid being located. So now that Wren has locked all the doors behind him on his way to the Betty, Call must attempt to patch in manually to the *Auriga*'s computer to help the group get out. Call and the clone go into the nearby chapel so the android can use its terminals. Call crosses herself before sitting down, causing the clone to react in disbelief: Call has been programmed to be religious. Ironically, the plug Call needs is connected to an electronic Bible. At first, the android does not want to go into Father, because, she whines, she feels as if her "insides are all liquid." The Ripley clone will not stand for such nonsense; after all, once Call takes command of the ship, she can initiate a self-destruct sequence. Clearly embarrassed to expose her body, Call inserts the plug into her forearm and uploads herself to the mainframe. The scene is a marvel of posthuman displacement: God the Father has been replaced by the ship's computer, Father; the Bible has been replaced by the android, Call; and the human who seeks communion with the higher power has been replaced by the Alien-human hybrid clone, Ripley.

Call then takes over Father, occasionally coming back into her self to speak to the Ripley clone. Their first action is to ensure the elimination of the Aliens: because Call finds she cannot blow up the *Auriga* (her initial plan), the clone suggests to change the ship's trajectory to make it crash into Earth. In a reprisal of Mother's role in *Alien*, the android opens doors and starts the ship for the humans. But Call proves that she has a personality beyond mere programming: when she realizes Wren is about to get to the *Betty*, she closes his exit door. When he cries for help to Father, she answers: "Father's dead, asshole." The "Mother" Call is in charge and does not hesitate to repay the evil doctor: she calls over the ship's loudspeakers for the

Aliens to go get Wren as if she could order them about. Tellingly, Wren flees in panic, clearly believing that if Father is dead and the females have taken over, he is finally in *real* peril.

For a moment, the Ripley clone and Call share the joy of the joke on Wren, but the android winces in pain from her wound. The clone offers to help, causing Call to reject her once again, saying in an accusing voice what she thinks is on the clone's mind: "You must think this is pretty funny" (meaning, of course, that the clone would find *her* pretty funny—talk about low self-esteem). The clone looks at her earnestly and responds, "I'm finding a lot of things funny lately—but I don't think they are." Mollified somewhat, Call lets the clone touch her. She looks at the clone as if for the first time while she ministers the wound, and asks rudely, "How can you go on living, knowing what you are?" For the clone is, like Call, an aberration, a disgusting body. "Not much choice," the clone responds quietly. Call's look softens: "At least there's part of you that's human," she says, as if being human were some kind of boon. She then looks at her own open body and recoils in disgust: "I'm just . . . look at me. I'm disgusting." Two proclamations are attendant in this last statement: (1) "Look at me"—I need attention and feel that I am not seen for who or what I really am; and (2) "I'm disgusting"—I do not fit the societal norm, I am a mess. Even the clone is better than I am, because she is part human. That this discussion happens under a cross is doubly damning, as Christianity has long held that the female body is inherently filthy.

Ironically, one female outsider (an android) tried to kill the other female outsider (a hybrid) in order to save a humanity—represented by the men outside the chapel—that rejects her. Call's altruistic motive may be expressed only through self-loathing (I am not "human"; therefore, I am "disgusting") and prejudice against those like her (all other "nonhumans" who are also "disgusting"). The thinly veiled feminist narrative here is hard to miss. It is appropriate that the base of the discussion focuses on Call's "messy," open body. The juxtaposition, then, between the body we see (Winona Ryder as Call) and her self-description as "disgusting" (the abject) reveals the multilayered dialogues that intersect in the body of the female: she can be simultaneously one thing and its opposite. This juxtaposition of opposite and irreconcilable positions on the body of the female resonates with the mythical virgin-whore dyad and draws upon images of the teen girl who is anorexic-bulimic, depressed, or suicidal, a role that Ryder would play shortly thereafter in *Girl, Interrupted* (1999).

By cutting her connection to the panoptical net, Call has become an independent agent, but she has also broken contact with other androids like herself: the cost of individual survival when faced with the destructive force of the patriarchy is the loss of the collective consciousness. Call, like a postfeminist claiming that collective action is passé, is alone in her quest to save humanity. Notably, no other autons are with her, nor does she speak of being on a mission for some auton secret society. By deciding to "pass" in the mainstream rather than forming a coalition of her peers—no matter how noble her goals from the human perspective—Call has abandoned collective action of the feminist mode in favor of individual sacrifice and heroism of the patriarchal hero. She is James Bond, not Betty Friedan.

Now it is the clone's turn to ask questions: Why does Call care about what happens to anyone, particularly the *Betty*'s pirates? She replies, simply, "Because I'm programmed to." Call's claim that she cares about humans, about the men, because she is "programmed to" clearly alludes to the main purpose of the female androids in *The Stepford Wives* (1975): to behave and devote themselves to caring for their husbands. However, unlike the Stepford androids, Call is disobedient and breaks human law for the higher good. Her "humaneness" is couched in terms of her origin as a Second Gen: just as God created man and man created the machine, the machines begat Call. She is, therefore, the fulfillment of the human goal of evolution through creation. She is more humane than humans presumably because she is more evolved.

Disturbingly, however, Call seems to have internalized a pattern of self-loathing that points to the more generalized oppression of women. Just as she has been "programmed to care," she has been "programmed to hate herself," and the two seem to be tied to one another. Unlike the good android Bishop, who never seems to worry that he is not a human male (he is so passive that he even refuses a gun Vasquez offers him), Call clearly cares that she is less than a human woman. What Call's "programming" has done to her is to equate caring for others with abjection of her self. Call's motives, therefore, are not so much heroic as pathetic (from the Latin *pathētos*, meaning "liable to suffer"). She does not want to save the world because she loves the world; she saves the world so it will love her—even though it never will, as Ripley knows all too well.

No wonder the Ripley clone finds her devotion truly funny: "You're programmed to be an asshole! You're the new asshole model they are putting out?" The clone's amazement makes perfect sense as a mature feminist's admonition of the young woman's folly of caring for those who emotionally and verbally abuse her—as the men just bluntly did. This admission, then, undermines Call's earlier postfeminist position: she has been protecting and trying to fit in with humans (men) who discuss her penetrability behind her back. The absurdity of it all makes them share a smile, though Call looks away. The moment is lost when Distephano comes to get them.

Their comradeship is sealed in the next fight between the Ripley clone and Johner. Johner, furious because Call has tampered with the *Auriga* so that now they have less time to escape, threatens to kill her. The clone grabs him by the neck with one hand, choking him, and with the other hand she grabs his tongue. She then looks at Call and asks, "Want another souvenir?" Call smiles, a bit afraid but definitely amused at the clone's method for shutting Johner up. Just as Call took over the ship run by Father, the macho Johner can be silenced. His "it must be a chick thing" tongue is clearly connected to the toothed phallus of the Alien tongue. Both can "kill" and "wound," but the Ripley clone is not taking either any longer. She is fed up with men and Aliens. Once again, our protagonist has demonstrated her ability to handle dangerous and abusive phallic tongues.

(S)Mothering

> This thing of darkness I / Acknowledge
> mine.
>
> —Prospero, *The Tempest*, 5.1

As the ragtag gang of fugitives gets near the *Betty*, the Ripley clone suddenly feels the call of the Alien Queen and halts dead in her tracks. An Alien hand grabs the grate she is on, and she is pulled through into the abyss. Call looks down to see where the clone fell, and sees her lying on what seems a cross between a snake pit and a cesspool, her smooth white flesh against a teeming mass of Alien brown-black slithering tails and glistening heads, her body slowly being pulled down by the creatures' movements, as if she were being consumed. Again we see an image of woman as the abject—though the clone is serene, this pulling from below is the pull of the unconscious. As with Ripley's descent into Fiorina's "basement" in *Alien³*, this is the clone's required visit to the land of the monstrous.

The Ripley clone's journey to the lair of the Alien Queen is portrayed in a series of shots interspersed with darkness that resembles the sequence of her emergence from the diaphanous bag at the beginning of the film, only this time the clone is nestled in the arms of an Alien. She is being taken back into the womb. Like a little girl, the clone presses her forehead against the Alien's shoulder, relieved for the moment of the pressures and confusions of her hybrid nature.

She regains consciousness in the Queen's nursery. Gediman, cocooned high above, explains that the Alien Queen has had a second cycle, in which she developed a womb with a creature inside it. Now she is giving birth, according to Gediman, "for" Ripley, and that makes the Queen "perfect" (and an obvious allusion to his labeling of the Ripley clone at the opening of the narrative). Once again, what the doctor sees as perfect, the film reveals as monstrous. The camera focuses on the Queen's grotesque womb, a dark pod-looking thing reminiscent of *Invasion of the Body Snatchers*, making it a literal synecdoche of the Alien Queen. She is no longer presiding, as in *Aliens*, but supine and immobilized—a horrible, crippled image of imposed motherhood that reminds us of Ripley-7 in the lab of horrors. That the powerful Alien Queen, which for two films in the series served as the horrific foe, has been reduced by the machinations of the human doctors to little more than a vast pulsating immobilized womb is, perhaps, as clear a referent as possible to the malicious damage the medico-industrial complex inflicts on the female. Had we not seen the lab of clones, and not seen the horribly deformed and immobilized form of Ripley-7 reduced to nothing more than a womb, we might not recognize the immensity of the accusation implied here. We must read this moment as the culmination of the locus of horror in the series: here, in full color, is how the patriarchy hystericizes the female body.

The scene is appropriately climactic: the camera stays on the throbbing womb, while the Queen's screams and the musical score punctuate the surfacing of a new horror. Significantly, as Catherine Constable notes, the "translucent layer of mucus" covering the terrible apparition brings to mind the image of the Ripley clone emerging from her chrysalis after the surgery: the being rising from the monstrous womb is Ripley's equal.[31] The creature (nicknamed the Newborn) stands roughly nine feet tall, a slimy, sickly pinkish skeletal figure displaying a swollen stomach and hanging breasts.[32] Its sunken eyes and protruding jaw give its face the look of a terrifying human skull that contrasts with its soulful baby-blue eyes. The Newborn alternatively roars and mews, giving the impression of an aggressive but also helpless infant. Its first actions are to inspect and then kill its mother, shattering the allegiance that all Aliens (including the Ripley clone) show toward the Queen. It then advances, faces the clone, smells her, clacks its teeth (playfully?), and, in a grotesque imitation of an adoring pet, proceeds to lick her face with an enormous pink tongue. "Ooooh," coos Gediman from above. "It thinks you're its mother."

The reappearance of the phallic tongue motif associates the Newborn with the aggression displayed by the Aliens and Johner, positing it as the clone's new antagonist. The old foe, the Alien species as represented by its (now somewhat human) Queen, has been quickly dispatched and replaced by a creature whose hybrid body epitomizes human-created evil. Fusing human and Alien, male and female, child and peer, ferocity and innocence in one image, the Newborn is unpredictable and therefore dangerous. Its apparent loathing and subsequent destruction of its birth mother, for example, do not stem from any obvious reason, and neither does its affection for the Ripley clone (discounting the fact that she seemingly "smells" right). The effect of its actions, on the other hand, is clear: by killing the Alien Queen and transferring its affection to the clone, it confirms her claim to the title of *the* monster's/ monstrous mother of the narrative. The fact that its acceptance of the Ripley clone mirrors the well-known scene in *Alien³* where the Alien recognizes Ripley as the carrier of an Alien Queen further substantiates the image of the clone as the new Queen. She once again has "one inside of her," but this time it will not be coming out. The Ripley clone, unable to endure the creature, flies in horror when it turns on the immobilized Gediman and bites off his head.

In the meantime, the rest of the group has boarded the *Betty*, only to find that the enterprising Wren managed to get there first. Taking Call hostage, he intends to force her to call off the order to crash the *Auriga*, but suddenly Purvis begins to spasm: the Alien is coming. This is the first time since *Alien* that the male body is the site of birthing fear. The twist is that, thanks to the honesty of the Ripley clone, Purvis knows what is happening to him, and he can appropriate his own death by turning the Chestburster into a weapon. He grabs Wren and, after some requisite violence, pulls Wren's head against his chest just as the Chestburster launches itself free. The sequence, then, borrows the chest-bursting scene to create a rape-revenge narrative by including Wren's body as Purvis's "target." In other words, Wren infected Purvis with an Alien (rape #1), that now bursts from Purvis's chest as Purvis forces Wren's head into its path (rape #2 and Purvis's revenge). The moment also incorporates several visual puns: Purvis's death scream mirrors the Chestburster's birth scream (seen in a shot that goes down Purvis's throat into his chest) and recalls Junior's victory scream in *Alien³* as he gets ready to rape Ripley. Also, Wren is not only "mind fucked" but dies at the hand of his "brain child"—his "pet science project," as Christie termed it. The scene then twists into a mock gang rape when Distephano, Johner, and Call, horrified at the sight of the screeching Alien trapped by Wren's head, riddle the joined Purvis, Wren, and Alien with bullets.

The clone boards the *Betty* as it pulls away from the *Auriga*. They cannot fly to safety because the door of the cargo hold will not close. Call goes down to close it and discovers that the Newborn has boarded the *Betty* after the clone. In the flashing blue light of the cargo hold the Newborn's face looks like a death mask. Call, displaying the wisdom of a horror-film survivor, promptly hides. Distephano enters, looking for Call, only to get his head mashed as the angry Newborn tries to grab him. Call comes out of hiding but is intercepted by the Newborn, who caresses her head carefully, perhaps having learned caution from its experience with Distephano. Suddenly cruel, it probes the hole in her side, making her scream in pain.

The Ripley clone steps in. "Put it down," she commands, as if it had been playing with some fragile knickknack. The contrite Newborn obeys. The clone goes to it, and they embrace. She caresses its head and face, losing herself in this intimate moment. But a shot of the porthole reminds her (and us) of the necessary end for all monsters. The realization is painful: she, who of all beings is closest to the Newborn, must betray its trust and become its executioner. At the same time, we become aware that no one else would experience its death more properly than the clone. We are reminded of the climactic scene in *Bram Stoker's Dracula*: Mina, the reincarnation of Dracula's only love, slays the vampire to save the world from his presence, only after giving him a kiss of unconditional love that allows him to make his peace with God.[33] Similarly, the Ripley clone will take personal responsibility for the fate of the Newborn in a way the human doctors did not for any of their creations. In an intimate moment that Peter Travers describes as a "close erotic encounter,"[34] the clone gently opens the Newborn's mouth, and, moaning, cuts her hand on its teeth. She throws the resulting acidic blood onto the porthole's window, causing a small hole in the glass. The suction of the escaping pressure pulls the Newborn to the bulkhead with its back against the window, a small part of its flesh acting as stopper. It tears, and an abortion drama ensues: the Ripley clone, a woman who has made an emotionally difficult but necessary choice, represents the pro-choice position. She watches the Newborn's destruction in obvious distress, even telling it she is sorry. The Newborn's painful piecemeal death represents the pro-life position, vividly illustrating the rhetoric of the horrors of the vacuum aspiration abortion: the Newborn writhes in agony as its torn body flies into space in a continuous stream of bloody pieces. Its face is left for last, one lingering image of its half-bred monstrosity hanging on to the window.

Once the Newborn is gone, the vacuum threatens the Ripley clone. Call, strapped to a bar on the wall, extends her arm to help her. The clone catches it, confirming her bond with the android. The pro-choice, pro-life dialectic of the abortion scene is resolved by an alternative family of choice—Ripley and Call. They spoon together, the Ripley clone behind Call, to wait for the *Betty* to clear the atmosphere.

Off into the Sunrise: Postutopian or Posthuman?

> To live with the alien, the freak, and the monster is to come to terms with *ourselves*.
>
> —Jeffrey A. Weinstock, "Freaks in Space"

When the Ripley clone and Call finally can look up, and out, the *Betty* is coasting over Earth, and a golden sun bathes the clouds surrounding them. We get a shot of the *Betty*'s insignia, a Vargas-style pinup girl riding on a bomb, an image associated most frequently with World War II B52 bombers and literally replicated at the end of *Dr. Strangelove* (1964), when Major Kong (Slim Pickens) rides the bomb on home like a bucking bronco. The camera pans down, framing Ripley and Call in the open, spherical porthole of the *Betty*, suggesting a connection between the babe on the bomb and the film's protagonists: Ripley and Call are not simple heroes, but Bomber Girls joyously riding destruction down toward Earth. After all, however well-intentioned their motives, they have caused an atomic explosion of undetermined magnitude on Earth. We cannot but wonder—did Call pick an uninhabited part of Earth? Is there such a thing? How many people died in the crash?

The explosion, it seems, is irrelevant. Or at least it is to the clone: she looks at Call and says, somewhat cynically, "Well, you did it. You saved the Earth." The Ripley clone seems happy to pass the baton Ripley has been carrying for three films; as far as she is concerned, Call can be the new hero of the series—wherever that may lead her. In response, Call wonders what will happen to them now that they are here, but the clone cannot figure it out either: she, too, is a stranger in this world.

As the movie credits roll, we realize—or we should—that the happy ending implied is a joke on us. From the crashing of the *Auriga* into Earth in a massive atomic explosion, to the bringing of an Alien organism into the biosphere (the Ripley clone) there can be no happy ending. Every member of the surviving crew is wanted for one reason or another. Call is an illegal android, Ripley is an illegal Alien-hybrid clone, and Johner and Vriess are smugglers who hijacked bodies and sold them for profit. Can Earth, described by Johner as "a shithole," be the location of our happy ending? Given the ways humans behave in the narrative, we can only expect that the four survivors either will be detained and destroyed or will go underground. But this is the stuff of sequels.

Alien Resurrection clearly fails (intentionally or unintentionally) to answer the question it repeatedly asks of its protagonist: "Who are you?" The clone seems to have chosen imperfect humans over her own genetic offspring for whom she feels not only affinity but affection. At the same time, by referring to herself as a stranger to Earth, she pointedly differentiates herself from humanity. She is not technically human, and neither is Call, who saved humanity from itself. In the end, the Ripley clone chooses, not humanity in general, but Call and the humane. As humans, the psychologically and physically crippled

Johner and Vriess are excluded from the final scene; only the two females look to the dawn of the future. They, it is clear, are the future.

The future of the humane: the android and the Alien-human hybrid look to the future.

We are left with a final scene that mimics the "riding off into the sunset" ending of the western genre. But this new dawn, however hopeful in tone, cannot escape the fact that the hope is not for humanity. As a hybrid, the clone is the equivalent to *Species'* Sil. Who is to say whether or not she can reproduce? Because the Alien Queen clone was able to reproduce alone with "just her womb," is it possible that the Ripley clone can reproduce in the same fashion? We could easily assume, based on the overwhelming reproductive compulsion of the Alien species, that the clone must reproduce. This time she knowingly carries within herself the potential destruction of the patriarchy. In allowing herself to survive—and we must remember that Ripley rejected this very same option in *Alien³*—the Ripley clone has become the Alien in more ways than one, the most important being that she no longer considers the goals of, or the survival of, the patriarchy, over her own self-survival. That, apparently, is Call's role. This Ripley now has more than the two obvious choices of the previous films: to fight the Alien and thereby the patriarchal death drive or to sacrifice herself for the system. Both these options, of course, aid the ends of patriarchy, as each serves the needs of power by validating its reality. By giving the protagonist of the franchise a third option—appropriating the Alien—Whedon and Jeunet have liberated her from the dichotomy of human and Alien. In choosing herself, she chooses both human and Alien without choosing one over the other. Our Ripley, the old Ripley, has become the shadow superhero who sheds the heart of gold for acceptance of the power and necessity of the dark soul within us all. There is no longer a need for the destroying mother to be externalized, for this Ripley admits that the destructive potential of the all-consuming mother resides within her. In *Alien*, *Aliens*, and *Alien³*, Ripley is attempting to save the human race, but in *Alien Resurrection* her clone is trying to save herself. She is the end of the human, a complex posthuman female of choice and action.

More power to her.

Alien Woman

Woman is not born: she is made. In the making, her humanity is destroyed. She becomes symbol of this, symbol of that: mother of the earth, slut of the universe; but she never becomes herself because it is forbidden for her to do so.

—Andrea Dworkin, *Pornography*

Oophobia

In the beginning, there was the egg . . . The advertising poster for *Alien* is a marvel of juxtaposition. Floating in space above the alien plain, the egg is the familiar made grotesque: its enlarged surface is covered in bumps and craters, the narrower end at the top seems a bit too pointed, and of course there is the matter of the crack emanating a poisonous green light and gas. The combination of the egg and the word *Alien* radically defamiliarizes a common object to horrific effect.

198

The poster also implies the mixing of science fiction and horror in the vein of *Them!* or *It!* or *The Thing from Another World*. The image of the egg further complicates this cross-genre impulse by replacing the masculine rocket with the ovoid form, which connects the film with monstrous birth films like *Rosemary's Baby* and *The Omen*. One does not need to see the film at all to know that what emerges from that egg will be a monstrous evil freak (at least by human standards) bent on the destruction of any human within reach. And, worst of all, it will be coming for us, as the viewer of the poster is the only human in sight.

As if the combination of science fiction, bug-eyed monster horror, and monstrous birth were not enough, *Alien*'s masterstroke is its invocation of the monstrous mother, for it is not Giger's biomechanoid that we see in the poster but the evil, acidic womb. The womb, as we have argued, is infinitely more dangerous than the solitary killer because the womb can produce more killers—after all, Victor Frankenstein's fear and envy of the womb are what lead him to compete with Mother Nature.

Also referencing the monolith in *2001*, the *Alien* poster offers the monstrous womb as a religious symbol from an unknown culture. Like the Venus of Willendorf, the egg represents a fertility goddess reduced to the bare essentials of womb and vaginal cleft. And like *2001*'s monolith, the *Alien* egg seems to be demanding fear and obeisance.

The intent of *Alien*'s poster was frightfully clear: this is an alien womb up to no good. Whereas in *2001* the "Star Child" was the site of wondrous fascination, in *Alien* the monstrous birth is the site of horror. What the studio was selling was the horror of reincorporation and dissolution into the womb-tomb: "In space," the poster assures us, "no one can hear you scream." That the pro-life movement will adopt a similar rhetoric for projects such as the film *The Silent Scream* speaks to the sacred horror of the womb. The tag line also evokes the image of astronaut Frank Poole's death in space (again, *2001*), his body silently flying away from the *Odyssey* into the darkness. Space, the poster is telling us, is the most terrifying and lonely place of all. The imminent confrontation with the Alien egg, with this monstrous motherhood, this Otherness personified, will be—like birth, like death—a solitary experience.

The advertising poster for *Alien* tells the whole tale—except for the part about the protagonist being a woman. How ironic, then, that while we may have been buying a menacing extraterrestrial, we ended up with a female hero facing the monstrous feminine.

Last Stand

The poster for *Aliens* supplants the horrific egg with a central image of mother and child, and it would be hard to miss the fact that the mother is carrying some serious weaponry. Unlike the poster for *Alien*, where the threat of the monstrous feminine was aimed at the viewer's own person, *Aliens* clearly posits the threat to the family. Even more importantly, the implied threat of the monstrous mother from *Alien* is literalized—this film is not just about the horror of the monstrous offspring, but the rivalry between the good mother and the bad mother.

Although we do not see the horrible creature lurking just outside our vision—in fact, right behind the viewer when looking at the poster, the signs of monstrous motherhood are everywhere: directly above Ripley's head, for example, the letter *I* of the title is opened like a reptilian eye or a vagina. Considering both images, one might expect a monstrous female dragon–like creature, the origin of the monstrous proliferation of Alien eggs surrounding Ripley's feet. In case the viewer did not get the hint, the eggs mimic both the color and shape of the "I" opening: although Giger was asked to redesign the eggs for *Alien* to make them less obviously vaginal, the eggs in *Aliens'* poster have been consciously redesigned to suggest the vagina more strongly. Blue light emanates from the seams as if they are in the process of opening—threatening to explode like so many bombs.

Thus, the good woman and the bad woman meet on the battlefield of the reproductive plain. Ripley is rescuing the little girl from the poisonous womb of death. What is at stake are mothering styles. The tag line for the film, "This time it's war," speaks not to the worthless macho Marines with their useless guns and even more useless bombs, but to the war between the women, the battle for the body, the battle for the children. The good woman will do whatever it takes to save the little girl from death at the hands of the monstrous mother. She will wear fatigues, learn to shoot, strap a gun and a flamethrower together, enter the slime of the ghetto, and reach into the dire depths of the very womb of the monstrous mother herself. The war is on the female who does not conform to patriarchal norms of motherhood and the nuclear family.

Enemy Mine

The bitch is back in the poster for Fincher's *Alien³*. The central image of the mother and child is replaced with Ripley and the Alien. Creeping into the side of the frame, the Alien extends its lethal jaws just inches from Ripley's exposed neck. Her abject terror is evident. The implied threat of rape and death from previous films now visits upon the body of Ripley *for real*. Whereas the poster for *Alien* focused on monstrous motherhood as the source of the creature and *Aliens*  on the rivalry between mothering styles, *Alien³* focuses on the horrid, perverse, and permanent connection between torturer and victim, between Death and the sacrificial maiden.

Rather than advertise either the hero or the monstrous creature (as *Alien* and *Aliens* had done), this joining of the two in a single frame already belies the dynamic tension between the protagonist and the Alien that was hinted at in *Aliens*. The juxtaposition of the two faces is a study in dramatic similitude: white and black, left and right, attacking and defending, alien and human, one would be hard pressed to imagine anything so different, and yet so similar. Not only are the heads of both characters framed together in a loose mirror image (Ripley facing front, while the Alien faces her), but their open mouths, slick shiny skin, and rigid lines all suggest an odd affinity between these two beings. Evil and good, darkness and light, they could be opposites, or perhaps two complementary parts of one self.

Sisterhood

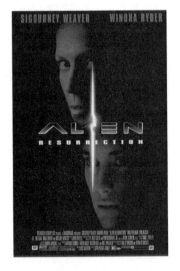

Drawing on the poster for *Aliens*, the poster for *Alien Resurrection* places two females as the dominant image of the film. However, the Alien is not simply out of the shot; it has been relegated to the background entirely, suppressed behind the symbolic surface of the image.

Like the poster for *Alien³*, two faces are juxtaposed. The words of the title separate them. The Alien, the tear caused by the Other, joins them. Two protagonists, two female heroes, separated by time, space, perspective, and death, are joined by the Alien. Of course, it is not insignificant that the faces we see are not just two unnamed women: these are Sigourney Weaver and Winona Ryder, and the viewer knows, she just *knows*, that the film is a buddy picture in the vein of *Thelma and Louise*.

For *Alien Resurrection* is in many ways about the relationship between these two women, about what ties them together and what separates them. Ripley died trying to kill the Alien species once and for all, yet she lives; and with her comes her own personal demon, a monstrous shadow lurking in the background, fighting to make itself known. Call is bent on being a new Ripley. Thus, in *Alien Resurrection*, the myth of the monstrous feminine has become both a threat and a promise, that which threatens to divide women also has the power to bind them together: the shadow of the monstrous mother, of the castrating vagina dentata, of the monstrous birth is not simply a specter to be expelled, but embraced. Not even death could save Ripley from the monster—she killed it in *Alien*, killed its mother in *Aliens*, killed the mother and herself in *Alien³*—but she can save both the monster and herself and, by so doing, sacrifice the human in the name of the humane.

What Is an *Alien* Film?

Like any horror film, the four films of the *Alien* series sell us the manifestation of our own fear, and, like any science-fiction film, they give us a word of warning. We fear the loss of the primacy of the rational-humanist subject symbolized by the closed male body. The warning: the monstrous bitch at the door may have already gotten in, and we somehow failed to notice.

But, like the best of both science fiction and horror, the series also sells hope: the transformative power of the monstrous feminine Other may lead us, not to death, but to something else, and maybe that something else will be the ticket to our future survival. Being something other than human (an android or hybrid or clone), something other than man or woman, good or evil, self or Other, father or mother, something other than all those dichotomies we live with every single day just might not be so bad after all. That possibility of difference is what makes the *Alien* series truly remarkable.

Selected Bibliography

The *Alien* Saga

"Alien." In *The Science Fiction Film Sourcebook*, ed. David Wingrove. Essex, UK: Longman, 1985, 22–23.

"Alien." In *Variety's Complete Science Fiction Reviews*, ed. Donald Willis. New York: Garland, 1985, 343.

"Alien 3 [sic]," *Time*, 1 June 1992, 87.

"Alien Experience." 2001. http://www.alienexperience.com/. Accessed 17 August 2003.

"The Alien Lair." 2000. http://welcome.to/alienlair. Accessed 17 August 2003.

"Alien Legend." 1997. http://www.planetavp.com/al/. Accessed 17 August 2003.

"ALIEN Movies Resource." 1997. http://www.planetavp.com/amr/. Accessed 17 August 2003.

"Alien Resurrection." http://www.alien-resurrection.com/. Accessed 17 August 2003.

"Aliens Archive." 1996. http://aliensarchive.tripod.com/aliens/. Accessed 17 August 2003.

"alienscollection.com." http://www.alienscollection.com/. Accessed 17 August 2003.

Alleva, Richard. "Alienated." *Commonweal*, 17 July 1992, 19.

Anderson, Craig. "Alien." In *Science Fiction Films of the Seventies*. Jefferson, NC: McFarland, 1985, 217–224.

Ansen, David. "Saint Ripley and the Dragon." *Newsweek*, 1 June 1992, 73.

———. "Terminating the Aliens." *Newsweek*, 21 July 1986, 64–65.

———. Martin Kasindorf, and Katrine Ames. "Hollywood's Scary Summer." *Newsweek*, 18 June 1979, 54–59.

Bell-Metereau, Rebecca. "Woman: The Other Alien in *Alien*." In *Women Worldwalkers: New Dimensions in Science Fiction and Fantasy*, ed. Jane B. Weedman. Lubbock: Texas Tech Press, 1985, 9–24. (Reprinted in *Hollywood Androgyny*. New York: Columbia University Press, 1985, 209–224).

SELECTED BIBLIOGRAPHY

Benton, Mike. "Aliens." In *Science Fiction Comics: The Illustrated History*. Vol. 3, Taylor History of Comics. Dallas: Taylor Publishing, 1992.

Berenstein, Rhona. "Mommie Dearest: Aliens, Rosemary's Baby and Mothering." *Journal of Popular Culture* 24, no. 2 (1990): 55–73.

B.G. "Flying High." *The New Yorker*, 11 June 1979, 154.

Billy, Ted. "A Curious Case of Influence: *Nostromo* and *Alien(s)*." *Conradiana* 21, no. 2 (1989): 147–157.

Bischoff, David F. *Aliens: Genocide*. New York: Bantam, 1994.

———. *Aliens vs. Predator: Hunters Planet*. New York: Bantam, 1994.

Bisson, Terry, and Joss Whedon. *Alien Resurrection: The Official Junior Novelization*. New York: HarperPrism, 1997.

Blackmore, Tim. "'Is this going to be another bug hunt?': S-F Tradition versus Biology-as-Destiny in James Cameron's *Aliens*." *Journal of Popular Culture* 29, no. 4 (Spring 1996): 211–226. Available from EBSCOHOST; accessed 20 December 2001.

Bowman, James. "*Alien* Menace." *National Review*, 26 January 1998, 35–36.

Bradshaw, Peter. "Alien: The Director's Cut." *The Guardian*, 31 October 2003. http://film.guardian.co.uk; accessed 3 November 2003.

Brooker, Will. "Internet Fandom and the Continuing Narratives of *Star Wars, Blade Runner*, and *Alien*." In *Alien Zone II: The Spaces of Science Fiction Cinema*, ed. Annette Kuhn. New York: Verso, 1999, 50-73.

Bundtzen, Lynda K. "Monstrous Mothers: Medusa, Grendel, and Now Alien." *Film Quarterly* 40, no. 3 (1987): 11–17.

Byars, Jackie. "Introduction to Some Ideological Readings of *Alien*." In "Symposium on *Alien*," ed. Charles Elkins. *Science-Fiction Studies* 7, no. 3 (1980): 278–282.

Byers, Thomas B. "Commodity Futures." In *Alien Zone: Cultural Theory and Contemporary Science Fiction Cinema*, ed. Annette Kuhn. New York: Verso, 1990, 39–51.

Canby, Vincent. "HAL, If You're Still Out There, Here's a Computer-Friendly Sequel." *New York Times*, 22 May 1992, C1, C19.

———. "Screen: 'Alien' Brings Chills from the Far Galaxy." *New York Times*, 25 May 1979, C16.

Caryn, James. "Sequels Battle Monsters, Villains and Burnout." *New York Times*, 31 May 1992, H20.

Constable, Catherine. "Becoming the Monster's Mother: Morphologies of Identity in the *Alien* Series." In *Alien Zone II: The Spaces of Science Fiction Cinema*, ed. Annette Kuhn. New York: Verso, 1999, 173-202.

Creed, Barbara. "*Alien and the Monstrous Feminine*." In *Alien Zone: Cultural Theory and Contemporary Science Fiction Cinema*, ed. Annette Kuhn. New York: Verso, 1990, 128-141.

Crispin, A. C. *Alien Resurrection* (novelization). New York: Warner, 1997.

Croatto, Pete. "Alien: The Director's Cut." www.filmcritic.com; accessed 8 November 2003.

Doherty, Thomas. "Genre, Gender, and the Aliens Trilogy." In *The Dread of Difference: Gender and the Horror Film*. Austin: University of Texas Press, 1996, 181–199.

Eaton, Michael. "Born Again." *Sight and Sound* (December 1997): 6–9.

Edelstein, David. "Mother of the Year." *Rolling Stone*, 28 August 1986, 31–42.

Elkins, Charles, ed. "Symposium on *Alien*." *Science Fiction Studies* 7, no. 3 (1980): 278–304.

Eyers, Jonathan A. "The Alien Encyclopedia." http://www. absoluteavp.com/enc/. Accessed 18 August 2003.

Fitting, Peter. "The Second Alien." In "Symposium on *Alien*," ed. Charles Elkins. *Science Fiction Studies* 7, no. 3 (1980): 285–293.

Foster, Alan Dean. *Alien 3* [sic]: *The Novelization*. New York: Warner Books, 1992.

———. *Aliens: A Novelization*. New York: Warner Books, 1986.

———. *Alien: A Novel*. New York: Warner Books, 1979.

"Fox Store: The Alien Legacy." 20th Century Fox Home Entertainment. 1999. http://www.foxhome.com/ alienlegacy/index_frames.html. Accessed 17 August 2003.

Frank, Alan. "Alien." In *The Science Fiction and Fantasy Handbook*. London: Batsford, 1982, 10–11.

Giger, H. R. *Giger's Alien*. Beverly Hills, CA: Galerie Morpheus International, 1999.

———. *H. R. Giger's Necronomicon*. London: Big O Publishing, 1978.

Goldberg, Lee, et al. "Aliens (1986)." In *Science Fiction Filmmaking in the 1980s*. Jefferson, NC: McFarland, 1995, 7–22.

Goodall, Jane. *"Aliens." Southern Review* 23 (1990): 73–82.

Goodman, Walter. "Film: Sigourney Weaver in *Aliens*." *New York Times*, 18 July 1986, C11.

Gould, Jeff. "The Destruction of the Social by the Organic in Alien." In "Symposium on *Alien*," ed. Charles Elkins. *Science Fiction Studies* 7, no. 3 (1980): 278–285.

Graham, Paula. "Looking Lesbian: Amazons and Aliens in Science Fiction Cinema." In *The Good, the Bad and the Gorgeous: Popular Culture's Romance with Lesbianism*, eds. Diane Hamer and Belinda Budge. London: Pandora, 1994, 197–217.

Greenberg, Harvey R. "Fembo: *Aliens'* Intentions." *Journal of Popular Film and TV* 15, no. 4 (Winter 1988): 165–171.

———. "Reimagining the Gargoyle: Psychoanalytic Notes on *Alien*." In *Close Encounters: Film, Feminism and Science Fiction*, ed. Constance Penley et al. Minneapolis: University of Minnesota Press, 1991, 83–104. First published as "The Fractures of Desire: Psychoanalytic Notes on *Alien*, the Contemporary 'Cruel' Horror Film." *Psychoanalytic Review* 70, no. 2 (1983): 241–267.

Gross, Edward, and Jon Snyder. "Alien IV: The Movie You'll See . . . and the one you won't," *Sci-fi Universe Magazine* 1 (July 1994); http://www.planetarp.com/ amr/films/a4/inta95.html; accessed 12 January 2004.

Harmetz, Aljean. "A Sequel to 'Alien' Ready to Go into Production." *New York Times*, 9 July 1985, C16.

SELECTED BIBLIOGRAPHY

Hochman, David. "Beauties and the Beast." *Entertainment Weekly*, 5 December 1997, 18–24.

"HR Giger—The Official Website." http://www.hrgiger.com/. Accessed 17 August 2003.

Jeffords, Susan. "The Battle of the Big Mamas: Feminism and the Alienation of Women." *Journal of American Culture* 10, no. 3 (1987): 73–84.

Jennings, Ros. "Desire and Design—Ripley Undressed." In *Lesbians and the Moving Image*, ed. Tamsin Wilton. London: Routledge, 1995, 193–206.

Johnson, Brian D. "Holiday Treats from Hollywood." *Maclean's*, 29 December 1997/5 January 1998, 103–105.

Kael, Pauline. "Aliens." In *Hooked*. New York: Penguin, 1989, 192–193.

Kavanagh, James H. "Feminism, Humanism and Science in *Alien*." In *Alien Zone: Cultural Theory and Contemporary Science Fiction Cinema*, ed. Annette Kuhn. New York: Verso, 1990, 73–81.

Lee, Clayton. "Cognitive Approaches to *Alien*." In "Symposium on *Alien*," ed. Charles Elkins. *Science Fiction Studies* 7, no. 3 (1980): 299–302.

Maslin, Janet. "Invading Theaters: Bugs, Drugs and Thugs." *New York Times*, 28 November 1997, E1, E17.

———. "Ripley, Believe It or Not, Has a Secret, and It's Not Pretty." *New York Times*, 26 November 1997, E1, E10.

Matheson, T. J. "Triumphant Technology and Minimal Man: *The Technological Society*, Science Fiction Films, and Ridley Scott's *Alien*." *Extrapolation* 33, no. 3 (1992): 215–229.

Miller, Mark. "You Say You Want a Resurrection? Done." *Newsweek*, 9 June 1997, 75.

Mullhall, Stephen. *On Film*. New York: Routledge, 2002.

Murdock, Andrew, and Rachel Aberly. *The Making of Alien Resurrection*. New York: HarperPrism, 1997.

Murphy, Kathleen. "The Last Temptation of Sigourney Weaver." *Film Comment* 28, no. 4 (July–August 1992): 17–20.

Navarro, Yvonne. *Aliens: Music of the Spears*. New York: Bantam Spectra, 1996.

Newton, Judith. "Feminism and Anxiety in *Alien*." In *Alien Zone: Cultural Theory and Contemporary Science Fiction Cinema*, ed. Annette Kuhn, 82–90. New York: Verso, 1990. First published in *Science Fiction Studies* 7, no. 3 (1980): 293–297.

O'Hehir, Andrew. "The Horror, The Horror." www.salon.com, 1 November 2003.

Perry, S. D. *Aliens vs. Predator: War*. New York: Bantam Spectra, 1999.

———. *Aliens: Berserker*. New York: Bantam Spectra, 1998.

———. *Aliens: Labyrinth*. Reprint. New York: Bantam, 1996.

Perry, Steve. *Aliens: Nightmare Asylum*. New York: Bantam, 1993.

———. *Aliens: Earth Hive*. New York: Bantam Spectra, 1992.

Perry, Steve, and Stephani Perry. *Aliens vs. Predator: Prey*. New York: Bantam Spectra, 1994.

———. *The Female Wars*. New York: Bantam, 1993.

"Planet Alien." 2002. http://www.planet-alien.co.uk/. Accessed 17 August 2003.

Roberts, Robin. "Adoptive versus Biological Mothering in *Aliens.*" *Extrapolation* 30 (1989): 353–363.

Rushing, Janice H. "Evolution of 'The New Frontier' in *Alien* and *Aliens*: Patriarchal Co-optation of the Feminine Archetype." *Quarterly Journal of Speech* 75, no. 1 (1989): 1–24.

Safford, Tony. "Alien/Alienation." In "Symposium on *Alien,*" ed. Charles Elkins. *Science Fiction Studies* 7, no. 3 (1980): 297–299.

Sheckley, Robert. *Aliens: Alien Harvest*. New York: Bantam Spectra, 1995.

Schickel, Richard. "Alien Resurrection." *Time*, 1 December 1997, 84.

———. "Help! They're Back!" *Time*, 28 July 1986, 54–58.

Schlesinger, Arthur. "Of Blobs and Banalities." *Saturday Review*, 4 August 1979, 51.

Schofield, Sand. *Aliens: Rogue*. New York: Bantam, 1995.

Schwarzbaum, Lisa. "Alien Resurrection." *Entertainment Weekly*, 5 December 1997, 47–49.

Scobie, Stephen. "What's the Story, Mother?: The Mourning of *Alien.*" *Science Fiction Studies* 20, no. 1 (1993): 80–93.

Sobchack, Vivian. "The Virginity of Astronauts: Sex and the Science Fiction Film." In *Alien Zone: Cultural Theory and Contemporary Science Fiction Cinema*, ed. Annette Kuhn. New York: Verso, 1990, 103–115.

Speed, Louise. "*Alien₃*[sic]: A Postmodern Encounter with the Abject." *Arizona Quarterly* 54, no. 1 (Spring 1998): 125–151.

Syonan-Teo, Kobayashi. "Why Sigourney Is Jesus: Watching *Alien3* [sic] in the Light of *Se7ven.*" *Vidiocy*. 1998. http://inkpot.com/film/alien.htm. Accessed 17 August 2003.

Taubin, Amy. "Invading Bodies: Aliens³ [sic] and the Trilogy." *Sight and Sound* (July–August 1992): 8–10. (Reprinted as "The 'Alien' Trilogy: From Feminism to Aids." In *Women and Film: A Sight and Sound Reader*, ed. Pam Cook and Philip Dodd. Philadelphia: Temple University Press, 1993, 93–100.)

Thomson, David. *David Thomson on the Alien Quartet*. New York: Bloomsbury, 1998.

———. "The Bitch Is Back." *Esquire*, December 1997, 56–57.

Torry, Robert. "Awakening to the Other: Feminism and the Ego-Ideal in *Alien.*" *Women's Studies* 23 (1994): 343–363.

Travers, Peter. "Twisted Sisters in Space." *Rolling Stone*, 11 December 1997, 83–85.

Vaughn, Thomas. "Voices of Sexual Distortion: Rape, Birth, and Self-Annihilation Metaphors in the *Alien* Trilogy." *Quarterly Journal of Speech* 81, no. 4 (November 1995): 423–435.

Williams, Anne. "Inner and Outer Spaces: The *Alien* Trilogy." In *Art of Darkness: A Poetics of Gothic*. Chicago: University of Chicago Press, 1995, 249–252.

Wopat, Chris. "Alien Collectors Homeworld." 1997. http://www.xenomorph.org/. Accessed 17 August 2003.

Cultural Criticism and Theory

Alan, Frank. *The Science Fiction and Fantasy Handbook*. London: Batsford, 1982.
Bakhtin, Mikhail. *Rabelais and His World*. Trans. Helene Iswolsky. Bloomington: Indiana University Press, 1984.
Balsamo, Anne. *Technologies of the Gendered Body: Reading Cyborg Women*. Durham, NC: Duke University Press, 1996.
Barr, Marleen, ed. *Future Females, The Next Generation: New Voices and Velocities in Feminist Science Fiction Criticism*. Boulder, CO: Rowman & Littlefield, 2000.
Bartokowski, Frances. *Feminist Utopias*. Lincoln: University of Nebraska Press, 1989.
Baudrillard, Jean. *Simulations*. Trans. Paul Foss, Paul Patton, and Philip Beitchman. New York: Simiotext[e], 1983.
Beauvoir, Simone de. *The Second Sex*. Trans. and ed. H. M. Parshley. New York: Vintage, 1989.
Bell-Metereau, Rebecca. *Hollywood Androgyny*. New York: Columbia University Press, 1985.
Broderick, Mick. "Heroic Apocalypse: Mad Max, Mythology and the Millennium." In *Crisis Cinema: The Apocalyptic Idea in Postmodern Narrative*, ed. Christopher Sharrett. Washington, DC: Maisonneuve, 1993, 251–272.
Broege, Valerie. "Electric Eve: Images of Female Computers in Science Fiction." In *Clockwork Worlds: Mechanized Environments in SF*, ed. Richard D. Erlich and Thomas P. Dunn. Westport, CT: Greenwood, 1983, 183–194.
Brooke-Rose, Christine. *A Rhetoric of the Unreal: Studies in Narrative and Structure, Especially of the Fantastic*. Cambridge: Cambridge University Press, 1992.
Brosnan, John. *The Primal Screen*. London: Hazell, 1991.
Brownmiller, Susan. *Against Our Will: Men, Women, and Rape*. New York: Fawcett Columbine, 1993.
Butler, Judith. *Antigone's Claim: Kinship between Life and Death*. New York: Columbia University Press, 2000.
———. *Bodies That Matter: On the Discursive Limits of "Sex."* New York: Routledge, 1993.
———. *Gender Trouble: Feminism and the Subversion of Identity*. New York: Routledge, 1990.
Campbell, Joseph. *The Masks of God: Primitive Mythology*. New York: Penguin, 1991.
———. *The Masks of God: Oriental Mythology*. New York, Penguin, 1991.
———. *The Power of Myth*. New York: Doubleday, 1988.

SELECTED BIBLIOGRAPHY

———. *The Hero with a Thousand Faces*. Bollingen Series XVII. Princeton, NJ: Princeton University Press, 1973.

Cartwright, Frederick F., and Michael D. Biddiss. *Disease and History*. New York: Barnes & Noble, 1991.

Chodorow, Nancy. *The Reproduction of Mothering*. Berkeley: University of California Press, 1978.

Chunovic, Louis. *One Foot on the Floor: The Curious Evolution of Sex on Television from* I Love Lucy *to* South Park. New York: TV Books, 2000.

Cirlot, J. E. *A Dictionary of Symbols*. 2nd ed. Trans. Jack Sage. New York: Philosophical Library, 1971.

Clover, Carol J. *Men, Women, and Chainsaws: Gender in the Modern Horror Film*. Princeton, NJ: Princeton University Press, 1992.

Cohen, Jeffrey J., ed. *Monster Theory: Reading Culture*. Minneapolis: University of Minnesota Press, 1996.

Connerton, Paul. *How Societies Remember*. Cambridge: Cambridge University Press, 1989.

Creed, Barbara. *The Monstrous Feminine: Film, Feminism, Psychoanalysis*. New York: Routledge, 1997.

———. "Lesbian Bodies: Tribades, Tomboys and Tarts." In *Sexy Bodies: The Strange Carnalities of Feminism*, ed. E. Grosz and E Probyn. London: Routledge, 1995, 86–103.

———. "Gynesis, Postmodernism and the Science Fiction Horror Film." In *Alien Zone: Cultural Theory and Contemporary Science Fiction Cinema*, ed. Annette Kuhn. New York: Verso, 1990, 128–144.

Daniels, Les. *Wonder Woman: The Life and Times of the Amazon Princess*. San Francisco: Chronicle Books, 2000.

———. *DC Comics: Sixty Years of the World's Favorite Comic Book Heroes*. Boston: Bulfinch Press, 1995.

———. *Marvel: Five Fabulous Decades of the World's Greatest Comics*. New York: Harry N. Abrams, 1993.

Davies, Jude, and Carol R. Smith. *Gender, Ethnicity and Sexuality in Contemporary American Film*. Edinburgh: Keele University Press, 1997.

Davies, Philip John, and Paul Wells, eds. *American Film and Politics from Reagan to Bush Jr*. New York: Manchester University Press, 2002.

De Lauretis, Teresa. *Technologies of Gender: Essays on Theory, Film, and Fiction*. Bloomington: Indiana University Press, 1987.

Duchet-Suchaux, G., and M. Pastoreau. *The Bible and the Saints*. New York: Flammarion, 1994.

Dworkin, Andrea. "Pornography: Men Possessing Women." In *Feminism in our Time: The Essential Writings, World War II to the Present*, ed. Miriam Schneir. New York: Vintage, 1994: 419–427.

Fernbach, Amanda. *Fantasies of Fetishism: From Decadence to the Posthuman*. New Brunswick, NJ: Rutgers University Press, 2002.

Fiedler, Leslie. *Freaks: Myths and Images of the Secret Self*. New York: Touchstone, 1978.

Fischer, Lucy. *Cinematernity: Film, Motherhood, Genre*. Princeton, NJ: Princeton University Press, 1996.

Foster, Gwendolyn A. *Captive Bodies: Postcolonial Subjectivity in Cinema*. Albany: State University of New York Press, 1999.

Foucault, Michel. *The History of Sexuality: Volume 1: An Introduction*. Trans. Robert Hurley. New York: Vintage, 1996.

———. *Discipline and Punish: The Birth of the Prison*. Trans. Alan Sheridan. New York: Vintage, 1995.

———. *The Birth of the Clinic: An Archeology of Medical Perception*. Trans. A. M. Sheridan Smith. New York: Vintage, 1994.

———. *This Is Not a Pipe*. Trans. James Harkness. Berkeley: University of California Press, 1983.

Freud, Sigmund. *The Standard Edition of the Complete Psychological Works of Sigmund Freud*. 24 vols. Ed. James Strachey. New York, W.W. Norton & Co., 2000.

Goldberge, Lee, et al. *Science Fiction Filmmaking in the 1980s*. Jefferson, NC: McFarland, 1995.

Gould, George M., and Walter L. Pyle. *Anomalies and Curiosities of Medicine*. Electronic Text Center, University of Virginia Library. http://etext.lib.virginia.edu/toc/modeng/public/GouAnom.html.

Grant, Barry Keith. *The Dread of Difference: Gender and the Horror Film*. Austin, TX: University of Texas Press, 1996.

Graham, Elaine L. *Representations of the Post/Human: Monsters, Aliens and Others in Popular Culture*. New Brunswick, NJ: Rutgers University Press, 2002.

Grossberg, Lawrence, Cary Nelson, and Paula Treichler, eds. *Cultural Studies*. New York: Routledge, 1992.

Grosz, Elizabeth. "Freaks." *Social Semiotics* 1, no. 2 (1991): 25.

Haraway, Donna J. *Simians, Cyborgs and Women: The Reinvention of Nature*. New York: Routledge, 1991.

Hartouni, Valerie. "Containing Women: Reproductive Discourse in the 1980s." In *Technoculture*, ed. Constance Penley and Andrew Ross. Minneapolis: University of Minnesota Press, 1991, 26–56.

Haskell, Molly. *Holding My Own in No Man's Land: Women and Men and Film and Feminists*. New York: Oxford University Press, 1997.

———. *From Reverence to Rape: The Treatment of Women in the Movies*. New York: Holt, Rinehart and Winston, 1974.

Hayles, N. Katherine. *How We Became Posthuman: Virtual Bodies in Cybernetics, Literature, and Informatics*. Chicago: University of Chicago Press, 1999.

Helford, Elyce Rae. "Postfeminism and the Female Action-Adventure Hero: Positioning *Tank Girl*." In *Future Females, the Next Generation: New Voices and Velocities in Feminist Science Fiction Criticism*, ed. Marleen S. Barr. Lanham, MA: Rowman & Littlefield, 2000, 291–308.

Hollinger, Veronica, and Joan Gordon, eds. *Edging into the Future: Science Fiction and Contemporary Cultural Transformation*. Philadelphia: University of Pennsylvania Press, 2002.

Horsley, Jake. *The Blood Poets: A Cinema of Savagery, 1958–1999*. 2 vols. Lanham, MD: Scarecrow, 1999.

Jameson, Frederic. *Postmodernism, or the Cultural Logic of Late Capitalism*. Durham, NC: Duke University Press, 2001.

Jancovich, Mark. *Horror*. London: Batsford, 1992.

Jeffords, Susan. *Hard Bodies: Hollywood Masculinity in the Reagan Era*. New Brunswick, NJ: Rutgers University Press, 1994.

Jung, Carl Gustav. *The Archetypes and the Collective Unconscious*. Trans. C. F. Hull. Bollingen Series XX. Princeton, NJ: Princeton University Press, 1990.

Klock, Geoff. *How to Read Superhero Comics and Why*. New York: Continuum, 2002.

Kristeva, Julia. *Powers of Horror: An Essay on Abjection*. Trans. Leon S. Roudiez. New York: Columbia University Press, 1982.

Kroker, Arthur and Marilouise, eds. *The Hysterical Male: New Feminist Theory*. New York: St. Martin's, 1991.

———, eds. *Body Invaders: Panic Sex in America*. CultureTexts Series. Montreal: New World Perspectives, 1987.

Kuhn, Annette. *Women's Pictures: Feminism and Cinema*. New York: Verso, 1993.

———, ed. *Alien Zone II: The Spaces of Science Fiction Cinema*. New York: Verso, 1999.

———, ed. *Alien Zone: Cultural Theory and Contemporary Science Fiction Cinema*. New York: Verso, 1990.

Laqueur, Thomas. *Making Sex: Body and Gender from the Greeks to Freud*. Cambridge, MA: Harvard University Press, 1990.

Leonard, Linda Schierse. *Meeting the Madwoman: An Inner Challenge for Feminine Spirit*. New York: Bantam: 1993.

Lewis, Lisa A. *Gender Politics and MTV: Voicing the Difference*. Philadelphia: Temple University Press, 1990.

Macdonald, Myra. *Representing Women: Myths of Femininity in the Popular Media*. New York: Edward Arnold, 1995.

Marks, Elaine, and Isabelle de Courtivron, eds. *New French Feminisms: An Anthology*. New York: Schocken, 1981.

Mayne, Judith. *Cinema and Spectatorship*. New York: Routledge, 1993.

Menville, Douglas, and R. Reginald, with Mary A. Burgess. *Futurevisions: The New Golden Age of the Science Fiction Film*. San Bernadino, CA: The Borgo Press, 1985.

Modeleski, Tania. *Feminism without Women: Culture and Criticism in a "Postfeminist" Age*. New York: Routledge, 1991.

Mulvey, Laura. *Visual and Other Pleasures*. Bloomington: Indiana University Press, 1989.

Murphy, Cullen. *The Word According to Eve*. New York: Mariner, 1999.

Myers, Richard. *S-F2: A Pictorial History of Science Fiction Films from "Rollerball" to "Return of the Jedi."* Secaucus, NJ: Citadel Press, 1984.

Pagels, Elaine. *Adam, Eve, and the Serpent*. New York: Vintage, 1988.

Paglia, Camille. *Sexual Personae: Art and Decadence from Nefertiti to Emily Dickinson*. New York: Vintage, 1991.

Penley, Constance. "Time Travel, Primal Scene and Critical Dystopia." In *Alien Zone: Cultural Theory and Contemporary Science Fiction Cinema*, ed. Annette Kuhn. New York: Verso, 1990, 116–127. (Reprinted in *Close Encounters: Film, Feminism and Science Fiction*, ed. Constance Penley et al. Minneapolis: University of Minnesota Press, 1991: 63–80.)

——, ed. *Feminism and Film Theory*. New York: Routledge, 1988.

——, Elisabeth Lyon, Lynn Spigel, and Janet Bergstrom, eds. *Close Encounters: Film, Feminism and Science Fiction*. Minneapolis: University of Minnesota Press, 1991.

Rapping, Elayne. *Media-tions: Forays into the Culture and Gender Wars*. Boston: South End, 1994.

Reynolds, Richard. *Super Heroes: A Modern Mythology*. Jackson: University Press of Mississippi, 1992.

Roberts, Adam. *Science Fiction: The New Critical Idiom*. New York: Routledge, 2000.

Roberts, Robin. *Sexual Generations: "Star Trek: The Next Generation" and Gender*. Urbana: University of Illinois Press, 1999.

——. *A New Species: Gender and Science in Science Fiction*. Urbana: University of Illinois Press, 1993.

Rogin, Michael Paul. *Ronald Reagan, the Movie: And Other Episodes in Political Demonology*. Berkeley: University of California Press, 1987.

Sabin, Roger. *Comics, Comix and Graphic Novels: A History of Comic Art*. New York: Phaidon, 1996.

Sammon, Paul M. *Ridley Scott: The Making of His Movies*. New York: Thunder's Mouth Press, 1999.

Scarry, Elaine. *The Body in Pain*. New York: Oxford University Press, 1985.

Sedgwick, Eve Kosofsky. *Epistemology of the Closet*. Berkeley: University of California Press, 1990.

Schwichtenberg, Cathy, ed. *The Madonna Connection*. Boulder, CO: Westview, 1993.

Scheir, Miriam, ed. *Feminism in Our Time: The Essential Writings, World War II to the Present*. NY: Vintage, 1994.

Seed, David. *American Science Fiction and the Cold War: Literature and Film*. Chicago: Fitzroy Dearborn, 1999.

Silver, Alain, and James Ursini. *The Vampire Film: From Nosferatu to Bram Stoker's Dracula*. New York: Limelight Editions, 1993.

Skal, David J. *The Monster Show: A Cultural History of Horror*. New York: Norton, 1993.

Sobchack, Thomas, and Vivian Sobchack. *An Introduction to Film*. 2nd ed. Boston: Scott, Foresman, 1987.

Sobchack, Vivian. *Screening Space: The American Science Fiction Film*. New York: Ungar, 1988.

Springer, Claudia. *Electronic Eros: Bodies and Desire in the Postindustrial Age*. Austin: University of Texas Press, 1996.

Stafford, Barbara Maria. *Body Criticism: Imaging the Unseen in Enlightenment Art and Medicine*. Cambridge, MA: MIT Press, 1991.

Tarrat, Margaret. "Monsters from the Id." In *Film Genre: Theory and Criticism*, ed. Barry K. Grant. Metuchen, NJ: Scarecrow Press, 1977, 161–181.

Tasker, Yvonne. *Working Girls: Gender and Sexuality in Popular Cinema*. New York: Routledge, 1998.

Telotte, J. P. *Science Fiction Film*. New York: Cambridge University Press, 2001.

———. *Replications: A Robotic History of the Science Fiction Film*. Urbana: University of Illinois Press, 1995.

———. "Human Artifice and the Science Fiction Film." *Film Quarterly* 36 (1983): 44–51.

Thompson, Rosemarie Garland, ed. *Freakery: Cultural Spectacle of the Extraordinary Body*. New York: New York University Press, 1996.

Traube, Elizabeth G. *Dreaming Identities: Class, Gender, and Generation in the 1980s Hollywood Movies*. Boulder, CO: Westview, 1992.

Vowell, Sarah. "Those Liberated Angels: How Farrah and and Her Friends Made Me a Feminist." *Time*, 6 November 2000, 8.

Walker, Jeff. "The Alien: A Secret Too Good to Give Away." *Rolling Stone*, 31 May 1979, 30–31.

Weinstock, Jeffrey A. "Freaks in Space: 'Extraterrestrialism' and 'Deep-Space Multiculturalism.'" In *Freakery: Cultural Spectacle of the Extraordinary Body*, ed. Rosemarie Garland Thompson. New York: New York University Press, 1996, 327–337.

William, Paul. *Laughing, Screaming: Modern Hollywood Horror and Comedy*. New York: Columbia University Press, 1994.

Wingrove, David, ed. *The Science Fiction Film Sourcebook*. Essex, UK: Longman, 1985.

Wood, Aylish. *Technoscience in Contemporary American Film: Beyond Science Fiction*. New York: Manchester University Press, 2002.

Wood, Robin. *Hollywood from Vietnam to Reagan*. New York: Columbia University Press, 1986.

Wright, Elizabeth, and Edmond Wright, eds. *The Žižek Reader*. Oxford: Blackwell, 1999.

Wurtzel, Elizabeth. *Bitch: In Praise of Difficult Women*. New York: Doubleday, 1998.

Film and Television

Due to multiple release formats of the same film (VHS, DVD, laser disc), we have included the original release date and the current copyright holder for purchase and rental release in the United States unless otherwise indicated.

2001: A Space Odyssey. 1968. Dir. Stanley Kubrick. Warner Studios.

Abyss, The. 1989. Dir. James Cameron. 20th Century Fox.

Alien. 1979. Dir. Ridley Scott. Writ. Dan O'Bannon and Ronald Shusset. 20th Century Fox.

Alien³. 1992. Dir. David Fincher. Writ. Vincent Ward (story), David Giler, Walter Hill, and Larry Ferguson (screenplay). 20th Century Fox.

Alien Resurrection. 1997. Dir. Jean-Pierre Jeunet. Writ. Joss Whedon (screenplay). 20th Century Fox.

Aliens. 1986. Dir. James Cameron. Writ. James Cameron (story), James Cameron, David Giler, and Walter Hill (screenplay). 20th Century Fox.

Alien Legacy, The: 20th Anniversary Edition. VHS. Five-tape boxed set. 20th Century Fox.

Alien Legacy, The: 20th Anniversary Edition. DVD. Four-disc boxed set. 20th Century Fox.

Alien Quadrilogy. 2003. Special Edition. DVD. Nine-disc boxed set. Fox Home Entertainment.

Android. 1982. Dir. Aaron Lipstadt. Jef Films International.

Bionic Woman, The. 1975–1978. Television. Sup. Prod. Kenneth Johnson. Universal Studios.

Blade. 1988. Dir. Stephen Norrington. New Line Studios.

Blade Runner. 1982. Dir. Ridley Scott. Columbia Tristar Home.

Boys from Brazil. 1978. Dir. Franklin J. Schaffner. Artisan Entertainment.

Bram Stoker's Dracula. 1992. Dir. Francis Ford Coppola. Columbia/Tristar Studios.

Bride of Frankenstein, The. 1935. Dir. James Whale. Universal Studios.

Buffy the Vampire Slayer. Film. 1992. Dir. Fran Rubel Kuzui. Writ. Joss Whedon. 20th Century Fox.

Buffy the Vampire Slayer. 1997–2003. Television. Created by Joss Whedon. Fox Studios, 1997–2001. UPN, 2001–2003.

"Buffy the Vampire Slayer." UPN. 2003. http://www.upn.com/shows/buffy/#.

Charlie's Angels. 1976–1981. Television. Columbia/TRI-Star Pictures Television.

Cherry 2000. 1987. Dir. Steve De Jarnatt. MGM.

Cité des enfants perdus, La [The City of Lost Children]. 1995. Dir. Marc Caro and Jean-Pierre Jeunet. Columbia/Tristar Studios.

Close Encounters of the Third Kind. 1977. Dir. Steven Spielberg. Columbia/Tristar.

Coffy. 1973. Dir. Jack Hill. MGM/UA Studios.

Coma. 1978. Dir. Michael Crichton. Warner Studios.

Crouching Tiger, Hidden Dragon. 2000. Dir. Ang Lee. Columbia/Tristar.

SELECTED BIBLIOGRAPHY

Dark Star. 1974. Dir. John Carpenter. VCI Home Video.

Delicatessen. 1991. Dir. Marc Caro and Jean-Pierre Jeunet. Paramount Studios.

Demon Seed. 1977. Dir. Donald Cammell. Warner Home Video.

Die Hard. 1988. Dir. John McTiernan. 20th Century Fox.

Dr. Strangelove or: How I Learned to Stop Worrying and Love the Bomb. 1964. Dir. Stanley Kubrick. Columbia/Tristar Studios.

Eve of Destruction. 1991. Dir. Duncan Gibbons. MGM/UA Studios.

Exorcist, The. 1973. Dir. William Friedkin. Warner Studios.

Fifth Element, The. 1997. Dir. Luc Besson. Columbia/Tristar.

Fight Club. 1999. Dir. David Fincher. Fox Home Entertainment.

First Blood. 1982. Dir. Ted Kotcheff. Artisan Entertainment.

Foxy Brown. 1974. Dir. Jack Hill. MGM/UA Studios.

Frankenstein. 1931. Dir. James Whale. Universal.

Freaks. 1932. Dir. Todd Browning. Warner Studios.

Friday Foster. 1975. Dir. Arthur Marks. MGM/UA Studios.

Futureworld. 1976. Dir. Richard T. Heffron. Goodtimes Home Video.

Galaxy Quest. 1999. Dir. Dean Parisot. Universal/MCA.

Ghostbusters. 1984. Dir. Ivan Reitman. Columbia/Tristar Studios.

G. I. Jane. 1997. Dir. Ridley Scott. Hollywood Pictures.

Halloween. 1978. Dir. John Carpenter. Anchor Bay Entertainment.

Heavy Metal. 1981. Dir. Gerald Potterton. Columbia/Tristar Studios.

Hunger, The. 1983. Dir. Tony Scott. Warner Studios.

Ice Pirates, The. 1984. Dir. Stewart Raffill. Warner Studios.

Invasion of the Body Snatchers. 1956. Dir. Don Seigal. Republic Studios.

Invasion of the Body Snatchers. 1978. Dir. Philip Kaufman. MGM/UA Studios.

I Spit on Your Grave [aka *Day of the Woman* et al.]. 1978. Dir. Meir Zarchi. Anchor Bay Entertainment.

It! The Terror from Beyond Space. 1978. Dir. Edward L. Cahn. MGM/UA Studios.

Jaws. 1975. Dir. Steven Spielberg. Universal Studios.

Jurassic Park. 1993. Dir. Steven Spielberg. Universal Studios.

Lethal Weapon. 1987. Dir. Richard Donner. Warner Studios.

Lifeforce. 1985. Dir. Toby Hooper. MGM/UA Studios.

Looker. 1981. Dir. Michael Crichton. Warner Studios.

Mad Max Beyond Thunderdome. 1985. Dir. George Ogilvie. Warner Studios.

Madonna: The Immaculate Collection. 1990. Dir. David Fincher ("Express Yourself," "Oh Father," "Vogue"), James Foley ("Papa Don't Preach"), Herb Ritts ("Cherish"). WEA/Warner Brothers.

Mary Shelley's Frankenstein. 1994. Dir. Kenneth Branagh. Columbia/Tristar Studios.

Matrix Revolutions, The. 2003. Dir. Andy Wachowski and Larry Wachowski. Warner Brothers.

Metropolis. 1927. Restored authorized ed. Dir. Fritz Lang. Kino International.

Navigator, The: A Medieval Odyssey. 1988. Dir. Vincent Ward. Hen's Tooth Video.

Omen, The. 1976. Dir. Richard Donner. 20th Century Fox.

Passion of Joan of Arc, The. 1928. Dir. Carl Theodor Dreyer. Home Vision Entertainment.

Piranha II: The Spawning. 1981. Dir. James Cameron and Ovidio G. Assonitis. Columbia Tristar Home.

Poseidon Adventure, The. 1972. Dir. Irwin Allen, Ronald Neame. 20th Century Fox.

Predator. 1987. Dir. John McTiernan. 20th Century Fox.

Predator 2. 1990. Dir. Stephen Hopkins. 20th Century Fox.

Psycho. 1960. Dir. Alfred Hitchock. Universal Studios.

Rambo: First Blood, Part 2. 1985. Dir. George P. Cosmatos. Artisan Entertainment.

Rapture, The. 1991. Dir. Michael Tolkin. New Line Studios.

Rosemary's Baby. 1968. Dir. Roman Polanski. Paramount Studio.

Se7en. 1995. Dir. David Fincher. New Line Studios.

Seventh Sign, The. 1988. Dir. Carl Schultz. Columbia/Tristar Studios.

Spaceballs. 1987. Dir. Mel Brooks. MGM/UA Studios.

Spacehunter: Adventures in the Forbidden Zone. 1983. Dir. Lamont Johnson. Columbia Tristar Home.

Species. 1995. Dir. Roger Donaldson. MGM/UA Studios.

Species II. 1998. Dir. Peter Medak. MGM/UA Studios.

Star Trek: First Contact. 1996. Dir. Jonathan Frakes. Paramount Studio.

Star Trek: Nemesis. Dir. Stuart Baird. Paramount Home Video, 2002.

Star Trek: The Motion Picture. 1979. Dir. Robert Wise. Paramount Studios.

Star Trek. 1966–1969. Television. Created by Gene Roddenberry. Paramount Network Television.

Star Trek: Deep Space Nine. 1993–1999. Television. Created by Gene Roddenberry. Paramount Network Television.

Star Trek: The Next Generation. 1987–1994. Television. Created by Gene Roddenberry. Paramount Network Television.

Star Trek: Voyager. 1995–2001. Television. Created by Gene Roddenberry. Paramount Network Television.

"startrek.com." Paramount Pictures. 2003. http://www.startrek.com/startrek/view/index.html. Accessed 18 August 2003.

Star Wars: Episode IV—A New Hope. 1977. Dir. George Lucas. 20th Century Fox.

Star Wars: Episode V—The Empire Strikes Back. 1980. Dir. Irvin Kershner. 20th Century Fox.

Star Wars: Episode VI—Return of the Jedi. 1983. Dir. Richard Marquand. 20th Century Fox.

Stepford Wives, The. 1975. Dir. Bryan Forbes. Anchor Bay Entertainment.

Starship Troopers. 1997. Dir. Paul Verhooven. Columbia/Tristar Studios.

Terminator, The. 1984. Dir. James Cameron. Artisan Entertainment.

Terminator 2: Judgment Day. 1991. Dir. James Cameron. Artisan Entertainment.

Terminator 3: Rise of the Machines. 2003. Dir. Jonathan Mostow.

Texas Chainsaw Massacre, The. 1984. Dir. Tobe Hooper. MPI Home Video.

SELECTED BIBLIOGRAPHY

Them! 1954. Dir. Gordon Douglas. Warner Studios.

Thing from Another World, The. 1951. Dir. Christian Nyby and Howard Hawks. Turner Home Video.

Thing, The [aka *John Carpenter's The Thing*]. 1992. Dir. John Carpenter. Universal Studios.

THX 1138. 1971. Dir. George Lucas. Warner Studios.

Velvet Vampire, The. 1971. Dir Stephanie Rothman. New World Pictures.

Westworld. 1973. Dir. Michael Crichton. Warner Studios.

Wonder Woman. 1976–1979. Television. Originally created by William M. Marston. Warner Brothers Television.

X-Files, The. 1993–2001. Television. Created by Chris Carter. Fox Studios.

"The X-Files." Fox.com. http://www.thex-files.com/ main_flash.html. Accessed 18 August 2003.

X-Men. 2000. Dir. Bryan Singer. 20th Century Fox.

Notes

Introduction: Can't Live with Them, Can't Kill Them

1. For a discussion of female roles and gender in *Star Trek: The Next Generation*, see Robin Roberts' book *Sexual Generations: "Star Trek: The Next Generation" and Gender* (Urbana: University of Illinois Press, 1999).

2. Interview with Winona Ryder for the *Alien Resurrection* digizine, www.alien-resurrection.com/digizine/int/b_wr_t.htm.

3. The nine-disc *Alien Quadrilogy (2003)* boxed set includes both versions.

Chapter 1: Men, Women, and an *Alien* Baby

1. Carol J. Clover, *Men, Women and Chainsaws: Gender in the Modern Horror Film*. (Princeton, NJ: Princeton University Press, 1992), 23.

2. See, for example, John Brosnan, *The Primal Screen* (London: Hazell, 1991), 102–103, 190. Other possible ancestors for the plot of *Alien* include A. E. Van Vogt's short stories "Black Destroyer" and "Discord in Scarlet," both published in *Astounding* in 1939 and reprised in Vogt's 1950 novel *The Voyage of the Space Beagle*.

3. Ronald Shusett reports on Yaphet Kotto's reaction to the Chestburster in the made-for-television documentary *The Alien Saga* (dir. Brent Zacky, 2002), and Ronald Shusett and Ron Cobb remember the crew's reaction to repeated viewings of the Chestburster scene in the documentary entitled *The Alien Legacy* (*The Alien Legacy: 20th Anniversary Edition*, VHS. 20th Century Fox, 1999; cat. no. 1417131).

4. David Thomson, *David Thomson on the Alien Quartet* (New York: Bloomsbury, 1998), 40.

5. Shusett, *The Alien Legacy*. There was some dispute as to whether writers O'Bannon and Shusett or producers Giler and Hill first suggested female roles in the film. On this point, Craig Anderson reports on Dan O'Bannon's interview with Marc Mancini of *Film Comment*, in which the screenwriter pulled out the original

NOTES

version of *Alien* to show Mancini the place where he had typed "The crew is unisex and all parts are interchangeable for men or women" (*Science Fiction Films of the Seventies*, Jefferson, NC: McFarland, 1985, 220).

6. David Giler, *The Alien Saga.*

7. Sarah Vowell, "Those Liberated *Angels*: How Farrah and Her Friends Made Me a Feminist," *Time*, 6 November 2000, 8.

8. Judith Newton, "Feminism and Anxiety in *Alien*," in *Alien Zone: Cultural Theory and Contemporary Science Fiction Cinema*, ed. Annette Kuhn (New York: Verso, 1990), 82–90.

9. John Hurt (narration), *The Alien Saga.*

10. Giler, *The Alien Saga.*

11. Ridley Scott, *The Alien Legacy.*

12. For *Alien* as a prime example of "cruel cinema," see Harvey R. Greenberg, "Reimagining the Gargoyle: Psychoanalytic Notes on *Alien*," in *Close Encounters: Film, Feminism and Science Fiction*, ed. Constance Penley et al. (Minneapolis: University of Minnesota Press, 1991), 83–104. For *Alien*'s symbolic enactment of the primal scene, see Daniel Dervin, "The Primal Scene in Film Comedy and Science Fiction," *Film/Psychology Review* 4, no. 1 (1980): 115–147.

13. Barbara Creed, *The Monstrous Feminine: Film, Feminism, Psychoanalysis* (London: Routledge, 1993), 16, 19–20, 27. Creed's study of the monstrous-feminine in horror film extends Julia Kristeva's discussion of abjection in *Powers of Horror: An Essay on Abjection*, trans. Leon S. Roudiez (New York: Columbia University Press, 1982).

14. Vincent Canby, "Screen: 'Alien' Brings Chills from the Far Galaxy," *New York Times*, 25 May 1979, C16; B.G., "Flying High," *The New Yorker*, 11 June 1979, 154; Douglas Menville and R. Reginald, with Mary A. Burgess, *Futurevisions: The New Golden Age of the Science Fiction Film* (San Bernadino, CA: The Borgo Press, 1985), 70; and Arthur Schlesinger, "Of Blobs and Banalities," *Saturday Review*, 4 August 1979, 51.

15. Rebecca Bell-Meterau, "Woman, The Other Alien in *Alien*," in *Women Worldwalkers: New Dimensions in Science Fiction and Fantasy*, ed. Jane B. Weedman (Lubbock: Texas Tech Press, 1985), 10–12.

16. Craig Anderson, "Alien," *Science Fiction Films of the Seventies* (Jefferson, NC: McFarland, 1985), 220.

17. Menville and Reginald, *Futurevisions*, 70.

18. James H. Kavanagh, "Feminism, Humanism and Science in *Alien*," in *Alien Zone: Cultural Theory and Contemporary Science Fiction Cinema*, ed. Annette Kuhn (New York: Verso, 1990), 79–81.

19. Newton, "Feminism and Anxiety in *Alien*," 82.

20. Clover, *Men, Women and Chainsaws*, 53.

21. H. R. Giger, *The Alien Legacy.*

22. All further references to O'Bannon's letter come from H. R. Giger's book *Giger's Alien* (Beverly Hills, CA: Galerie Morpheus International, 1999), 10.

23. Ibid., 34, 10, and 46, respectively.

24. Ibid., 9, 15, 47, 49.

25. Ibid., 11.

26. Ibid., 56.

27. The suggestion of the "over-sized, deformed baby" may have been taken up later by the designers of the Newborn in *Alien Resurrection*.

28. Giger, *Giger's Alien*, 58.

29. John Hurt (narrator), *The Alien Saga*.

30. Giger, *Giger's Alien*, 70.

31. Ibid., 54, 58, 62–66.

32. Ibid., 50.

33. Ridley Scott, *The Alien Legacy*.

34. For articles and press releases on this subject, see H. R. Giger's official Web site, www.hrgiger.com.

35. As Mikhail Bakhtin writes in *Rabelais and His World* (trans. Hélène Iswolsky, Bloomington: Indiana University Press, 281):

> Eating and drinking are one of the most significant manifestations of the grotesque body. The distinctive character of this body is its open unfinished nature, its interaction with the world. These traits are most fully and concretely revealed in the act of eating; the body transgresses its own limits: it swallows, devours, rends the world apart, is enriched and grows at the world's expense.

36. Ron Cobb explains that Mother's chamber was built to resemble "a cathedral full of votive candles" (*The Alien Legacy*).

37. As Kavanagh notes, although power on the *Nostromo* seems distributed based on ability rather than privilege, and although social disparity still exists in this "future" between the white-collar and blue-collar workers, the film directly addresses these inequities. Time and time again, the minority voices—the women and the proletariat workers (one a racial minority)—are proven right in their concerns. More importantly, their actions will lead them to survive the longest, while the white males will become the unwitting martyrs to capitalist greed ("Feminism, Humanism and Science in *Alien*," 73–74).

38. Newton, "Feminism and Anxiety in *Alien*," 86.

39. See, for example, Joseph Campbell, *The Masks of God: Primitive Mythology* (New York: Penguin, 1991), 68–70, and *The Masks of God: Oriental Mythology* (New York: Penguin, 1991), 164–168.

40. See, for example, Joseph Campbell, *Primitive Mythology* (New York: Penguin, 1991), 68–70; Carl Gustav Jung, *Alchemical Studies*, trans. R. F. C. Hull, *Bollingen Series XX* (Princeton, NJ: Princeton University Press, 1967), 324; and J. E. Cirlot's *The Dictionary of Symbols*, trans. Jack Sage (New York: Philosophical Library, 1971), 173–175.

41. Many reviewers report the astronauts' entry into the alien ship as taken from Mario Bava's *Planet of the Vampires* (1965). See, for example, Menville and Reginald, *Futurevisions*, 71.

42. Creed argues that by looking "into the egg/womb in order to investigate its mysteries," Kane "becomes a 'part' of the primal scene, taking up the place of the mother, the one who is penetrated, the one who bears the offspring of the union" (*The Monstrous-Feminine*, 19).

43. See, for example, Sigmund Freud, "Lecture 23: Some Thoughts on the Development and Regression-Aetiology," in *The Standard Edition* (vol. 7, pt. 3).

44. The term *hysteria* derives from the Greek *hyster* or *hystero*, meaning "womb," and the suffix *-ia*, indicating either an illness or, interestingly enough, a territory. Thus, one who is described as "hysterical" may be variously described as suffering from a womb-induced illness and wandering the domain of the womb (a hysteric is mentally ill and lost in the womb world). We use the term *hysteria* here not in the sense of a psychological illness (what is now called "conversion anxiety") but in its common definition, as an excessive emotion or reaction.

45. Ridley Scott mentions raw oysters as one of the seafoods making up the Facehugger's innards (*Alien, The Alien Legacy: 20th Anniversary Edition*, DVD. 20th Century Fox, 1999).

46. In *Rabelais and His World*, Mikhail Bahktin describes the feast as an interaction between the bodies of the participants and the world, an act that signals the state, not of being, but of becoming something new: "The grotesque body . . . is the body in the act of becoming. It is never finished, never completed; it is continually built, created, and builds and creates another body. Moreover, the body swallows the world and is itself swallowed by the world. . . ." (317).

47. Members of the cast, crew, and audience have interpreted the Chestburster as a penis. In *The Alien Saga*, actress Veronica Cartwright remembers what she thought at the sight of the creature: "[It was] quite a shock, actually. I mean, we are looking at this sort of gray . . . penis." The Alien was also spoofed in *The Ice Pirates* (1984) as a "space herpe." Comedy thus reveals that the Alien is a sexual infection of the ship.

48. In her analysis of the *Alien* trilogy, Amy Taubin writes of this scene in *Alien*: "Looking for a warm host for their eggs, the aliens didn't bother about the niceties of sexual difference. When the baby alien (or as one 42nd Street moviehouse denizen exclaimed, 'little-dick-with-teeth') burst from John Hurt's chest, it cancelled the distinction on which human culture is based." See Taubin, "Invading Bodies: Aliens[3] [sic] and the Trilogy," *Sight and Sound* (July–August 1992): 9. On how birth is the prime site of abjection, see Kristeva, *Powers of Horror*, 154–156.

49. Of the abjection inherent in the cadaver, Kristeva (*Powers of Horror*, 3) writes:

> The corpse (or cadaver: *cadere*, to fall), that which has irremediably come a cropper, is cesspool, and death; it upsets even more violently

the one who confronts its as fragile and fallacious chance. A wound with blood and pus, or the sickly, acrid smell of sweat, of decay, does not *signify* death. In the presence of signified death—a flat encephalograph, for instance—I would understand, react, or accept. No, as in true theater, without makeup or masks, refuse and corpses show me what I permanently thrust aside in order to live. These body fluids, this defilement, this shit are what life withstands, hardly and with difficulty, on the part of death. There, I am at the border of my condition as a living being. My body extricates itself, as being alive, from that border. Such wastes drop so that I might live, until, from loss to loss, nothing remains in me and my entire body falls beyond the limit—cadere, cadaver. If dung signifies the other side of the border, the place where I am not and which permits me to be, the corpse, the most sickening of wastes, is a border that has encroached upon everything.

50. On the multiple connections between Jones, the Alien, and Ripley, see Tony Safford, "Alien/Alienation," in "Symposium on *Alien*," ed. Charles Elkins, *Science Fiction Studies* 7, no. 3 (1980): 297–299.

51. Tellingly, both the poster for the Polish and Latin American release of *Alien* subtitled the film *The Eighth Passenger*.

52. H. R. Giger, *H. R. Giger's Necronomicon* (London: Big O Publishing, 1978), 64.

53. Ibid., 16–17.

54. Donna J. Haraway, *Simians, Cyborgs, and Women* (New York: Routledge, 1991), 166. In "'Fully Functional': Machines and Gender," Robin Roberts argues that all machines in science fiction are feminized, none more so than the android—the robot made in the likeness of man. Thus, although in *Star Trek: The Next Generation* the android Data is outwardly gendered as masculine (his human creator even supplied Data with a "fully functional" penis and programming in "multiple techniques . . . of pleasuring"), the show nonetheless codes him as a feminine Other. For example, in several episodes Data is treated as a possession (i.e., "The Most Toys," episode 70, and "The Measure of a Man," episode 35, both directed by Larry Shaw and David Carson and aired in 1987). In the one instance where he clearly has a sexual encounter, he is the passive partner to the aggressive, usually masculinized human female, Tasha Yar. Data is often visually associated with the feminine as well: one notable instance has him practicing his smile in front of the *Mona Lisa* as if the frame were a mirror (*Sexual Generations: "Star Trek: The Next Generation" and Gender* (Urbana: University of Illinois Press, 1999), 91–107.

55. "Ripley Reassures Lambert," Extra Features: Deleted Scenes, *Alien*, DVD.

56. Ridley Scott, audio commentary, *Alien*, DVD.

57. At least, that was how Ridley Scott conceived of the Alien: "If the Alien had originally jumped on the cat—it would be a version of the cat" (audio commentary, *Alien*, DVD).

58. Croatto, "Alien: The Director's Cut." www.filmcritic.com

59. See Ros Jennings, "Desire and Design—Ripley Undressed," in *Lesbians and the Moving Image*, ed. Tamsin Wilton (London: Routledge, 1995), 195, 198.

60. Clover, *Men, Women, and Chainsaws*, 31.

61. Greenberg, "Reimagining the Gargoyle," 93.

62. Dworkin, "Pornography: Men Possessing Women," in *Feminism in Our Time: The Essential Writings, World War II to the Present*, ed. Miriam Schneir (NY: Vintage, 1994), 427.

63. See, for example, *Behind the Green Door* (1972).

64. Thomson, *David Thomson on the Alien Quartet*, 50.

Chapter 2: Ripley Gets Her Gun: *Aliens* and the Regan Era Hero

1. Harvey R. Greenberg, "Fembo: *Aliens'* Intentions," *Journal of Popular Film and Television* 15, no. 4 (Winter 1988): 166.

2. Internet Movie Database (IMDb) user "alx.kdd" declares *Xenogenesis* a microcosm of the themes and characters present in later Cameron films, including the strong female hero ("Fascinating look at the early work of James Cameron," *IMDb user comments for Xenogenesis* [http://us.imdb.com/Title?0251488. 3 January 2001]). As of this writing, we have not been able to obtain a copy of the short film.

3. Paula Parisi, "In the Beginning," *The Hollywood Reporter*, 7 March 1995. Cited in *Joshua's James Cameron Web Site*, http://www.sweetbomb.com/cameron/articl33.htm.

4. David Edelstein, "Mother of the Year," *Rolling Stone* 28 (August 1986): 31–42.

5. Greenberg, "Fembo," 164–171.

6. James Cameron and Gayle Anne Hurd, "Aliens (1986)," in *Science Fiction Filmmaking in the 1980s*, ed. Lee Goldberg (Jefferson, NC: McFarland, 1995), 8–9.

7. Susan Jeffords, *Hard Bodies: Hollywood Masculinity in the Reagan Era* (New Brunswick, NJ: Rutgers University Press, 1994), 1–25.

8. Ibid., 140–177.

9. See Susan Jeffords's discussion of Riggs and McClane, *Hard Bodies*, 55.

10. James Cameron, interview, *Aliens: Special Edition, The Alien Legacy: 20th Anniversary Edition*, DVD (20th Century Fox. 1999).

11. Human birth has always contained an element of horror. See, for example, Lucy Fischer's *Cinematernity: Film, Motherhood, Genre* (Princeton, NJ: Princeton University Press, 1996), 79.

12. In an ironic reversal, just two years later Weaver played a corporate bitch who abuses her ambitious working-class secretary in *Working Girl* (1988). For an analysis of the "working girl" character, see "Transforming Heroes: Hollywood and

the Demonization of Women" in Elizabeth G. Traube's *Dreaming Identities: Class, Gender, and Generation in 1980s Hollywood Movies* (Boulder, CO: Westview, 1992).

13. Edelstein, "Mother of the Year," 481.

14. Scenes deleted from the cinematic release demonstrate the depth of the film's forgetfulness, as well as Cameron's attempt to recast the danger into a well-known psychological terrain. As Harvey R. Greenberg ("Fembo," 167) describes:

> Ripley's ablated memory is diagnostic of the effacement practiced by Cameron upon Scott's script. *Aliens* deals with the Company's former scheming much as the unconscious of the Freudian hysteric processes past trauma: the plot against *Nostromo* is rendered *non arrivée*, so that it exists under the sign of erasure. In the script's fictive work, the fear and loathing Ripley should rightly feel toward the Company's past and present directors are displaced upon the Alien itself.

15. Cameron, interview, *Aliens: Special Edition.*

16. Greenberg, "Fembo," 167.

17. Cameron, interview, *Aliens: Special Edition.*

18. Carol J. Clover, *Men, Women, and Chainsaws: Gender in the Modern Horror Film* (Princeton, NJ: Princeton University Press), 154, 159.

19. As Ann Balsamo, argues, "Women who use bodybuilding technology to sculpt their bodies are doubly transgressive; first, because femininity and nature are so closely aligned, any attempt to *reconstruct* the body is transgressive against the 'natural' identity of the female body." Second, because acquiring muscles is a "male body prerogative" that transgresses "the 'natural' order of gender identity" See Balsamo, *Technologies of the Gendered Body* (Durham, NC: Duke University Press, 1997).

20. For a discussion of what Thomas Vaughn terms "reciprocal rather than one-way rape" in *Aliens*, see his "Voices of Sexual Distortion: Rape, Birth, and Self-Annihilation Metaphors in the *Alien Trilogy*," *Quarterly Journal of Speech* 4, no. 81 (November 1995): 427–429.

21. *Poontang* is a slang word for prostitute or vagina common in the Vietnam War era (and Vietnam films) that may originate from the French *putain* (prostitute).

22. Harvey R. Greenberg ("Fembo," 168) notes that Cameron has incorporated Isaac Asimov's First Law of Robotics into the narrative.

23. Cameron (interview, *Aliens: Special Edition*) labeled the attacking Aliens as "Warriors" "in the sense of warrior ants."

24. Jeffords, *Hard Bodies*, 56.

25. Ibid., 58.

26. It is worth noting that only the female Marines are indirectly or accidentally responsible for the death of three of their comrades: Dietrich flames Frost when she is snatched by an Alien, Vasquez shoots an Alien that sprays acid blood all over Drake, and Ferro causes her own and Spunkmeyer's death by not listening to his warning about the Alien slime on the ramp of the drop ship.

NOTES

27. Edelstein, "Mother of the Year," 42.

28. According to Robin Roberts, "nuclear winter landscapes frequently are caused by masculine science or war" and may echo "flawed mother/daughter relationships." See Roberts, *A New Species: Gender and Science in Science Fiction*, (Urbana: University of Illinois Press, 1993), 108.

29. Cameron and Hurd, "Aliens (1986)," 19.

30. Robin Roberts, "Adoptive versus Biological Mothering in *Aliens*," *Extrapolation* 30, no. 4 (Winter 1989): 360–361.

31. Greenberg, "Fembo," 167.

32. Elaine Scarry posits that war is "a contest where the participants arrange themselves into two sides and engage in an activity that will eventually make it possible to designate one side the winner and one side the loser (or more precisely, makes it possible for the loser to identify itself so that the other side will recognize itself the winner by default)." See Scarry, *The Body in Pain: The Making and Unmaking of the World* (Oxford: Oxford University Press, 1985), 87.

33. Interestingly, Ridley Scott originally imagined the Alien species as an extraterrestrial bioweapon run amok (audio commentary, *Alien*, DVD).

34. Cameron and Hurd, "Aliens (1986)," 10.

35. See Barbara Creed, *The Monstrous-Feminine: Film, Feminism, Psychoanalysis* (London: Routledge, 1993), 43–58. As Julia Kristeva writes: "Excrement and its equivalents (decay, infection, disease, corpse, etc.) stand for the danger to identity that comes from without: the ego threatened by the non-ego, society threatened by its outside, life by death." See Kristeva, *Powers of Horror: An Essay on Abjection*, trans. Leon S. Roudiez (New York: Columbia University Press, 1982), 71.

36. Edelstein, "Mother of the Year," 42.

37. Amy Taubin, "Invading Bodies: Aliens[3][sic] and the Trilogy," *Sight and Sound* (July–August 1992): 9.

38. Susan Jeffords appropriated Pauline Kael's phrase (from *The New Yorker*) for the title of her feminist analysis of *Aliens*: " 'The Battle of the Big Mamas': Feminism and the Alienation of Women," published in the *Journal of American Culture* 10, no. 30 (1987): 73–84.

39. Cameron and Hurd, "Aliens (1986)," 15.

40. Tim Blackmore, " 'Is this going to be another bug hunt?': S-F Tradition versus Biology-as-Destiny in James Cameron's Aliens." *Journal of Popular Culture* 29, no. 4 (Spring 1996): 211–226. Available from EBSCOHOST.

41. Tim Blackmore references an interview with Cameron, where the *Aliens* director reprises his view of Ripley as having been married (" 'Is this going to be another bug hunt?' ").

42. Judith Newton, "Feminism and Anxiety in *Alien*," in *Alien Zone: Cultural Theory and Contemporary Science Fiction Cinema*, ed. Annette Kuhn (New York: Verso, 1990), 86–87.

43. Jeffords, *Hard Bodies*, 34.

44. Greenberg, "Fembo," 170.

Chapter 3: "The Bitch Is Back": The Iconoclastic Body in *Alien³*

1. "Alien 3 [sic]," *Time*, 1 June 1992, 87; David Ansen, "Saint Ripley and the Dragon," *Newsweek*, 1 June 1992, 73.

2. Richard Alleva, "Alienated," *Commonweal*, 17 July 1992, 19.

3. Stephen Mulhall, *On Film* (New York: Routledge, 2002), 101.

4. Steve Perry and Stephani Perry, *The Female Wars* (New York: Bantam, 1993).

5. David Thomson, *David Thomson on the Alien Quartet* (New York: Blooms-bury, 1998), 97–101.

6. In her analysis of the first three *Alien* films, Amy Taubin writes of *Alien³*: "AIDS is everywhere in the film. It's in the danger surrounding sex and drugs. It's in the metaphor of a deadly organism attacking an all-male community. It's in the iconography of the shaven heads." See Taubin, "Invading Bodies: Aliens3 [sic] and the Trilogy," 9–10. Several outside factors support Taubin's reading. David Thomson (*The Alien Quartet*, 97), for example, reports that during the early stages of the film's production, producers Giler and Hill discussed the Alien as representing cancer or HIV. Certainly AIDS was becoming a hot topic in Hollywood: that same year, *Bram Stoker's Dracula* alluded to HIV by including a scene where Van Helsing discusses syphilis and other "diseases of the blood"; one year later, *Philadelphia* made its debut.

7. See, for example, Kathleen Murphy, "The Last Temptation of Sigourney Weaver," *Film Comment* 28, no. 4 (July–August 1992): 17–20.

8. Julia Kristeva, *Powers of Horror: An Essay on Abjection*, trans Leon S. Rou-diez (New York: Columbia University Press, 1982), 4. For an analysis of abjection in *Alien³*, see Louise Speed, "*Alien₃* [sic]: A Postmodern Encounter with the Ab-ject," *Arizona Quarterly* 54, no. 1 (Spring 1998): 125–151.

9. See Lisa Lewis, "Chapter Six: Female Address Video (1980–1986)," in *Gender Politics and MTV: Voicing the Difference* (Philadelphia: Temple University Press, 1990), 109–147.

10. In a deleted scene, Dr. Clemens finds Ripley lying on the beach after she apparently left the EEV and swam to the shore (one of the trailers actually shows Clemens carrying her body from the shore into the compound). See, for example, "Alien Legend-Alien 3—Deleted Scenes," http://www.planetavp.com/al/Alien3/DeletedScenes/; accessed 2 August 2003.

11. Freud defined the fetish object as a substitute for the penis. The young male, traumatized by the realization that his mother does not have a penis, assumes that she was castrated by the father. Unwilling to admit his own subsequent fear of castration, the boy surmises that her penis must be somewhere else about her body and, therefore, focuses on other body parts (the nose, hands, feet, or what have you) as the site of erotic desire. The fetishist, like the homosexual, desires the penis, but

the site of that object is the heterosexual object, the female: it is the *woman's* penis he desires. See Sigmund Freud, "Fetishism (1927)," *The Standard Edition* (vol. 21, *The Future of an Illusion, Civilization and Its Discontents and Other Writings*, 1927E 21/152). In *Alien³*, when the camera is confronted with the fact of Ripley's nudity (no penis), the film mimics castration anxiety and displacement by focusing on Ripley's feet, hands, and, particularly, face and head. The film, like a fetishist, refuses to admit the castrating power of the father and thus does not accept alignment with the male, heterosexual viewpoint, but rather locates the phallus (the source of power) on the female body through fetish.

12. Again Kristeva (*Powers of Horror*, 4) on the abjection of the corpse:

In that compelling, raw, insolent thing in the morgue's full sunlight, in that thing that no longer matches and therefore no longer signifies anything, I behold the breaking down of a world that has erased its borders: fainting away. The corpse, seen without God and outside of science, is the utmost of abjection. It is death infecting life. Abject. It is something rejected from which one does not take part, from which one does not protect oneself as from an object. Imaginary uncanniness and real threat, it beckons to us and ends up engulfing us.

13. The text of *The Book of Common Prayer* continues "through our Lord Jesus Christ; who shall change our vile body, that it may be like unto his glorious body, according to the mighty working, whereby he is able to subdue all things to himself" ("The Burial of the Dead" *The Book of Common Prayer*, 1662, from Lynda M. Howell's *The 1662 Book of Common Prayer Website*, http://www.eskimo.com/~lhowell/bcp1662/occasion/burial.html; accessed 2 August 2003).

14. This is the first confirmation in the series that the Alien is modified by its host, incorporating the host's DNA. The implication, of course, is that the Alien Queen "born" of Ripley is truly a creature to be feared, as it would incorporate her survivability, tenacity, and resolve (a thread picked up in *Alien Resurrection*).

15. Thomas Laquer, *Making Sex: Body and Gender from the Greeks to Freud* (Cambridge, MA: Harvard University Press, 1990), 214–215. Kristeva (*The Powers of Horror*, 71) elucidates on how the female's internal bleeding signals the threat within: "Menstrual blood . . . stands for the danger issuing from within the identity (social or sexual); it threatens the relationship between the sexes within a social aggregate and, through internalization, the identity of each sex in the face of sexual difference."

16. See, for example, Thomas Doherty's "Genre, Gender, and the Aliens Trilogy," in *The Dread of Difference: Gender and the Horror Film* (Austin: University of Texas Press, 1996), 197.

17. Ros Jennings, "Desire and Design—Ripley Undressed," in *Lesbians and the Moving Image*, ed. Tamsin Wilton (London: Routledge, 1995), 203.

18. Andrew Lichtenstein adds the following explanation to his photographs of prisoners sporting the teardrop tattoo under an eye: "Originally each teardrop represented a murder committed. More recently they have begun to represent each of the family or gang members who have died while a prisoner is locked up. Because of the location of the tear on the face, these tattoos are about commitment, an unabashed declaration of the inmate experience" ("Texas Prison Tattoos," http://www.foto8.com/issue09/reportage/AndrewLichtenstein/prisontattoos01.html; accessed 24 July 2003).

19. Mulhall, *On Film*, 98.

20. Vivian Sobchack, "The Virginity of Astronauts: Sex and the Science Fiction Film," in *Alien Zone: Cultural Theory and Contemporary Science Fiction Cinema*, ed. Annette Kuhn (New York: Verso, 1990), 103–115.

21. The scene reappropriates Weaver's original screen test for *Alien* and rejects the voyeuristic display of her body at the end of *Alien*. As in the screen test, Weaver expresses sexual desire in a straightforward and voluntary manner.

22. See Paula Graham's "Looking Lesbian: Amazons and Aliens in Science Fiction Cinema," *The Good, The Bad and the Gorgeous:* Popular Culture's Romance with Lesbianism, eds. Diane Hawer and Belinda Budge (London: Pandora, 1994), 197–217, and Jennings, "Desire and Design."

23. For an argument on how rape is about domination and violence rather than sex, see Susan Brownmiller, *Against Our Will: Men, Women, and Rape* (New York: Fawcett Columbine, 1993).

24. Camille Paglia, *Sexual Personae: Art and Decadence from Nefertiti to Emily Dickinson* (New York: Vintage, 1991), 11.

25. Dillon's fight with the Alien alludes to Samson's fight with the lion (Judges 14:6) and Michael's fight with the dragon (Rev. 12:7–9).

26. Jean Baivel, "Devotion to the Immaculate Heart of Mary" and "Devotion to the Sacred Heart of Jesus," *The Catholic Encyclopedia* (http://www.newadvent.org/cathen/07168a.htm; accessed 28 July 2003). On how Christianity embraces abjection, see Kristeva, ". . . Qui Tollis Peccata Mundi," *Powers of Horror*, 113–132.

27. See, for example, Valerie Hartouni, "Containing Women: Reproductive Discourse in the 1980s," in *Technoculture*, ed. Constance Penley and Andrew Ross (Minneapolis: University of Minnesota Press, 1991), 27–56.

28. David J. Skal, *The Monster Show: A Cultural History of Horror* (New York: Norton, 1993), 302.

29. For a reading of Antigone as transgressive feminism, see Judith Butler, *Antigone's Claim: Kinship between Life and Death* (New York: Columbia University Press, 2000).

30. Taubin, "Invading Bodies," 10.

31. Elizabeth Wurtzel, *Bitch: In Praise of Difficult Women* (New York: Doubleday, 1998), 414.

Chapter 4: "Who Are You?":
Alien Resurrection and the Posthuman Subject

1. Janet Maslin, "Ripley, Believe It or Not, Has a Secret, and It's Not Pretty," *New York Times*, November 26 1997, E1, E10.

2. Brian D. Johnson, "Holiday Treats from Hollywood," *Maclean's*, 29 December 1997/5 January 1998, 105.

3. Richard Schickel, "Alien Resurrection," *Time*, 1 December 1997, 84.

4. Peter Travers, "Twisted Sisters in Space," *Rolling Stone*, 5 December 1997, 83, 85.

5. Lisa Schwarzbaum, "Alien Resurrection," *Entertainment Weekly*, 5 December 1997, 47–49.

6. Knowing, for example, that Sigourney Weaver has never played a "ditzy blonde with cleavage"—in fact, that she is a thin brunette who is best known in science fiction for killing nasty Aliens—deepens our enjoyment of a film like *Galaxy Quest* (1999), where she is transformed into a dumb, large-breasted, blond "fluff" actress named Gwen DeMarco who finds aliens "cute." For more on cinematic parody, see, for example, Thomas Sobchack and Vivian Sobchack, *An Introduction to Film*, 2nd ed. (Boston: Scott, Foresman, 1987), 11.

7. Geoff Klock, *How to Read Superhero Comics and Why* (New York: Continuum, 2002), 38.

8. Ripley's hybrid nature anticipates the dark, superhero films to follow in the late 1990s such as *Blade* (1998) and *X-Men* (2000).

9. Andrew Murdock and Rachel Aberly, *The Making of Alien Resurrection* (New York: HarperPrism, 1997), 6.

10. Travers, "Twisted Sisters," 85.

11. The theme of nightmares forced upon the innocent pervades Jeunet's *City of Lost Children*, where the created man, Krank, visits nightmares upon abducted children in his quest to experience a real dream.

12. Mary Shelley, *Frankenstein*, (Reprint, New York: Dover, 1994), 18.

13. J. E. Cirlot, *A Dictionary of Symbols*, 233.

14. French psychoanalyst Jacques Lacan argues that the castration anxiety felt by the child as described by Freud is essentially a linguistic anxiety rather than a physical one. The child, noting the power of the father (men) over the mother (women) realizes that the woman is "castrated" in the sense that she is disempowered. As all language is masculine, we all must enter the "Law of the Father" (or "Name of the Father") when we enter into language (begin to speak) and become subjects. To learn to speak is therefore inherently to come under the control of the Father. See Jacques Lacan, *Ecrits: A Selection*, trans. Bruce Fink (New York: Norton, 1999), particularly chapters 1: "The Mirror Stage as Formative of the *I* Function, as Revealed in Psychoanalytic Experience," 3: "The Function and Field of Speech and Language in Psychoanalysis," and 9: "The Subversion of the Subject and the Dialectic of Desire in the Freudian Unconscious."

15. As Paul Connerton writes in *How Societies Remember* (Cambridge: Cambridge University Press, 1989), "All totalitarianisms behave in this way; the mental

enslavement of the subjects of a totalitarian regime begins when their memories are taken away" (14).

16. Once again, the female reproductive body is the cause for fear. This echoes Victor Frankenstein's fear of the female creature he is constructing at the request of his male creature; through her "a race of devils would be propagated upon the earth who might make the very existence of the species of man a condition precarious and full of terror" (Shelley, *Frankenstein*, 121).

17. At first, Victor Frankenstein is quite enthusiastic about the consequences of creating a human being: "A new species would bless me as its creator and source; many happy and excellent creatures would owe their being to me. No father would claim the gratitude of his child so completely as I should deserve theirs" (ibid., 32).

18. See, for example, Edward Gross and Jon Snyder's "ALIEN IV: The Movie You'll See . . . and the one you won't," *Sci-Fi Universe Magazine* 1 (July 1994).

19. In *Buffy the Vampire Slayer*'s third season, the vampire-with-a-soul Angel throws a sharp letter opener at the evil mayor of Sunnydale, who stops it with his open hand, transfixing his palm. After removing the blade, the mayor's wound heals almost instantly, revealing his invulnerability and underscoring his malevolent freakishness ("Enemies," dir. David Grossman, writ. Douglas Petrie, Fox, 16 March 1999).

20. In season three of *Buffy the Vampire Slayer*, Willow meets her vampire döppelganger from an alternate universe. The Willow vampire attempts to seduce Willow but is eventually captured, sent back to her own universe, and killed ("Doppelgangland," dir. Joss Whedon, writ. Joss Whedon. Fox, 23 February 1999).

21. Elyce Rae Helford, "Postfeminism and the Female Action-Adventure Hero: Positioning *Tank Girl*," in *Future Females, The Next Generation: New Voices and Velocities in Feminist Science Fiction Criticism*, ed. Marleen S. Barr (Lanham, MA: Rowman & Littlefield, 2000), 300.

22. Given Gediman's earlier comment that "she is something of a predator," this feat connects the Ripley clone to the figure of the extraterrestrial hunter, the Predator, who, in *Predator 2* (1990), has what appears to be an Alien skull in its trophy room.

23. A similar scene in *The City of Lost Children* shows four identical cloned fetuses in square glass chambers. The context for the existence of these fetuses is worded as a grotesque fairy tale: an inventor sought to create a family for himself, but his creations were genetically imperfect (and freakish). He fights with his oldest "son," Krank, who throws him into the sea. Not having known their "father," the four identical clones continually dispute as to which of them is "the original," when they are, in fact, mere copies of the inventor.

24. For the human models for these bodies, see George M. Gould and Walter L. Pyle's *Anomalies and Curiosities of Medicine*, chapter 5, "Major Terata." Electronic Text Center, University of Virginia Library (http://etext.lib.virginia.edu/toc/modeng/public/GouAnom.html; accessed 2 August 2003).

25. Leslie Fiedler, *Freaks: Myths and Images of the Secret Self* (New York: Touchstone, 1978), 225.

26. Elizabeth Grosz, "Freaks," *Social Semiotics* 1, no. 2 (1991): 25. Another film that explored dark doubling and the freakish, transgressive body is *Total Recall* (1990). In this film, the protagonist, while undergoing a procedure to implant "vacation memories" of Mars, recovers suppressed memories of his previous life as a spy. He then travels to Mars, where he becomes the liberator of its mutated humans, who, due to radiation poisoning, are all freaks of one sort or another. Some have physical deformities, some mental powers, others both. Their leader, Kuato, is parasitic, being joined with a man named George (a phenomenon named the One-and-a-Half). Kuato is able to hide himself within George's body to avoid detection (his emergence takes time and apparently causes George great pain). In this case, however, the secret sharer, though clearly physically freakish and boasting a strong intellect and mental powers, is not evil. Rather, Kuato is a savior-prophet of sorts.

27. In season 1 of *The X-Files*, Special Agent Mulder discovers a storeroom containing tanks with human bodies immersed in a clear liquid. These humans, he later learns, are terminally ill experimental subjects being injected with extraterrestrial viruses ("The Erlenmeyer Flask," dir. R. W. Goodwin, writ. Chris Carter, Fox, 13 May 1994).

28. J. P. Telotte, *Replications: A Robotic History of the Science Fiction Film* (Urbana: University of Illinois Press, 1995), 190.

29. Susan J. Wolfe, "Star Trek's Data: Humanity as the Last Frontier" (paper presented at the annual meeting of the Popular Culture/American Culture Association of the Southwest and Texas, Albuquerque, NM, 15 February 2003).

30. Interestingly, Call's masquerade points, however obliquely, to another pastiche performance popular in recent film—drag. Drag is, essentially, not impersonation, which seeks to copy as perfectly as possible, nor parody, which seeks to imitate in order to expose, but a pastiche, which openly imitates previous drag performances. In *To Wong Foo, Thanks for Everything! Julie Newmar* (1995), for example, only by entering a rural town where drag, as such, is not recognized as a discursive mode, could Miss Noxema Jackson (Wesley Snipes), Miss Vida Boheme (Patrick Swayze), and Miss Chi-Chi Rodriguez (John Leguizamo) be taken as female. And, of course, it is the fact that they are "too female" that eventually gives them away to the women.

31. Catherine Constable, "Becoming the Monster's Mother: Morphologies of Identity in the *Alien* Series," in *Alien Zone II: The Spaces of Science Fiction Cinema*, ed. Annette Kuhn (New York: Verso, 1999), 195.

32. Chris Hall's early conceptual art for the Newborn's body was morphologically female. Andrew Murdock and Rachel Aberly, *The Making of Alien Resurrection* (New York: HarperPrism, 1997), 124.

33. Joss Whedon would use a similar scene in the cliffhanger episode for the second season of *Buffy the Vampire Slayer*. In it, Buffy must sacrifice her vampire lover, Angel, to stop Acathla, an ancient demon, from sucking Earth into the Demon Dimension. Angel is sucked into Acathla's vortex ("Becoming, Part Two," dir. Joss Whedon, writ. Joss Whedon, Fox, 19 May 1998).

34. Travers, "Twisted Sisters," 85.

Index

INDEX